NATIONAL DEVELOPMENT

Dedicated to the government agencies in which
win–win analysis workshops have been conducted:
Africa, countries such as Ghana, Kenya, Malawi, Morocco and
South Africa;
Asia, countries such as China, India, Korea, the Philippines, and Sri Lanka;
Europe, countries such as Croatia, France, Germany, Italy and Russia;
Latin America, countries such as Argentina, Brazil, Mexico and Panama.

National Development

Being more effective and more efficient

STUART S. NAGEL
University of Illinois

Ashgate

Aldershot • Burlington USA • Singapore • Sydney

Published by
Ashgate Publishing Limited
Gower House
Croft Road
Aldershot
Hants GU11 3HR
England

Ashgate Publishing Company
131 Main Street
Burlington, VT 05401-5600 USA

Ashgate website: http://www.ashgate.com

British Library Cataloguing in Publication Data
National development : being more effective and more
    efficient. – (Policy Studies Organization series)
    1. Policy sciences 2. Conflict management
    I. Nagel, Stuart S., 1934–   II. Policy Studies Organization

Library of Congress Cataloging-in-Publication Data
Nagel, Stuart S., 1934–
    National development : being more effective and more efficient / Stuart S. Nagel.
        p.   cm. – (Policy studies organization series)
    ISBN 1–8401–4024–0
    1. Policy sciences.   I. Title.

H97.N3327   2000
320'.6 21–dc21   99–043344

ISBN 1 84014 024 0

Typeset by Manton Typesetters, Louth, Lincolnshire, UK.
Printed and bound in Great Britain by MPG Books Ltd, Bodmin, Cornwall

Summary Table of Contents

Detailed Table of Contents

PART III INSTITUTION BUILDING IN DEVELOPMENTAL POLICY STUDIES

List of Tables

Introduction

SUPER-OPTIMIZING ANALYSIS AND POLICY STUDIES

Super-optimizing analysis refers to dealing with public policy problems by finding an alternative that enables conservatives, liberals and other major viewpoints all to come out ahead of their best initial expectations simultaneously.

Super-optimum solutions (SOS) in public controversies involve solutions that exceed the best expectations of liberals and conservatives simultaneously. We are primarily concerned with public or governmental controversies, not controversies among private individuals, such as marriage, consumer, employment or other disputes. We are, however, interested in controversies over what statutes, judicial precedents or administrative regulations should be adopted governing marriage, consumer, employment, or other such relations.

An optimum solution is one that is best on a list of alternatives in achieving a set of goals. A super-optimum solution is one that is simultaneously best on two separate sets of goals: one set a liberal, the other set conservative. The sets may share many or all of the goals, but they are likely to differ in terms of the relative weights they give to the same goals.

An example

For example, in the minimum wage controversy, both liberals and conservatives endorse the goal of paying a decent wage and the goal of not overpaying to the point where some workers are unnecessarily laid off because their employers cannot afford the new higher minimum. Liberals, however, give relatively high weight to the first goal and relatively low but positive weight to the second goal, and vice versa for conservatives.

The liberal alternative in the minimum wage controversy might be $4.40 an hour and the conservative alternative might be $4.20 an hour. The liberal alternative would thus score higher on the 'decent wage' goal, and the conservative alternative lower. On the goal of 'avoiding overpayment', the

1

liberal alternative would score lower, and the conservative alternative higher. These real data would thus provide a classic tradeoff controversy.

The object in this example is to find a solution that is simultaneously better from a liberal perspective than $4.40 an hour and better from a conservative perspective than $4.20 an hour. One such super-optimum solution would be to provide for a minimum wage supplement by the government of 22 cents an hour to each unemployed person who is hired. The worker would receive $4.41 an hour, but the employer would pay only $4.19 an hour. The liberal–labor interests would be getting more than their best expectation of $4.40 an hour, and the conservative–business interests would be paying less than their best expectation of $4.20 an hour. The government and taxpayers would be benefitting by virtue of (1) the money saved from otherwise providing public aid to unemployed people, (2) the money added to the gross national product which provides income to others, increases taxes and an increased base on which to grow in subsequent years, (3) better role models for the children of people who would otherwise be unemployed, and (4) an upgrading of skills if qualifying for the wage subsidy means business has to provide on-the-job training and workers have to participate.

SOS contrasted with other types of solutions

Solutions to public controversies can be classified in various ways. First, there are super-optimum solutions in which all sides come out ahead of their initial best expectations, as mentioned above. At the opposite extreme is a super-malimum solution in which all sides come out worse than their worst initial expectations. This can be the case in a mutually destructive war, labor strike or highly expensive litigation.

In Pareto-optimum solutions, nobody comes out worse off and at least one side comes out better off. This is not a very favorable solution compared to a super-optimum solution. A Pareto-malimum solution would be one in which nobody is better off and at least one side is worse off.

In a win–lose solution, what one side wins the other side loses. The net effect is zero when the losses are subtracted from the gains. This is the typical litigation dispute scenario when one ignores the litigation costs. A lose–lose solution is one where both sides are worse off than they were before the dispute began. This may often be the typical litigation dispute outcome, or close to it when one includes litigation costs. These costs are often so high that the so-called winner is also a loser. This is also often the case in labor–management disputes that result in a strike, and even more so in international disputes that result in going to war.

Finally, there is the so-called win–win solution. At first glance this sounds like a solution where everybody comes out ahead. What it typically refers to, though, is an illusion, since the parties are only coming out ahead relative to their worst expectations. In this sense, the plaintiff is a winner no matter what the settlement is because he could have won nothing if liability had been rejected at trial. Likewise, the defendant is a winner no matter what the settlement is because he could have lost everything the plaintiff was asking for if liability had been established at trial. The parties are only fooling themselves, in the same sense that someone who is obviously a loser tells himself he won because he could have done worse.

Ways of arriving at super-optimum solutions

Having a third party benefactor is one of many ways of arriving at super-optimum solutions. Other ways include (1) expanding the resources available, (2) setting realistically higher goals than what was previously considered the best, (3) having big benefits for one side but only small costs for the other side, (4) combining alternatives that are not mutually exclusive, (5) removing or decreasing the source of the conflict, and (6) developing a package of alternatives that would satisfy both liberal and conservative goals.

One procedure for arriving at super-optimum solutions is to think in terms of what is in the conservative alternative that liberals might like and, likewise, what is in the liberal alternative that conservatives might like, then to think whether it is possible to make a new alternative that will emphasize these two aspects. Another technique is to emphasize the opposite. This involves saying what is in a conservative alternative that liberals especially dislike and what is in the liberal alternative that conservatives especially dislike, then to think about making a new alternative that eliminates these two aspects. A variation on this is to add new goals. The usual procedure starts with the conservative goals as givens in light of how they justify their current best alternative, and it starts with the liberal goals as given in light of how they justify their current best alternative. This technique involves thinking about the goals conservatives tend to endorse that are not currently involved in the controversy, but that could be brought in to justify a new alternative. Likewise, what goals do liberals tend to endorse that are not currently involved in the controversy, but that could also be brought in? For this technique, a good example is the free speech controversy, where liberals want virtually unrestricted free speech in order to stimulate creativity, and conservatives want restrictions on free speech in order to have more order in the legal system. However, liberals also like due process, equal protection and right to privacy. That raises questions as to whether it might be permissible to restrict free speech in order to satisfy those constitutional rights, where the restrictions are not so great but the jeopardy of those other rights might be great. Likewise, conservatives like policies that are good for business. They might therefore readily endorse permissive free speech that relates to advertising, to trying to convince workers that they should not join unions, or to lobbying.

One problem with super-optimum solutions is that they look so good that they may cause some people to think they might be some kind of a trap. An example is the Camp David Accords, a classic super-optimum solution where Israel, Egypt, the United States and everybody involved came out ahead of their original best expectations. According to the *New York Times* for 26 March 1989, however, Israeli intelligence at least at first opposed Anwar Sadat's visit to Israel and the Camp David Accords until close to the signing on the grounds that it all sounded so good that it must be a trap. The Israeli intelligence felt that Israel was being set up for a variation on the Yom Kippur war whereby Israel got into big trouble by relaxing its guard because of the holidays. They viewed this as an attempt to get them to lower their guard again, and then any minute the attack would begin. They were on a more intense alert at the time of the Camp David negotiations than they were at any other time in Israel's history. This nicely illustrates how super-optimum solutions can easily be viewed by people as a trap because they look so good that they are unbelievable. Traditional solutions are not so likely to be viewed as traps, and they are taken more at their face value, which is generally not much.

Relations to decision-aiding software

Super-optimizing is an approach to public policy analysis. Policy analysis or policy evaluation can be defined as processing a set of goals to be achieved, alternatives available for achieving them, and relations between goals and alternatives in order to arrive at a best alternative, combination, allocation or predictive decision rule. Policy analysis can be facilitated by decision-aiding software. Such software involves showing goals on the columns of a table, alternatives on the rows, and relations as words or numbers in the cells. The overall totals can be shown in a column on the far right, with an analysis that can quickly show how the totals would change if there were changes in the goals, alternatives, relations or other inputs.

This kind of decision-aiding software also facilitates the finding of super-optimum solutions. It can quickly determine the liberal and conservative totals for each alternative. It can quickly test to see if a proposed super-optimum solution does score better than the best liberal and conservative alternatives using the liberal and conservative weights. Such software also facilitates finding SOS solutions by enabling one to work with many alternatives and many criteria simultaneously. Each side can thereby give on some criteria which are not so important to it and receive on other criteria, in order to arrive at solutions where both sides come out ahead of their initial best expectations.

The key literature on decision-aiding software includes Patrick Humphreys and Ayleen Wisudha, *Methods and Tools for Structuring and Analysing Decision Problems* (London School of Economics and Political Science, 1987); Saul Gass *et al.* (eds), *Impacts of Microcomputers on Operations Research* (North-Holland, 1986); and S. Nagel and Lisa Bievenue, *Teach Yourself Decision-Aiding Software* (University Press of America, 1992).

Relations to dispute resolution and growth economics

Another stream of inspiration has come from people in the field of mediation and alternative dispute resolution. The key literature here includes Lawrence Susskind and Patrick Field, *Dealing with an Angry Public: The Mutual Gains Approach to Resolving Disputes* (The Free Press, 1996); William Ury, Jeanne Brett and Stephen Goldberg, *Getting Disputes Resolved: Designing Systems to Cut the Costs of Conflict* (Jossey-Buss, 1988); and S. Nagel and M. Mills, *Multi-Criteria Methods for Alternative Dispute Resolution* (Quorum, 1990).

Still another stream of inspiration has come from people who are expansionist thinkers. It includes the conservative economist Arthur Laffer and the liberal economist Robert Reich, who have in common a belief that policy problems can be resolved by expanding the total 'pie' of resources or other things of value available to be distributed to the disputants. The expansion can come from well-placed subsidies and tax breaks, with strings attached to increase national productivity. This kind of thinking can apply to disputes involving blacks–whites, rich–poor, males–females, North–South, urban–rural and other categories of societal disputants. Some of the key literature here is Robert Reich, *The Work of Nations: Preparing Ourselves for 21st Century Capitalism* (Knopf, 1991); and Paul Roberts, *The Supply Side Revolution* (Harvard University Press, 1984); David Levine, *Reinventing the Workplace: How Business and Employees Can Both Win* (Brookings Institution, 1995).

When the idea of super-optimum solutions was first proposed in the 1980s, people thought it was some kind of funny trick to think one could arrive at solutions to public policy problems that could exceed the best expectations of both liberals and conservatives simultaneously. Since then, the ideas have been presented in numerous workshops where skeptical and sometimes even cynical participants would divide into groups to try to develop SOS solutions to problems within their field of interest. They found that, by opening their minds to the possibilities and by following some simple procedures, they could succeed in arriving at reasonable SOS solutions. It is hoped that this research will contribute in the long run to decreasing the glamour and excitement of super-optimum solutions by making such solutions almost a matter of routine thinking. There is joy in creating new ideas, but there is more joy in seeing one's new ideas become commonplace.

APPENDIX: THE GENERIC SOS SOLUTION FROM A SPREADSHEET PERSPECTIVE

A   The alternatives
1   Conservative alt.
2   Compromise
3   Liberal alt.
4   SOS1 (dominating SOS)
5   SOS2 (non-dominating SOS)
6   SOS3 (new-goal SOS)

B   The criteria

		Meas. unit	Conservative weights	Liberal weights
1	Conservative goal	1–5 scale	3.00	1.00
2	Liberal goal		1.00	3.00
3	Neutral goal		2.00	2.00

C   Scores of alternatives on criteria

	Cons. goal	Lib. goal	Neut. goal
Conservative alt.	5.00	1.00	3.00
Compromise	3.10	3.10	3.00
Liberal alt.	1.00	5.00	3.00
SOS1	5.10	5.10	3.10
SOS2	4.50	4.50	2.90
SOS3	4.00	4.00	4.00

D   Initial analyses

		Conservative combined raw scores	Liberal combined raw scores
1	Conservative alt.	16.00	8.00
2	Compromise	12.40	12.40
3	Liberal alt.	8.00	16.00
4	SOS1	20.40	20.40
5	SOS2	18.00	18.00
6	SOS3	16.00	16.00

Notes:
  1   The conservative alternative is shown first because it tends to be the current alternative on which we would like to improve. The conservative alternative or set of alternatives in a policy problem tends to differ from the liberal alternatives in the relative extent to

which it favors those who are relatively well off in a society, whereas the liberal alternative tends to favor those who are not so relatively well off.

2   The first super-optimum solution (SOS1) (and the most difficult to achieve) is to find an alternative that is better than the conservative, liberal and compromise alternatives on all the goals. The second super-optimum solution (SOS2) is an alternative that is not better on all the goals than the other alternatives, but is better on the overall or combined score adding across the goals. The third super-optimum solution (SOS3) is not better on all the goals and is not better on the overall score with the initial goals, but it is better on the overall score than the non-SOS alternatives when another goal is added.

3   The conservative goals or goals in this context are by definition goals that conservatives disproportionately favor, as indicated by the fact that those goals are given relatively high weight by conservatives. The liberal goals are likewise given relatively high weight by liberals. Note, however, that, in a typical policy problem, conservatives tend to give positive weight to liberal goals (although relatively less weight than to conservative goals) and vice versa with liberals.

4   The scores of the alternatives on the criteria are based on a 1–5 scale for the sake of simplicity, although that does not have to be. Under a 1–5 scale, 5 means highly conducive to the goal, 4 means mildly conducive, 3 means neither conducive nor adverse, 2 means mildly adverse and 1 means the alternative is highly adverse to the goal.

5   The conservative alternatives logically score high on the conservative goals and low on the liberal goals, and vice versa for the liberal alternatives. The compromise alternative scores slightly above the middle on each goal. That avoids ties in this analysis, and that is the general nature of compromises.

6   The scores of the super-optimum solutions on the conservative, liberal and neutral goals are consistent with their definitions. Likewise, the scores of the alternatives on the neutral goal are consistent with the definition of the neutral goal as being between the conservative goal and the liberal goal in its normative direction.

7   The combined raw scores are determined by adding the weighted relation scores together. For example, the conservative alternative receives 16 points using the conservative weights by adding (3 times 5) to (1 times 1). Using the liberal weights, the conservative alternative receives only 8 points by adding (1 times 5) to (3 times 1). For the sake of simplicity in this generic analysis, only the conservative goal and the liberal goal are used. The neutral goal has to be activated to enable the 'new-goal SOS' to be a super-optimum solution.

8   Using the conservative weights, the conservative alternative logically comes out ahead of the liberal alternative, and vice versa using the liberal weights. The compromise alternative is the winner among those three alternatives with an aggregate score of 24.80 versus 24.00 for either the conservative or the liberal alternative, but the compromise alternative is only the second choice of both groups.

9   The three super-optimum alternatives all do better than the traditional compromise. What is more important, the three super-optimum alternatives all simultaneously do better than the conservative alternative using the conservative weights and they do better than the liberal alternative using the liberal weights. That is the essential characteristic of a super-optimum alternative. It is the new first choice of both groups.

10   Even the worst of the three super-optimum solutions comes out so far ahead of the traditional compromise that the only way the traditional compromise could be a winner is (1) if one or more of the goals were to be given a negative weight, or (2) if one or more of the relation scores were to go above 5, below 1, or otherwise be unreasonable.

PART I
DOMESTIC POLICY PROBLEMS

1   Poverty and the Economy

POVERTY AND ECONOMIC POLICY

Unemployment and inflation

Evaluating policies for dealing with unemployment and inflation

Doing nothing is not likely to worsen unemployment or inflation, but it is not likely to help either. Decreasing the money supply and increasing interest rates may decrease inflation, but increase unemployment. The same is true of decreasing government spending and increasing taxes. The Reagonomics approach involved decreasing taxes to stimulate employment, and decreasing domestic spending to reduce inflation. The Democratic counterpart of the 1990s was to increase employment through government jobs and decrease inflation through price control.

Increasing the money supply and decreasing interest may stimulate employment, but increase inflation. The same is also true of increasing government spending and reducing taxes.

The SOS is to stimulate greater productivity through well-placed subsidies with strings attached, big money and competent administration. See Table 1.1.

A simplified analysis of inflation and unemployment

Raising interest rates to decrease inflation may have the effect of decreasing prices by reducing spending from borrowed money. Those benefits may be more than offset by the undesirable effects of reducing the ability of business to borrow for expansion, inventory and other purposes. The reduction in spending may also have an adverse effect on employment.

Lowering interest rates to decrease unemployment may have little impact because businesses are reluctant to borrow when they are reducing their operations and sales are down. Likewise, consumers are reluctant to borrow when they are already heavily in debt and fearful of a reduction in employment or hours.

11

Table 1.1 Evaluating policies for dealing with unemployment and inflation

Criteria Alternatives	L Goal Cut unemploy-ment to 3%	C Goal Cut inflation to 3%	L Goal Equal distribution of inflation & unemploy-ment	C Goal Free enterprise	N Total (neutral weights)	L Total (liberal weights)	C Total (conservative weights)
C Alternative Do nothing	3	3	2	4	24	22	26

C Alternative
  Less money
  More interest
	2	4	3	3	24	22	26

C Alternative
  Reduce spending
  Raise taxes
	2	4	3	3	24	22	26

C Alternative
  Reduce taxes
  Reduce domestic spending
	4	4	3	3	28	28	28*

L Alternative
  More money
  Less interest
	4	2	3	3	24	26	22

L Alternative
  Increase spending
  Reduce taxes
	4	2	3	3	24	26	22

L Alternative							
Job creation	4	4	4	1	26	29 ⎤	23
Price control							
L Alternative							
Tax breaks & subsidies	4	4	3	3	28	28 ⎦	28
Cut defense spending							
N Alternative							
Combine	3.5	3.5	3	3	26	26	26
SOS Alternative							
Strings attached							
Big subsidies	5	5	5	4	38	39**	37**
Objective allocation							

13

Notes to SOS tables in general:
1. C = conservative, L = liberal, N = neutral, S = super-optimum.
2. The 1–5 scores showing relations between alternatives and goals have the following meanings: 5 = the alternative is highly conducive to the goal, 4 = mildly conducive, 3 = neither conducive nor adverse, 2 = mildly adverse, 1 = highly adverse.
3. The 1–3 scores showing the relative weights or multipliers for each goal have the following meanings: 3 = this goal has relatively high importance to a certain ideological group, 2 = relatively middling importance, and 1 = relatively low but positive importance.
4. A single asterisk shows the winning alternative on this column before considering the SOS alternative. A double asterisk shows the alternative that simultaneously does better than the conservative alternative on the conservative totals, and better than the liberal alternative on the liberal totals.

Raising taxes and decreasing spending to fight inflation may not be politically feasible. It would also reduce the ability of the government to give tax breaks and well-placed subsidies to increase productivity. Lowering taxes and increasing spending to fight unemployment may not be politically feasible when the national debt and deficit are already too high.

Increasing the adoption of new technologies and raising the skills of workers help to reduce inflation by (1) increasing the productivity of labor to offset increased wages, (2) increasing the quality of goods to offset increased prices, and (3) increasing the GNP and domestic income to further offset increased prices. Increasing the adoption of new technologies and raising the skills of workers help to reduce unemployment by (1) making the workers more employable, (2) increasing the GNP and domestic spending to stimulate the creation of more jobs, and (3) increasing the productivity and wage rates, thereby offsetting a possible reduction in hours.

The conservative alternative of having interest rates up in time of inflation and down in time of unemployment does not make sense if inflation and unemployment are problems simultaneously. That would be so if both were over 3 per cent. Likewise, the liberal alternative of having a budget

Table 1.2   A simplified SOS analysis of the unemployment–inflation problem

Criteria Alternatives	L Goal Reduce unemploy- ment	C Goal Reduce inflation	N Total (neutral weights)	L Total (liberal weights)	C Total (conservative weights)

C Alternative
  Fight inflation
  (e.g. 6% to 10%
  on interest)
	5	2	14	11	17*

L Alternative
  Fight
  unemployment
  (e.g. 6% to 4%)
	2	5	14	17*	11

N Alternative
  Compromise
  (e.g. 6% to
  7%)
	<3	>3	12	12	12

SOS Alternative
  Well-placed
  subsidies
	5	5	20	20**	20**

surplus in time of inflation and a budget deficit in time of unemployment does not make sense when both inflation and unemployment are over 3 per cent or so. One can, however, stimulate new technologies and upgrade skills when inflation and unemployment are occurring simultaneously. See Table 1.2.

Rural agriculture policy

Evaluating policies for dealing with the farm income problem

The conservative alternative would win on the conservative total if more weight were given to farmer income. The importance of farmer income has been lessening even among conservatives, along with the lessening of the political power of farmers.

American farmers are potentially capable of competing well in the world marketplace given their efficient technology, land and agricultural methods. The value of the dollar since 1980 has been relatively high as a result of government borrowing to meet the national debt. This has interfered with other countries being able to get dollars to buy American farm products as easily as obtaining the kind of money needed to buy farm products from Canada, Australia, Argentina or elsewhere. See Table 1.3.

Food prices in developing nations: an SOS spreadsheet perspective

Table 1.4 shows that high farm prices is the conservative alternative in this context and low prices is the liberal alternative. The liberal weights involve a 3 for urban desires, a 1 for rural desires, and a 2 for all the other goals. With the liberal weights, the SOS wins 76 to 48 for all the other alternatives. We then go back and put in the conservative weights. The conservative weights give a 2 to all the neutral goals just as liberal weights do but, as regards urban and rural desires, for the conservative in the context, rural desires get a 3 rather than a 1, and urban desires get a 1 rather than a 3. The SOS is a winner even with the conservative weights, although now the high prices do better than they did before, but still not as well as the SOS.

The neutral perspective is not to give everything a weight of 1, but rather a weight of 2. If the neutrals gave everything a weight of 1, they would be giving neutral goals less weight than either the liberals or the conservatives give them. Thus, the neutral picture is that rural desires get a weight of 2, and so do urban desires. The SOS wins with the neutral weights too. It is super-optimum, because it is out in front over both the conservative and liberal alternatives using both the conservative and liberal weights. It also

Table 1.3 Evaluating policies for dealing with the farm income problem

Criteria / Alternatives	C Goal Raise farmer income	L Goal Raise consumer benefits	N Goal Reduce tax costs	L Goal Equity	N Total (neutral weights)	L Total (liberal weights)	C Total (conservative weights)
C Alternative Cut Supply Increase Govt demand	4.1	2	2	2	20.2	20.1	20.3
L Alternative Increase cons. demand Increase direct payments	3.9	4	2.5	4	28.8	32.9*	24.7
Fewer farmers Cut farm expense							
N Alternative All	4.5	2.9	2.2	3	21.2	26.6	23.8
SOS Alternative World market-place with $ deficit down	5	5	3	3.5	33	36.5**	29.5**

wins over the compromise. The SOS involves the farmers getting better than high prices and the urbanites paying lower than low prices, with the government providing a supplement like the minimum wage supplement, provided that administrative feasibility is satisfied.

Administrative feasibility involves the use of food stamps: they are given to urban food buyers; they cannot be easily counterfeited; food buyers give them to retailers, who in turn give them to wholesalers, who in turn give them to farmers, who turn them in for reimbursement. Criterion 8 only relates to political feasibility. There should be a separate criterion for administrative feasibility.

Of special importance is that no farmer gets the supplement without agreeing to adopt more modern farming methods: otherwise, it is just a handout for subsidizing inefficient farming. As a result of adopting more modern farming methods, productivity goes up. Food becomes available for export. Foreign exchange is then acquired for importing new technology. The new technology increases the GNP, and everybody is better off, including the taxpayers who pay the supplement. They are better off because, with the increased GNP, the government could even reduce taxes if it wanted to do so. It could reduce taxes below a 20 per cent level and still have more tax revenue if the GNP base has increased substantially.

Labor relations

Evaluating labor-management policies

In this context, 'workplace' refers to safety, minimum wages, maximum hours, child labor, environmental protection and non-discrimination; 'union' refers to the right to join a union without being fired, the right to bargain collectively, the right to strike, and other rules that increase the ability of unions to represent workers more effectively, 'working together' refers to labor and management seeking to increase productivity through new technologies, on-the-job training and incentives that are mutually arrived at. See Table 1.5.

The data in Table 1.6 come from Chapter 15, 'Finding a Super-Optimum Solution in a Labor–Management Dispute', in S. Nagel and M. Mills, *Multi-Criteria Methods for Alternative Dispute Resolution: with Microcomputer Software Applications* (Quorum Books, 1990). All the items are in thousands of dollars.

The illustrative example involves a leading grower in the Peoria, Illinois area (who employs approximately 7000 farmworkers a year) being sued by the Migrant Legal Counsel, which is a legal services agency that specializes

Table 1.4 Pricing food in developing nations

Criteria / Alternatives	C Goal Rural well being	L Goal Urban well being	N Goal Admin. feasibility	N Goal + Farming methods	N Goal + Export	N Goal Import technology	N Goal + GNP	N Goal Political feasibility	N Total (neutral weights)	L Total (liberal weights)	C Total (conserv. weights)
C Alternative High price	5	1	3	4	4	4	4	1	52 (18)	48 (14)	56* (22)
L Alternative Low price	1	5	3	2	2	2	2	5	44 (18)	48* (22)	40 (14)
N Alternative Compromise	3	3	3	3	3	3	3	3	48 (18)	48 (18)	48 (18)
S Alternative Price supplement	5.1	5.1	3	5	5	5	5	5	76.4 (26.4)	76.4** (26.4)	76.4** (26.4)

Notes:

1. The intermediate totals in parentheses are based on the first three goals. The bottom-line totals are based on all the goals, including the indirect effects of the alternatives.

2. The SOS of a price supplement involves farmers receiving 101 per cent of the price they are asking, but urban workers and others paying only 79 per cent, which is less than the 80 per cent they are willing and able to pay.

3. The difference of 22 per cent is made up by food stamps given to the urban workers in return for agreeing to be in programs that upgrade their skills and productivity. The food stamps are used to pay for staple products (like rice or wheat) along with cash. Farmers can then redeem the stamps for cash, provided that they also agree to be in programs that increase their productivity.

4. Food stamps have administrative feasibility for ease in determining that workers and farmers are doing what they are supposed to do in return for the food stamps. They cannot be easily counterfeited. They serve as a check on how much the farmers have sold.

5. By increasing the productivity of farmers and workers, the secondary effects occur of improving farming methods, increasing exports, increasing importing of new technologies, and increasing the GNP.

6. High prices are not politically feasible because of too much opposition from workers who consume but do not produce food. However, the high prices are acceptable if they can be met by way of price supplements in the form of food stamps.

C = conservative; L = neutral; and S = super-optimum solution.

* Conservative or liberal winner without the SOS.

** Conservative or liberal winner considering the SOS.

19

Table 1.5 Evaluating labor–management policies

Criteria / Alternatives	C Goal Stimulate business	L Goal Protect workers	N Goal Save taxpayers	L Goal Equity	N Total (neutral weights)	L Total (liberal weights)	C Total (conservative weights)
C Alternative Less workplace Less union	4	2	3	3	24	25	23*
L Alternative More Workplace More Union	2	4	3	3	24	29*	19
N Alternative Some union restrictions Some mgt restrictions	3	3	3	4	26	30	22
SOS Alternative Working together & OJT	5	5	2	5	34	39**	29**

in the legal problems of migratory farmworkers. The workers, as a large class action, were suing to recover approximately $3 million in wages that had been deducted to pay for loans, rents and other expenses without proper legal authorization. The money had actually been loaned or advanced to the workers, but the procedures designed to prevent illegal exploitation had not been followed.

The plaintiff's wildest initial expectation is to be repaid approximately $1 million in wages. This is a wild expectation since the money was deducted for goods, services and advances that had been provided to the workers by the grower, but not in accordance with the proper paperwork procedures. The defendant's wildest initial expectation is to have to pay nothing. That is a wild expectation since the defendant admittedly failed to comply with the proper deduction procedures, with no good defense other than that the money was owed. The defendant would thus be likely to lose on the issue of whether it complied with the proper procedures. A penalty is likely to be assessed to deter such improprieties on the part of the specific defendant and other potential defendants. The penalty is likely to be substantial in order to have deterrent value. There is also likely to be compensation to the named defendants for their efforts, plus considerable litigation costs if the case goes to trial.

The object is thus to arrive at a super-optimum solution whereby the workers in a sense receive more than $1 million and the defendant pays less than nothing. The key element in the super-optimum solution is the establishment of a credit union mainly consisting of $100,000 from the defendant to be deposited with interest for five years. That $100,000 can quickly generate $2 million worth of housing by serving as a 10 per cent down payment on a mortgage for existing or new housing units for the workers. The housing might be used as collateral for additional capital. It is also possible that a federal or state government agency will match the $100,000 as part of an economic development plan, thereby further increasing the lending opportunities.

The workers thereby obtain multiple family housing and a lending source for business opportunities that may be worth at least $2 million, plus the benefits of an improved grievance procedure, payments to named plaintiffs and compliance information. The total value is worth more than their wildest best expectation.

The growers thereby obtain the benefits of not having to provide housing for the workers. They also get interest on their savings and a subsequent return of the principal if requested. The grievance procedure can decrease friction. The compliance information can increase credibility. Payment to the named plaintiffs is a cost rather than a benefit, but it is more than offset by the benefits from the other relevant items of value. Therefore the growers

Table 1.6   Super-optimizing litigation analysis (using *Ramirez* v. *Rousonelos* as an illustrative example)

Criteria / Alternatives	Relevant items of value				Relevant totals
	Credit union, housing and business opportunities	Grievance procedure	Payment to named plaintiffs	Compliance information	
Plaintiff's SOS settlement (big benefits)	$2000	>$0	$50	>$0	>$1000
Plaintiff's best expectation = $1000	0	0	0	0	$1000
Likely compromise settlement = $500	0	0	0	0	$500
Defendant's best expectation = $0	0	0	0	0	$0
Defendant's SOS settlement	<$0	<$0	$50	~$0	<$0

are making a net gain as a result of this SOS settlement, which is the same as paying less than nothing.

Small business development

Africa's small business problem

The business development problem is very time-oriented in that it talks about small businesses as a stepping stone over time to big businesses. Shortsighted people say that there is a problem of unemployment, especially among women, and they must be given something to do. They give them dead-end jobs making clothes and selling clothes or, even worse, growing fruits and vegetables and selling these.

People with more of a time horizon say that the big problem is not eating a fish today but learning how to fish or doing some kind of activity that has some payoff beyond today or this week. In such a context this may involve sending the women to school to learn how to be computer operators. The business development context, as contrasted to the education and skills upgrading context, is to let them start out in a small machine shop where, for example, they make spark plugs. You cannot make spark plugs as fast as you can make dishcloths or as fast as you can go into the countryside and pick wild rhubarb to sell. To make spark plugs, first of all you have to get the machines to make them with and you have to learn to operate the machines. Maybe no income will come in for a couple of months, whereas income can be immediate when selling sweaters or casaba plants. In a few months, spark plugs are being made and sold, maybe with more income than with selling fruits and vegetables but also with more expense, so that at first it is even less profitable.

The key thing, however, is that making and selling spark plugs can lead to the creation of a factory. It can lead to the manufacturing of spark plugs on a larger scale or can lead to manufacturing of other auto parts. That in turn leads to the employment of more people, both men and women. It may even lead to producing more spark plugs than the local economy can buy because the local economy does not have many cars or trucks. That could mean exporting the surplus spark plugs to places that supply foreign money, hard currency for buying bigger machines for making, for example, bumpers, fenders, windshield wipers, maybe even cars eventually, although not necessarily.

Making cars in developing nations is frequently not productive; it is just a status symbol activity. Cars can be made better in Japan or even in the United States. Making cars is very complex, involving lots of components coming from different places. A spark plug may be nothing but some porcelain and some metal, with one machine making the whole article. There is no such thing as a machine that makes a whole car.

The super-optimum solution is deliberately choosing small businesses that have a high or, relatively speaking, higher capability of becoming big businesses even though it takes a while for even the small business form to pay off. (See Table 1.7.) That is part of long-term thinking, the idea of delayed gratification and also of taking one step back in order to take two steps forward later. It is a way of thinking that has not been particularly evident in equatorial countries, where there is a tradition that, if you want to eat, you do not have to do a lot of planting in the springtime and wait all the way until autumn to harvest something to eat. Instead, you just go out and shake a pineapple tree or coconut tree and you have food. That works fine for pineapples and coconuts. It does not work so well for pharmaceuticals. There is no pharmaceutical tree, although developing nations do sometimes make good use of herbs. What is certain is that there is no automobile tree.

Nobody worried about cars 100 years ago because they did not exist. Africa was blessed with being on the equator and having no need for heavy

Table 1.7   Business development and Africa

Criteria / Alternatives	C Goal Easy feasibility	L Goal Value to economy	N Total (neutral weights)	L Total (liberal weights)	C Total (conservative weights)
C Alternative Large business	2	4	12	10	14*
L Alternative Small business	4	2	12	14*	10
N Alternative Medium business	3	3	12	12	12
SOS Alternative Small to large (especially Mfg)	>3.5	>3.5	>14	>14**	>14**

clothes, heavy houses or heavy agriculture. The climate was warm all year round and wild food was plentiful. That has become something of a curse in the sense of creating limited time horizons with regard to delaying gratification. The concern of the African Development Bank for long-term development is well-placed. Africa is less concerned with long-term development than any other of the four world regions, partly because it has more land mass and more people along the equator than does Asia or Latin America, and certainly a lot more than eastern Europe, which is a long way from the equator. Eastern Europe may be confronted by almost the opposite problem, where it is so cold that people are incapable of doing much of anything. At the equator people are incapable of doing anything because in the past there has been so little need to do things.

One point to emphasize strongly is that this is not climatic determinism, because human beings are quite capable of overcoming whatever climate they happen to live in. Climate may have shaped things in prehistoric times, but modern people can live luxuriously in the Antarctic if they want to do so, or on the equator in central Africa. We have refrigerators for central Africa and we have effective heating devices for the Antarctic. It is a matter, to a considerable extent, of public policy stimulating the use of appropriate technology.

The term 'appropriate technology' is sometimes used by the backpackers to mean virtually no technology at all. It should be used to mean that what is good technology for the Antarctic may not be good technology for central Africa, but that humans have developed technologies that can deal with any climate or any kind of geographical factor. People could live luxuriously at the top of the Himalayas or well below sea level, as long as they are not under water. If necessary, we could even live under water and pump oxygen in, but that is rather unnecessary.

POVERTY AND SOCIAL POLICY

Public aid

Evaluating policies toward poverty and public aid

Reformed ADC (Aid to Dependent Children) includes (1) allowing recipients to keep a certain number of earned dollars per month as a work incentive, (2) allowing an impoverished family that has a father and mother present to receive aid, (3) providing for minimum levels on a nationwide basis, and (4) providing at least minimum due process. Minimum due process includes (a) being notified of wrongdoing, (b) a right to call witnesses, (c) a right to cross-examine opposition witnesses, (d) a judge who is not the complaining person, and (e) possibly a right to an appointed attorney.

NIT (negative income tax) involves a check in the mail to families whose annual income is below the poverty level. The amount of the monthly checks would supplement other income so as to bring the family up to a high percentage of the line between poverty and non-poverty. For example, a family of four is considered to be in poverty if their annual income is below $16,000. Bringing them up to 90 per cent level would mean bringing them up to $14,400. NIT is especially designed to eliminate the intrusiveness of the required caseworker. The approach through Old Age and Survivor's Insurance (OASI) in the United States would involve expanding the concept of survivor to include a child deserted by the family breadwinner, when the breadwinner is not necessarily deceased. The children's allowance involves a certain amount of money paid each month to each child until about age 18. This approach and OASI both apply to wealthy children as well as poor children, so removing the stigma of receiving aid.

The idea of job opportunities via subsidies to welfare recipients and employers relates mainly to upgrading skills and employability of welfare recipients. It also relates to subsidizing employers to be willing to hire such people, possibly through minimum wage vouchers. See Table 1.8.

A simplified SOS analysis of welfare policy

The notes to Table 1.1 are also applicable here. This simplified table eliminates the neutral goal of stimulating work.

Table 1.8   Evaluating policies toward public aid

Criteria Alternatives	C Goal Reduce taxes	N Goal Stimulate work	L Goal Dignity of poor	N Total (neutral weights)	L Total (liberal weights)	C Total (conservative weights)
C1 Alternative No public aid	4	3	1	16	13	19*

C2 Alternative
    Unreformed
    public aid
	4	2	2	16	14	18

L1 Alternative
    Aid regardless
    of need – OASI
	1	2	4	14	17	11

L2 Alternative
    Less restricted
    aid – NIT
	2	2	4	16	18*	14

N Alternative
    Compromise
    reforms
	3	3	3	18	18	18

SOS Alternative
    Work program,
    subsidies for
    employer &
    welfare recip.
	4	5	4	26	26**	26**

SOS Alternative SOS and N	3.5	5	4	25	25.5	24.5

The present table combines the conservative alternatives under the concept of ADC (Aid to Dependent Children) which is the main present form of public aid. The table also combines various liberal alternatives under the concept of reformed public aid. The various SOS components are combined under the concept of jobs.

Both conservatives and liberals are increasingly supporting the idea of jobs for welfare recipients. For conservatives, the motivation is partly the reduction of taxes for paying welfare, and the theory that welfare recipients should work, regardless of how useful the jobs might be. For liberals, the motivation is partly to increase the income and dignity of the poor. Whatever the motivation, the results are more programs to enable welfare recipients to obtain jobs. See Table 1.9.

Table 1.9   A simplified SOS analysis of welfare policy

Criteria Alternatives	C Goal Cut taxpayer burden	L Goal Dignity	N Total (neutral weights)	L Total (liberal weights)	C Total (conservative weights)
C Alternative ADC	4	2	12	10	14*

L Alternative
  Reformed
  public aid
	2	4	12	14*	10

N Alternative In between	3	3	12	12	12
SOS Alternative Jobs	5	5	20	20**	20**

Dealing with poverty due to not working

The conservative approach is to terminate welfare if the recipient does not obtain a job to partly offset or supplement the welfare payments. The liberal approach in the past has been to provide welfare without a work require-ment. The neutral position may provide for only partial termination. This means if a family of four receives $14,000, and the breadwinner earns $4,400, then partial termination would mean the family would only get $10,000. Another neutral position is have a work requirement but only where no preschool children are present.

The SOS alternative emphasizes the upgrading of the skills of people on welfare so that they can qualify for better jobs. There may also be an emphasis on providing wage supplements or subsidies for potential employ-ers to hire qualified people on welfare and provide them with on-the-job training. See Table 1.10.

Allocating an anti-poverty budget between education and public aid

Traditional liberals tend to endorse public aid as being especially important in dealing with poverty, as compared to conservatives who tend to endorse work-oriented education. Both may favor education or training over public aid as of 1999, but conservatives are less sympathetic to public aid than liberals.

Likewise, on the matter of goals, both conservatives and liberals may seek job opportunities and at least a minimum standard of living for the

Table 1.10 Dealing with poverty due to not working

Criteria \ Alternatives	C Goal Work	L Goal Decent income	N Total (neutral weights)	L Total (liberal weights)	C Total (conservative weights)
C Alternative Cut off welfare if don't work	4	2	12	10	14*
L Alternative Provide welfare, no strings	2	4	12	14*	10
N Alternative Some strings	3	3	12	12	12
SOS Alternative Upgrade skills of males & females	>3.5	>3.5	>12	>14**	>14**

poor. Relatively speaking, however, conservatives put more emphasis on job opportunities than liberals, and liberals put more emphasis on maintaining a minimum standard of living than conservatives.

Public aid may be more capable of providing a minimum standard of living than education, at least in the short run. The relations shown in the first column of Table 1.11 indicate that public aid does about twice as well on that goal. Education, on the other hand, may be much more capable of providing job opportunities than public aid. The relation shown in the second column of the table indicates that education does about three times as well on that goal.

If we were allocating only on the basis of the first goal, it would be logical to allocate 33 per cent of the budget to education and 67 per cent to public aid. If we were allocating only on the basis of the second goal, it would be logical to allocate 75 per cent to education and 25 per cent to public aid. If we were allocating on the basis of both goals equally, it would be logical to allocate the midpoint or average of 54 per cent to education and 46 per cent to public aid.

Using the liberal weights or multipliers, we would multiply the first goal by 3 in order to calculate the weighted averages shown in the liberal column of 44 per cent and 56 per cent. Using the conservative weights or multipliers, we would multiple the second goal by 3 in order to calculate the weighted averages shown in the conservative column of 65 per cent and 35 per cent.

Table 1.11   Allocating an anti-poverty budget to education and public aid

Criteria / Alternatives	L-Goal Minimum standard of living C=1 L=3	C-Goal Job opportunities C=3 L=1	N Total (neutral weights)	L Total (liberal weights)	C Total (conservative weights)	SOS
C Alternative Education	1 (33%)	3 (75%)	$108 (54%)	$88 (44%)	$130 (65%)	$131 (54%)
L Alternative Public Aid	2 (67%)	1 ($25)	$92 (46%)	$112 (56%)	$70 (35%)	$113 (46%)
Totals	3 (100%)	4 (100%)	$200 (100%)	$200 (100%)	$200 (100%)	$244 (100%)

The SOS column seeks to exceed the $130 that conservatives would allocate to education, and simultaneously exceed the $112 that liberals would allocate to public aid. Doing so means finding an extra $44 beyond the original $200 budget in order to arrive at those SOS allocations where both conservatives and liberals come out ahead of their best initial expectations simultaneously.

Another SOS approach would involve working within the $200 budget but increasing the effectiveness of education on either goal or increasing the effectiveness of public aid on either goal. Doing so is likely to mean more achievement on the first goal than the $130 allocation conservatives would provide, and more achievement on the second goal of public aid than the $112 allocation liberals would provide.

VA benefits policy: an SOS perspective

Conservatives approve of relatively low benefits for veterans in comparison to the benefits that liberals approve or advocate. The main conservative goal seems to be to keep taxes down. The main liberal goal is equity or fairness to those who have made sacrifices in defending the country.

The SOS for veterans seeking benefits might be to emphasize the upgrading of skills in order to provide better job opportunities. Doing so would be of more value to most veterans than having higher benefits in terms of health care or pensions. The job opportunities can also raise the national income, which provides a bigger tax base and thus allows for a possible lowering of the tax rate. See Table 1.12.

Table 1.12   VA benefits policy: an SOS perspective

Criteria / Alternatives	C Goal Low taxes	L Goal Equity	N Total (neutral weights)	L Total (liberal weights)	C Total (conservative weights)
C Alternative Low benefits	4	2	12	10	14*
L Alternative High benefits	2	4	12	14*	10
N Alternative In between	3	3	12	12	12
SOS Alternative Job opportunities	4	4	16	16**	16**

Education

Evaluating policies toward elementary and secondary education

The basic issue here is one of educational integration. It was found in the Coleman Report that peer-group interaction may be more important in determining education achievement than school facilities and teacher competence within the ranges that tend to exist. Bringing low-income white or black children into contact with middle-class children is more important in raising ambition levels than bringing black children into contact with white children.

The current conservative position is opposed to segregation by law, but is willing to tolerate segregation as a result of neighborhood housing patterns. The liberal position tends to advocate busing to enable poor children, especially black children, to go to school with white children. The neutral position is for public policy to play an active role by way of spending more money than has been spent in the past among inner-city schools. This tends to improve buildings, but they are less important than teachers and, especially, fellow students.

An SOS alternative may involve three parts. First would be a program of housing vouchers designed to facilitate economic class integration by enabling low-income children to move into better neighborhoods and thus attend economically integrated schools without busing. The second part involves bonus pay for teaching in the inner-city schools. The amount of the bonus would be just enough to equalize the average seniority between inner-city schools and outlying or suburban schools. The bonus money would probably have to come from federal funds, since teachers' unions would successfully object to using local funds to pay teachers' salaries on any basis other than the degree of advanced education and seniority.

The third part involves supplements to bring poor school districts up to a minimum threshold across each state and across the country. Such upgrading funds would probably also have to come from the federal government, since most states seem unwilling to appropriate the money, and most state and federal courts are unwilling to require them to do so. See Table 1.13.

Combining public and private higher education

The SOS alternative of combining public and private higher education is well represented by the American higher education system. Many major US universities are *state* institutions. Major private universities also receive large amounts of government money in the form of grants, scholarships and loans to students. Many major US universities are *private* institutions. Even the state universities are increasingly charging tuition. They are also increasing their admission standards, which makes them closer to elite private universities. The state universities are also increasingly relying on corporate and alumni contributions to supplement taxes.

Thus, the private universities are heavily state-supported and the state universities are heavily private-supported. They coexist at both a high-quality level and a lower level. This is a good example of the conservative and liberal alternatives flourishing simultaneously. See Table 1.14.

Adult education

The conservative position on federal funding involves a minimum of expenditures for adult education and on-the-job training (OJT), although there is no objection to the field houses of local parks or local schools providing adult education, or to private companies providing OJT. Liberals would like to see substantially increased federal expenditures for both adult education and OJT.

Conservatives might be pleased by a well-organized federal program that increases GNP and the tax base, and thereby reduces the tax rate, while at the same time it can be easily administered. Liberals might also be pleased with such a program, as contrasted to merely increasing expenditures without having a well-organized program.

A well-organized program needs such things as (1) plans regarding what kinds of skills need to be improved and how they can be improved, (2) monitoring of the funds that are made available so as to better ensure that the

Table 1.13 Evaluating policies toward elementary and secondary education

Criteria / Alternatives	N Goal Graduating high school	C Goal Reduce taxpayer burden: short-term	C Goal Reduce taxpayer burden: long-term	L Goal Minimum % for all neigh-borhoods	N Goal Political feasibility	L Goal Reduce middle class flight	N Total (neutral weights)	L Total (liberal weights)	C Total (conservative weights)
C Alternative Do nothing	2	5	1	1	2.5	2	27	24	30
L Alternative Busing	4	2.5	4	2.5	2	2	34	32	36
N Alternative Compensatory education	3.5	2	4	3.5	3	3.5	39	40*	38*
SOS Alternative Pay incentives, rent supplements & state supplements	5	1.5	4.5	4	2	4	42	44**	40**

Table 1.14 Combining public and private higher education

Criteria / Alternatives	L Goal Highly educated	L Goal Produce knowledge	C Goal Reduce tax cost	L Goal Equity	N Total (neutral weights)	L Total (liberal weights)	C Total (conservative weights)
C Alternative Private schools	2	2	4	1	18	19	17*
L Alternative State-owned schools	4	4	1	4	26	37*	15
N Alternative Some private	3	3	2.5	3	23	29.5	16.5
SOS Alternative Public $ to private/private $ to public	5	5	2	5	34	47**	21**

funds go toward achieving those plans and goals, and (3) being job-oriented in the sense of being designed to lead to specific needed and available jobs at the company where one is already working or at other expanding companies. The funds for such an OJT program can mainly be obtained from employers for upgrading their own workers. Federal funds can also be had for obtaining new technologies that are relevant to the new training. See Table 1.15.

Table 1.15   Adult education and on-the-job training

Criteria Alternatives	L Goal Increase GNP	C Goal Reduce tax burden	N Goal Adminis- trative feasibility	N Total (neutral weights)	L Total (liberal weights)	C Total (conservative weights)
C Alternative Keep as is	2	4	4	20	18	22*

L Alternative
   Money for OJT
   and adult ed.
	4	2	2	16	18*	14

N Alternative Middling	3	3	3	18	18	18

SOS Alternative
   1   Plans
   2   Strings
   3   Job-oriented
	5	5	5	30	30**	30**

A simplified SOS on elementary and secondary education

A recent new education proposal is contracting out the running of the public schools in a city or school district to a private enterprise firm. The contract provides that the firm receives payment equal to 90 per cent of the previous tax costs. The contract also provides for various standards designed to determine how well the students are learning at the beginning of the contract and at the end of each academic year. The contract can be awarded through open bidding, and is up for renewal or rebidding every few years. This arrangement may improve the quality of the schools, but generally does nothing for economic class integration of the students.

Another recent proposal is to provide vouchers that would enable public school students to go to other public schools, private schools or parochial schools. Such a system may generate some integration, but it is likely to decrease the quality of the public schools. There may also be a constitutional question if parochial schools are included.

A neutral goal could be added that relates to the quality of the schools. Both liberals and conservatives endorse this goal. They differ in this context mainly over the question of busing to provide for racial or economic integration. The quality of the schools is not so affected by busing. The quality may be enhanced through contracting out, and downgraded by encouraging the better students to go to private or parochial schools with government-provided vouchers. See Table 1.16.

Table 1.16   A simplified SOS on elementary and secondary education

Criteria Alternatives	L Goal Integration	C Goal Neighbor- hood schools	N Total (neutral weights)	L Total (liberal weights)	C Total (conservative weights)
C Alternative Do nothing	2	4	12	10	14*
L Alternative Busing	4	2	12	14*	10

N Alternative
  Compensatory
  education
	3	1	8	10	6

SOS Alternative
  Integration-
  oriented rent
  supplements with
  temporary
  subsidies for
  teachers and
  facilities
	5	5	20	20**	20**

Population control

Super-optimizing analysis applied to China's excess population problem

Relevant causes of excess children in the Chinese population context include the following:

1 the need for adult children to care for elderly parents, which could be better handled through social security and/or jobs for the elderly;

2   the need for extra children to allow for child mortality, which could be better handled through better child health care;
3   the need for male children in view of their greater value, which could be better handled through providing more opportunities for females;
4   the lack of concern for the cost of sending children to college, which could be better handled through a more vigorous program of recruiting rural children to college.

It is not a super-optimum solution to provide monetary rewards and penalties in this context because:

1   the monetary rewards for having fewer children enable a family to then have more children;
2   the monetary punishments for having more children stimulate a family to have still more family to provide offsetting income;
3   the monetary rewards and punishments are made meaningless by the simultaneous policies which are increasing prosperity in rural China.

See Table 1.17.

Table 1.17   Super-optimizing analysis applied to the Chinese excess population problem

Criteria / Alternatives	C Goal Small families	L Goal Reproductive freedom	N Total (neutral weights)	L Total (liberal weights)	C Total (conservative weights)
C Alternative Strict one-child policy	4	2	12	10	14*
L Alternative Flexible on family size	2	4	12	14*	10
N Alternative One child with exceptions allowed	3	3	12	12	12
SOS Alternative Reduce causes of excess children & productivity	5	5	20	20**	20**

The birth control controversy

See the more detailed section entitled 'Evaluating Alternative Birth Control Methods' for a set of ideas that are also applicable here. Those ideas deal in particular with the way the skin implant scores well on seven of the nine goals in Table 1.14.

The liberal goal of reducing births (see Table 1.18) only refers to unwanted births; liberals have been at the forefront of advocating new forms of reproduction to enable couples to conceive who otherwise cannot do so. The conservative goal of reducing oversexuality refers to becoming so obsessed or concerned with sex that one cannot be so productive in society in terms of one's responsibilities for obtaining an education, holding a job and being a good citizen. It is interesting to note that reducing oversexuality was also a goal of communist societies in eastern Europe, although it seems to be more of a conservative goal.

Table 1.18 The birth control controversy

Criteria / Alternatives	L Goal Reduce births	C Goal Reduce over-sexuality	N Goal Reduce teenage pregnancy	N Total (neutral weights)	L Total (liberal weights)	C Total (conservative weights)
C Alternative Abstinence	2	4	2	16	14	18*
L Alternative Pills & devices	4	2	2	16	18*	14
N Alternative Mixture	3	3	2	16	16	16
SOS Alternative Skin implant	5	2	5	24	27**	21**

Reducing teenage pregnancy is an especially important problem, regardless of whether the pregnancy was desired or whether it came from oversexuality or a single incident. It is an important problem because it can destroy lives with regard to (1) the teenage mother, who drops out of school and may become a chronic welfare recipient, (2) the baby, who may grow up in a home environment that is less conductive to future success than that of a baby born to an adult, and sometimes (3) a teenage father, who may be prematurely saddled with responsibilities, including many years of paternity payments.

Evaluating alternative birth control methods

The skin implant is highly effective because it is always present without requiring any special action. It is like an airbag in the context of car safety, as contrasted to other devices which require special action to be effective.

The skin implant also scores high marks on being easy to use, capable of being developed for both males and females, inexpensive, good for long intervals, reversible and safe. The present form does not have Catholic Church acceptability, but Catholic doctrines on birth control do not seem to be widely followed. The skin implant can facilitate non-reproductive sex, but its advantages outweigh its disadvantages, although this depends on how the criteria are weighted.

The skin implant may be especially valuable for preventing teenage pregnancies and abortion, since it can be made more effective for five years from puberty (at about age 13) to adulthood (at about age 18). Abstinence may be a better way to avoid teenage pregnancy, but it does not generally seem to be a realistically feasible alternative. The skin implant may be considered less than ideal by virtue of its facilitating non-reproductive sex, but its use seems better than all the costs that are associated with teenage pregnancy. See Table 1.19.

Families and children

Evaluating grounds for divorce

Incompatibility without fault is now the prevailing grounds for divorce in all 50 states in the United States. It is in conformity with public opinion, honest hearings, free choice, avoiding the error of wrongly staying married, and facilitating remarriage. On the other hand, no-fault divorce does not score well on avoiding the error of wrongly rushing into a divorce. It is contrary to the idea of promoting two parents in every family, and the idea of retaining all lawful marriages. See Table 1.20.

A simplified SOS on abortion

See the previous more detailed section on 'Evaluating Policies Toward Abortion' for a set of ideas that are also applicable here. The table below uses the main conservative goal of not killing a fetus and the main liberal goal of not killing a pregnant mother in a back-alley abortion.

The other two goals are the relatively conservative goal of reducing tax costs and the relatively liberal goal of equity for the poor. Those goals

Table 1.19   Evaluating alternative birth control methods

Criteria / Alternatives	L Goal Effective	L Goal Easy to use	L Goal Males & females	N Goal Inexpensive	N Goal Long intervals	N Goal Reversible	N Goal Safety	C Goal Church acceptability	C Goal Reduce non-productive sex	N Total (neutral weights)	L Total (liberal weights)	C Total (conservative weights)
C Alternative Abstinence, rhythm	2	2	4	4	2	4	4	4	4	60	60	60*
L Alternative Pills & devices	3	3	4	3	2	4	2	2	2	50	56	44
N Alternative Mixture SOS Alternative	2.5	2.5	4	3.5	2	4	3	3	3	55	58*	52
Skin implant	5	5	5	5	5	5	3	2	2	74	85**	63**

Table 1.20 Evaluating grounds for divorce

Alternatives \ Criteria	N Goal Equal public opinion	N Goal More honest hearings	N Goal Free choice	C Goal Fewer wrong divorces	L Goal Fewer wrongly staying married	N Goal More two parents	N goal Less taxpayer cost	N Goal More remarriage	N Total (neutral weights)	L Total (liberal weights)	C Total (conservative weights)
C1 Alternative No divorce allowed	1	1	1	5	1	5	5	1	40	36	44
C2 Alternative Adultery div. only	2	2	2	4	2	4	3	2	42	40	44
L1 Alternative Phys. cruelty required	3	3	3	3	3	3	3	3	48	48	48
L2 Alternative Mental cruelty	4	4	4	1	4	2	3	4	52	55*	49*
SOS Alternative Incompat. without fault	5	5	5	1	5	1	4	5	62	66*	58*

Note:
An additional conservative goal can be added of seeking to retain all lawful marriages. The alternative of no divorce allowed would score high on such a goal. The alternative of allowing divorces for mental cruelty would score low on such a goal. And so would the SOS alternative of allowing divorces for incompatibility without fault. The SOS alternative, however, wins by a big enough margin that it can afford to lose a bit to the more conservative alternatives and still come out the overall winner on both the conservative totals and the liberal totals. This is an example of sensitivity analysis whereby one sees how sensitive the tentative results are to adding an additional goal.

occur more when the issue is whether abortions should be covered by public aid or other government money. Even under those circumstances, the goals that relate to saving fetuses and saving pregnant mothers are more important.

Another pair of goals are symbolic goals that relate to effects on recreational sex and women's liberation. They include the conservative goal of prohibiting abortions because allowing them encourages sex for nonreproductive purposes. They also include the liberal goal of allowing abortions, at least in the first trimester, in order to communicate the idea that women should be able to control their own bodies, at least up to the time of a viable fetus.

POVERTY AND TECHNOLOGY POLICY

Housing

An SOS analysis of housing for the poor

The conservative approach to housing for the poor is to leave it up to the marketplace (see Table 1.21). The liberal approach is to provide for public housing that is owned or subsidized by the government and rented to low-income people at rents below the market level. The neutral position is to budget more for public housing than conservatives would, but less than liberals would.

When it was first developed in the 1930s, public housing meant large projects owned by the government. In the 1960s, liberals turned against such projects because they became unpleasant places in which to live, given the congestion of so many poor people and juveniles in a small area. The major modifications involved requiring future public housing to be low-rise rather than high-rise and to give the tenants more control over the management process.

In the context of housing for the poor, conservatives are interested in keeping tax expenditures down and in aiding private sector housing. The liberal goal is decent housing for the poor. The marketplace may be able to provide some housing for the poor, but not above a minimum level of decency and quality.

The SOS alternative might be rent supplements or vouchers. These involve, for example, a low-income recipient paying $300 toward a $400 apartment and the government providing a $100 voucher to make up the difference. The voucher can only be used for private sector housing. This system involves less tax expenditure than traditional public housing, and it

Table 1.21 Evaluating policies for providing housing for the poor

Criteria / Alternatives	L Goal Decent housing for poor	C Goal Stimulate housing development	N Goal Reduce tax costs	L Goal Equity race & class	N Total (neutral weights)	L Total (liberal weights)	C Total (conservative weights)
C Alternative Marketplace	1	4	4	2	22	21	23*
L Alternative Large-scale public housing	3.1	3	1	2	18.2	20.3	16.1
N Alternative Low rise public housing, condos & home ownership	4	3.5	2	4	27	31.5?	22.5
SOS Alternative Rent supplements & skills upgrade	5	5	2	5	34	39**	29**

Note:
? The former liberal alternative of large-scale public housing is being abandoned by liberals because of its adverse relations to goals that liberals formerly thought benefitted from large-scale public housing.

does put money into the private sector marketplace. It can also provide better quality housing than public housing.

Along with rent supplements can go a program for upgrading the skills of recipients, who can then increase their incomes and eventually no longer need the rent supplements. The skills upgrading may be especially important for the homeless, who may have virtually no income.

The voucher system also has the extra benefit of facilitating economic class integration. A requirement in using the vouchers might be that one has to use them in neighborhoods that are above the concentrated poverty level, so facilitating school integration in terms of low-income children going to school with middle-class children. This also stimulates ambition on the part of the parents more than living in public housing.

Disputes between conflicting urban economic classes with international implications: landlords versus tenants

Rent supplements   The housing problem easily lends itself to a super-optimum solution where both the landlords and tenants are better off through a voucher system which liberals and conservatives now endorse. This is a good example of a program that is in effect, rather than one that just sounds like a good idea for the future. Nearly all these programs are in effect to some extent, including housing vouchers, but not enough. It is far less expensive to provide a housing voucher supplement than it is to provide public housing, crime costs, welfare costs and lost GNP. The emphasis on the Reagan administration on reducing costs, though, failed to come forth with the money for the rent supplements, even though the Reagan administration talked about rent supplements as the ideal way of dealing with housing for the poor.

On the matter of land use, conservatives (except the extremists) have long since accepted the idea of zoning. Conservatives should do so more readily than liberals, since they are the property owners who will be most affected by having a glue factory or a stable moved next door to property they own. Opposition comes from only a small segment of highly mercenary conservatives who would like to be able to sell their house to a glue factory regardless of what it does to the neighborhood. There are also some conservatives who are ideologically opposed to all rules and are basically anarchists, rather than conservatives. They are likely to be opposed to basic zoning laws.

Points to note on the housing problem   This is a good example of a situation where both liberals and conservatives have been wrong. Liberals were wrong in advocating low-cost high-rise public housing. It has turned out to be very expensive to maintain, even with the low cost to build; it is especially undesirable for raising children; it has also resulted in highly segregated clustered housing. Conservatives were wrong in thinking that the marketplace would remedy the problem. It has resulted in the United States having the worst homeless problem of any industrialized country. The problem would be even worse if it were not for a hodgepodge of government shelters to supplement the marketplace.

The SOS solution is rent supplements. It has the potential for working well and is endorsed by both conservatives and liberals. Liberals like rent supplements because they preserve the dignity of poor people; they result in racial integration and economic class integration; they result in adequate affordable housing for the poor. Conservatives like rent supplements because they encourage being a landlord; they rely heavily on the marketplace, with no government ownership and minimal government activity; they stimulate ambition on the part of poor people. The big problem has been the lack of money to have a well-financed rent supplement program.

Home ownership for the poor did not work out well with private real estate administration. There was a great deal of corruption in the assessing of the value of property, to get the government to pay off more than the property was worth on the foreclosure; there was deception on a grand scale of potential owners regarding maintenance costs, leading to excessive payments and foreclosures.

The problem of the new homelessness   This is not a totally new problem. One section of the homeless consists of people who formerly lived on 'skid rows' that were less visible. Skid rows have now been wiped out by a good deal of expansion of downtown areas and urban renewal. The new element is that a good many of the homeless are people who are not winos, but aged people or even young mothers with little children, who cannot afford adequate housing. There are also people who, back in the days of mental institutions, might have been institutionalized instead of being handled on an out-patient drug therapy basis.

The key problems or the key remedies relate to the following.

1   In the case of the unemployed skid row types, there is a possibility of providing some educational employment opportunities, with the right kind of subsidies to them and potential employers.
2   In the case of people who are simply impoverished, the rent supplement program does not work so well because they have no adequate incomes to supplement. They, too, need skills development and job opportunities, although it is a different type of skills development from that of skid row types. If they have children, it means providing for daycare.

3   The third category, the mentally disturbed, can also benefit from skills development and jobs that they can handle. All three programs require money: not just money for housing, but money for skills development and job opportunities. That is more important in the long run than housing, but short-run housing is also needed.

An important point, though, is that these three categories of people may have virtually no income at all and thus the rent supplement idea is not so meaningful, even if it is a 100 per cent rent supplement. The drawback with the 100 per cent supplement is that it is only a short-term solution. We do not want to be putting people on a 100 per cent dole for the rest of their lives if they have some skills that can be developed and that are marketable, which virtually everybody has. One finds no homeless people who are quadriplegics, incapable of doing anything. Homeless people frequently have well above average stamina if they can survive sleeping on sidewalks and in parks. It is a shame that such stamina and survival ability isn't put to more constructive use.

Health care

Evaluating health care policies

Doing nothing means leaving health care to the marketplace. Poor people and most middle-class people cannot afford the expensive marketplace charges. Thus doing nothing may lack political feasibility because of voter opposition and the inequities.

Socialized medicine means that most doctors are salaried employees of the government, providing health care in government hospitals. Such a system may lack economic feasibility because it is so expensive, especially with a lack of economic incentives to keep costs down. Government reimbursement is the system under Medicaid, for the poor, and Medicare, for the aged. It is also highly expensive, handling reimbursement on a case-by-case basis.

It made more sense prior to about 1980 to talk about only poor people having a problem paying for reasonable health care. The cost of health care since 1980 has become high enough so that it is a serious problem for middle class people as well. The increase is partly due to (1) newer more expensive forms of diagnosis or treatment such as cat scans and MRIs; (2) a greater quantity and percentage of elderly middle class people who have many health care problems; and (3) the higher costs of medical administration due to insurance bookkeeping, Health Management Organization (HMO) administration, and nursing homes. The most efficient system might be for groups of doctors to agree to provide full medical service for a flat insurance premium of about $2,000 a year. The doctors then, in effect, pay out of their own pockets all expenses per patient above $2,000. That is the HMO insurance system.

As of 1999, a better SOS alternative might be to privatize health care for the poor, the aged and the middle class, but to provide vouchers that can be used to pay for all or part of the insurance in health management organizations or other types of organized clinics. Doing this can provide universal coverage while keeping costs down through competition and insurance per patient rather than per case. See Table 1.22.

Health care policy: an SOS perspective

Medicare and Medicaid involve individuals who go to whatever doctor will service them, with the government then paying all or a high percentage of each case-by-case bill. Such a system tends to be much more expensive than the system of salaried government doctors and is inequitable if it only covers the poor and the aged.

Government-owned hospitals or salaried government doctors tend to be inefficient owing to lack of competition. Such a system is also inequitable if it only applies to veterans or poor people, since health care expenses can no longer be easily afforded by lower middle-class people or middle-class people in general.

Subsidized HMOs in this context means that the government provides health care vouchers to poor people, aged people and middle-class people who can qualify. Such vouchers supplement the premiums which HMOs require in order to provide HMO coverage. The HMOs compete with each other, thereby generating lower prices and better quality service. The money for the vouchers can come mainly from employers to cover their own employees, with a provision for covering the self-employed and the non-employed.

Energy

Providing heat for the poor

The problem here is how to provide heat for the poor in the winter time when poor people cannot afford the heating bills which power companies charge. The conservative alternative of leaving it up to the marketplace is not likely to provide adequate heat for the poor if this means selling heat

Table 1.22   Evaluating health care policies

Criteria / Alternatives	C Goal Expand medical profession	L Goal Quality of care	N Goal Reduce tax cost	L Goal Access and equity	N Goal Political feasibility	N Total (neutral weights)	L Total (liberal weights)	C Total (conservative weights)
C Alternative Do nothing	4	1	5	1	1	24	22	26
L Alternative Socialized medicine	3	3	1	3.5	2	25	28.5	21.5
N Alternative Private enterprise with govt reimbursement	4	3	2	4	4	34	37*	31*
SOS Alternative Govt doctors for poor, medicare supplements	4	4	3	4	4	38	42**	34**

47

below cost. The marketplace, however, may stimulate more efficiency than a socialistic power company that is tax-supported, and more efficiency than a regulated utility that is guaranteed a profit in return for accepting regulation.

Socialistic power companies can provide heat below cost as part of their equity obligations, just as the post office delivers mail to rural houses, charging less than the actual cost of the mail delivery. Private ownership with price regulation may lead to inefficiency because the government guarantees a profit in return for artificially low prices. These prices may be lower than those of the marketplace, but still not low enough to provide adequate heat for the poor.

An SOS alternative might be to provide poor people with energy vouchers whereby they can supplement what they can afford to pay to the power company. These vouchers take into consideration both the prices of the power company and the ability to pay of the low-income consumer. The voucher system does not interfere with efficient private profit-making companies, but it is capable of providing adequate heat for the poor. See Table 1.23.

Table 1.23   Providing heat to the poor

Criteria / Alternatives	C Goal Efficient operation	L Goal Heat for the poor	N Total (neutral weights)	L Total (liberal weights)	C Total (conservative weights)
C Alternative Marketplace	2	2	8	8	8
L Alternative Socialistic power companies	4?	2	12	14*	10
N Alternative Private ownership with regulation	3?	2	10	9	11*
SOS Alternative Renewable franchise with competition	>3.5	>3.5	>14	>14**	>14**

Note:
It is questionable whether either socialistic or capitalistic power companies can be efficient if they are monopolies. When customers have no choice between electric power companies, then the electricity sellers have little incentive to be efficient with regard to adopting the latest technologies or to reducing prices to attract customers.

POVERTY AND POLITICAL POLICY

Electoral reform

Electoral reform

Low-income people need to be empowered to shift more for themselves and be less dependent on public-aid systems. Both conservative and liberals use concepts like empowerment and power to the people. Conservatives sometimes use such concepts in an overly paternalistic way. Liberals sometimes use such concepts in an unnecessarily frightening revolutionary way. Both sides are likely to agree that enfranchising poor people (at least in theory) is a good thing for society and especially democracy. In the context of voting, that means making it easier for qualified low-income people to vote as a minimum form of political participation. They are frequently in effect disenfranchised because they find it more difficult to register at the time of voting, as is done in some countries and states. Low-income people also find it difficult to lose time from work in order to vote. A simple solution is to make election day a holiday as some countries do, or at least to hold major elections on Sunday or on multiple days. One should also be allowed to vote at one's home precinct, workplace, precinct, or any precinct, so long as one passes the test of not having previously been exposed to a container of invisible ink while voting. If more low-income people participate in politics and voting, then more public policies would be adopted that relate to job facilitators, education, and merit treatment. See Table 1.24.

Conservative and liberal positions

The United States does not look good relative to the rest of the world when it comes to voter turnout. There are roughly two hundred million adults, of which approximately half are registered to vote, but only about half of those registered to vote actually do. That's about 50 million. That means if just 26 million out of the 50 million vote for a certain candidate for president, that candidate gets in. This can be a landslide if each state is hotly contested, even though it is only 26 million out of 200 million possible voters. It is not so good when, in effect, 12 per cent of the population can decide who will sit in the Oval Office. The U.S. is not undemocratic in the sense of prohibiting people from voting, but less democratic than it should be in the sense of facilitating voter turnout.

The true conservative goal might be to promote the election of conservative candidates but they are not going to say that. What they actually say, is that they want to avoid multiple voting. They do not want any schemes that

Table 1.24   Electoral reform

Criteria / Alternatives	C Non-eligible registration and voting	L Increase registration and voting
C Leave as is	+	−
L Postcard registration or tinker with motor voter	−	+
N Precinct registration, permanent registration	0	0

SOS
1. On site same day
     or census
     registration
2. Vote anywhere
3. Extended times
4. Invisible ink
	++	++

will allow cheating at the polls. Liberals, on the other hand, are very concerned about people who do not vote, so they want to decrease non-voting by adults who could be eligible. The conservative position promotes a decrease in multiple voting a number of ways. One of the most extreme positions is to purge the voter rolls every ten years and make people register again. This would guard against individuals still being present on the voter rolls who have moved or died. It greatly decreases the number of people who register when you have to do it again and again. Having advanced registration may make a difference with regard to decreasing multiple voting, but it also decreases voting in general. Liberals also want advanced registration, but they want to make the process easier. They support ideas like postcard registration, or registration at the time you get your driver's license – so called motor-vehicle legislation. They also support keeping the polls open a few hours later to make it easier to vote on election day. Unfortunately, the liberal solutions in total would not make much of a difference as more fundamental change is necessary.

A win-win alternative

What really needs to be adopted is the kind of system presently being used in many countries of the world, including Canada, South Africa, Mexico, and Mozambique, and states such as Wisconsin and Minnesota. It involves a few innovations. First of all, there is no requirement of advance registration. You can register in advance if you want to, but you can also register on-site, the day of election. Many people who don't vote on election day because they did not register in advance would probably vote if on-site registration on the day of election were possible. Also, if elections were to be moved to a non-working day instead of a Tuesday, more people would be able to participate. In catholic countries like Italy, France, and Mexico, election day is on a Sunday, when people don't work. Other nations hold their elections over a couple of days. Another improvement would allow people to vote in either their home precinct or district or their work precinct or district, or to even allow them to vote in any precinct provided there is some way of checking to make sure they haven't voted in another. Multiple precinct voting can make a large difference in voter turnout.

With all these facilitators, however, the conservative problem of multiple voting rises again. The way that problem is solved in South Africa, Mexico, Mozambique, and other countries, is by having voters dip their hand into a bowl of invisible ink. If you show up at a polling place anytime in the day after that, including your original polling place, your hand is viewed under an ultraviolet lamp, and if it shows that you have already voted, you are denied the right to vote again, and can possibly be arrested. The invisible ink method works much better than asking people to sign their names, because names can be forged much more easily than hands. It is a good example of a win–win solution because it would substantially decrease multiple voting and substantially decrease non-voting.

On-site registration, the non-working election day, multiple precincts, and the invisible ink method all have a political feasibility problem. This problem is political in the sense that it is very difficult to get such a measure through Congress or through a state legislature. This is because one political party is likely to have enough strength to block it, namely the party which thinks it will suffer as a result of expanded voter turnout. As long as it has enough power to stop these measures, they will never be adopted. If, however, they ever were adopted, they are not likely to be repealed. There is a kind of ratchet effect on new facilitators once they are adopted, because the party in power will look bad if it decreases the ability of people to register and vote. These measures are likely to be adopted when the Democrats have enough influence in the Congress or in the various state legislatures. The traditional thinking is that the Democratic party benefits more from expanded voter registration and turnout than the Republican party, due to the fact that a higher percentage of non-voters consist of the people who are poorer and less educated than average. Such voters are more likely to vote Democratic. The problem is political, but it may only be a temporary problem, as hopefully all the other feasibility problems may be temporary. For an analysis of electoral reform and SOS solutions, see Part II, chapter 5 on Reforming Electoral Procedures.

International relations

International refugees and super-optimum solutions

International refugees are people who have been forced out of their nations by war or natural disasters, and who are at least temporarily waiting to return, or to go on elsewhere. Emigrants are people who are voluntarily leaving their homes and going to other nations where they are considered immigrants.

The conservative position is to keep refugees out, partly to protect national purity, but also to avoid competition for jobs. The liberal position is to let refugees in, partly to help them, out of sympathy, but also in recognition that they may provide useful labor and innovative ideas themselves or through their children. The compromise is to let some refugees in, but on a selective basis, with restrictions.

The SOS solution might be to upgrade the skills of international refugees through organized international efforts, possibly under the direction of the United Nations. With greater skills, the refugees might be more acceptable to both conservatives and liberals, given their increased productivity and ability to enhance the economies of the countries to which they go. See Table 1.25.

POVERTY AND LEGAL POLICY

Criminal procedure

Evaluating alternative ways of handling pre-trial release

The conservative position is to set relatively high bonds in order to generate a high holding rate. Doing this increases the likelihood that arrested defendants will show up for trial and not commit another crime between arrest and trial. The liberal position is to set relatively low bonds in order to generate a

Table 1.25   International refugees and super-optimum solutions

Criteria Alternatives	C Goal Protect national purity	L Goal Promote quality of life of refugees & society	N Total (neutral weights)	L Total (liberal weights)	C Total (conservative weights)
C Alternative Refugees out	4	2	12	10	14*
L Alternative Refugees in	2	4	12	14*	10
N Alternative Between	3	3	12	12	12
SOS Alternative Upgrade skills	>3.5	>3.5	>14	>14**	>14**

low holding rate. Doing this increases the likelihood that arrested defendants will be able to continue their jobs, avoid the bitterness of being held in jail prior to trial, and avoid the expensive incarceration costs. The compromise position in many states, such as Illinois, is to have relatively high bonds but require the defendant to provide only 10 per cent of the total bond. This results in more defendants being released than the conservative alternative, but fewer defendants being released than the liberal alternative.

The SOS alternative is designed to raise the release rate possibly even higher than liberals advocate, but at the same time to get a high rate of defendants showing up for trial without committing crimes in the meantime. This can be done by (1) systematically screening arrested defendants to hold those who are relatively high risks, (2) requiring released defendants to report to the courthouse every week or so, (3) notifying defendants a few days before a hearing by mail, phone or in person, (4) prosecuting defendants who fail to show up for their court dates, and especially (5) reducing delay between arrest and trial, which otherwise leads to skipping out (failing to appear on one's court date) and to crime committing for those released and expensive incarceration costs for those held in jail pending trial. See Table 1.26.

Table 1.26 Evaluating policies toward pre-trial release

Criteria / Alternatives	C Goal High show-up rate	C Goal No crime committing	N Goal Lower tax costs	L Goal Less lost productivity	L Goal Less bitterness	N Total (neutral weights)	L Total (liberal weights)	C Total (conservative weights)
C Alternative High holding rate	4	4	2	2	2	28	24	32*
L Alternative Low holding rate	2	2	4	4	4	32	36*	28
N Alternative Middling holding rate	3	3	3	3	3	30	30	30
SOS Alternative Low holding, high appearance without crimes	5	5	5	5	5	50	50**	50**

Legal services

The alternative ways of providing the poor with legal counsel, as shown in Table 1.27, include (1) volunteer attorneys, favored by the White House, (2) salaried government attorneys, favored by Congress, and (3) a compromise that involves continuing the salaried system, but requiring that 10 per cent of its funding go to making volunteers more accessible and competent. The criteria are inexpensiveness, accessibility, political feasibility and competence. Each alternative is scored on each criterion on a 1–2 scale.

Table 1.27   An example of computer-aided mediation

		Inexpensiveness	Accessibility	Political feasibility	Competence
A	With unweighted criteria				
	Volunteer	2.00	1.00	2.00	1.00
	Salaried	1.00	2.00	1.00	2.00
	Compromise	1.50	2.00	2.00	2.00
B	With conservative values				
	Volunteer	4.00	1.00	4.00	1.00
	Salaried	2.00	2.00	2.00	2.00
	Compromise	3.00	2.00	4.00	2.00
C	With liberal values				
	Volunteer	2.00	2.00	2.00	2.00
	Salaried	1.00	4.00	1.00	4.00
	Compromise	1.50	4.00	2.00	4.00

Conservative values involve giving the weight of 2 to inexpensive and political feasibility on a 1–2 scale because those goals are important to conservatives. The other criteria of accessibility and competence only receive a weight of 1 under conservative values because they are not so important. Liberal values are the opposite with a high weight of 2 to accessibility and competence and a low weight of 1 to inexpensive and political feasibility. With conservative values, the volunteer system wins over the salaried system 10 points to 8. The compromise is an overall winner with 11.5 points. The 11 equals 3 + 2 + 4 + 2. With liberal values, the salaried system wins over the volunteer system 10 points to 8. The compromise is an overall winner with 11.5 points. The '10 per cent compromise' is thus a super-winner in being better than the original best solution of both the conservatives and the liberals. The 11.5 comes from adding 1.5 + 4 + 2 + 4.

As regards mandatory public interest work by lawyers, see Table 1.28. The SOS package involves five elements:

1   increase the benefits of mandatory *pro bono* by offering above-cost subsidies to the bar associations and provide them with favorable publicity;
2   decrease the costs by covering the coordination expenses and by allowing conservative causes to be counted;
3   increase the costs to non-compliers by threatening loss of one's license for not complying;
4   decrease the benefits to non-compliers by welcoming the overcrowded bar which gives lawyers free time to take on cases of the poor;
5   provide a good monitoring system so that the benefits and costs can be better allocated.

Evaluating policies regarding the right to counsel

The SOS alternative refers to having a base of salaried government lawyers but with lots of volunteers, possibly under a mandatory *pro bono* rule that will some day be adopted by the American Bar Association.

In order to use the volunteers more effectively, there is a need for clearinghouse activities to determine their times of availability, their specialties and the clients who need their help, and then to set up appointments at the regular legal aid offices. There is also a need for training the volunteers in the special problems that poor people have as tenants, consumers, family members, welfare recipients, and so on. See Table 1.29.

Table 1.28 Alternative policies toward mandatory public interest work by lawyers

Criteria / Alternatives	L Goal Increase representation	N Goal Reduce tax burden	C Goal Conservative causes	N Total (neutral weights)	L Total (liberal weights)	C Total (conservative weights)
C Alternative No mandatory 0 hours	2	4	3	18	17	18*
L Alternative Mandatory 40 hours	4	4	2	20	22*	18
N Alternative Partly 20 hours	3	3	2.5	17	17.5	16.5
SOS Alternative Package	5	4	4	26	27**	25**

Table 1.29 Evaluating policies regarding the right to counsel

Criteria / Alternatives	C Goal Politically feasible	L Goal Accessible to poor	L Goal Competent attorneys	N Goal Lower tax costs	N Total (neutral weights)	L Total (liberal weights)	C Total (conservative weights)
C Alternative No free counsel, or only volunteers	4	2	2	4	24	24	24*
L Alternative Salaried govt lawyers	2	4	3	3	24	29*	19
N Alternative Reimbursed Judicare, salaried criminal, volunteer civil	3	4	2	2	22	25	19
SOS Alternative Salaried base, clearinghouse, training prog.	4	5	4	4	34	39**	29**

2 Minorities and Public Policy

DISCRIMINATION IN GENERAL

Definitions

1 Discrimination: denying someone opportunities or government benefits for which he is qualified because of race, gender, age, economic class, religion, ancestral background or sexual orientation.
2 Segregation: keeping races separate involuntarily.
3 Separatism: voluntary separation.

Areas of activity in which discrimination may be present include:

1 voting and political rights,
2 courtroom discrimination and other aspects of the justice system,
3 schools and education,
4 employment,
5 housing,
6 public accommodations,
7 the area of domestic relations, such as whether blacks can marry whites, usually involves government interference or discrimination if it occurs.

When discrimination is desirable

One interesting item about how the world is changing with regard to what is considered permissible and is impermissible with regard to sexual activity. A generation ago it was quite acceptable to make sexist jokes and homophobic jokes just as racist jokes were acceptable. Many examples could be given. One such example is the Chicago columnist Mike Royko making fun of gay people. He said that gay pride marches or any gay marches are absurd because there is no reason for such a fuss to be made over people who have same-sex sexual preferences when no fuss is made over people who have any one of 200 or 300 kinds of sexual preferences that have been catalogued in sexual psychology books. More specifically, he said there are far more masturbators in the world than there are lesbians or male homosexuals. Why don't the masturbators have a parade and a masturbators' pride day?

In about 1990 in New York City there was a masturbators' pride parade held in support of Pee Wee Herman, the actor who was convicted of masturbating in a theatre. What did Mike Royko think about that? He probably said that there is nothing that one could possibly say is absurd anymore with regard to sexual activity. Actually, neither masturbation nor homosexuality should be matters of pride because they are not achievements one works at developing. They are sort of natural inclinations, unlike winning a Nobel Prize. But they never have a Nobel Prize winners' parade. Also, it might be pointed out that maybe 90 per cent of the sexual preferences he refers to are not harmless. A sexual preference for children is a harmful kind of sexual preference. We would not want to have a child rapists' day or an adult rapists' day, meaning people who rape adults. The kinds of sexual preferences that are catalogued in psychopathology books are by definition pathologies or obsessions that interfere with one's functioning, including heterosexual preferences. There is no likelihood of seeing a nymphomaniacs' pride parade.

One aspect of this whole thing is how easy it is to make jokes out of aspects of sexual discrimination. Any kind of discrimination that is not based on merit should not be a joking matter. One can make fun of some kind of strange fetish in the abstract, but to deny a person who is a foot fetishist a job teaching political science is discrimination. Presumably, there is nothing in teaching political science that is going to be interfered with by having a foot fetish. One could make an argument that a foot fetishist should not be hired in a shoe store, but even that is nonsense, unless the foot fetishist is doing something wrong. There was a letter to the editor of the *New York Times* (20 August 1991) about Professor Jeffries at CCNY who says outrageously obnoxious and abhorrent things about race relations. The author of the letter said how abhorrent he finds the statements, but that there has been no proof offered that this professor is a bad teacher or is in any way incapable of teaching his subject matter. Yet people want to fire him. He teaches African culture courses. It does not make any difference what he teaches. If he is doing it in a competent manner and, on the side, he advocates bestiality, or whatever, he can be called all kinds of names. But discriminating against him, meaning refusing to hire him or to fire him for something that is not related to his doing his job well does raise the question of freedom of speech.

One has to distinguish between discrimination or alleged discrimination against someone for speaking out bizarrely and against someone for behaving bizarrely. For sure, Mr Jones should not be fired as a physics teachers because he has been known to make a soapbox oration in favor of bestiality. What if he engages in bestiality? If it is a form of animal abuse, he should be prosecuted like any other animal abuser. If the job he has requires that he not be convicted of a felony, then he could be legitimately fired. It is legitimate in the sense that there is no federal or state law that says that employers have to keep people who are convicted of felonies, but just because it is legal does not necessarily make it right. Part of the issue would be whether Jones performs his obnoxious activities in private or in public. He has a certain right to privacy. If he engages in bestiality that does not qualify as sadistic animal abuse, in private, then one could make a case for saying he should not be fired from his job. If he engages in sadistic animal abuse in public or private, then the situation is more questionable. It is not speech activity. Torturing animals may not result in more than a year in prison, which would qualify as a felony, but it would be an imprisonable crime subject to jail time, as contrasted to a traffic violation.

Without getting into a lot of unnecessary details, the overall principle is that nobody should be fired from a job or refused a job who is capable of performing the job well, regardless of what non-job-related characteristics they might have that people find obnoxious, especially if these characteristics have something to do with advocacy rather than behavior, or relate to private behavior rather than public behavior, or to victimless behavior rather than behavior where somebody is getting hurt. All this is rather abstract because this is not what the Supreme Court has said when talking about discrimination. It never addresses the matter of people being fired for bestiality, just matters of race, union activity, gender, sexual preference, age or disability.

Some day the Supreme Court may decide that the Equal Protection Clause of the constitution is synonymous with merit treatment by governmental agencies. Thus, the Supreme Court will thereby elevate anti-discrimination to include all forms of non-merit treatment. As a practical matter this may mean a constitutional right to know why one is being fired or not promoted and maybe even not hired. This could mean a right to a hearing. If the government agency can truthfully establish only non-arbitrary grounds, then the treatment will probably be upheld.

On the matter of bestiality, it currently is grounds for dismissal from either government or non-government employment. If the above Supreme Court expansion occurs, it would probably be grounds for dismissal only if the government employer could show some relation to job performance and not just that the employee engages in obnoxious activities when not at work. If the bestiality involves the torturing of animals, this could easily reflect adversely on the character and fitness of the employee.

Perhaps the material dealing with discrimination in general should allow for an exception which says that, if a person has committed criminal behavior, he should be made to suffer so as to deter others. Such an attitude is manifested in denying jobs to ex-convicts, which seems to be counterproductive. If an ex-convict is capable of performing well a certain kind of job, the fact that the ex-convict may have been a child rapist, for example, should not mean that he is thereby deprived of productive work. The result is that society has to support him on some kind of welfare, a solution that hurts society, hurts the individual and hurts the beneficiaries of whatever kinds of work he could do. There should be negative sanctions, although a good society does not have to use them very often, given the positive incentives that should exist. The negative sanctions should include imprisonment, but in preparation for a more constructive life upon release, not subsequent discrimination.

RACIAL GROUPS

Anti-discrimination legislation and regulation

Points favoring such governmental activity

1   People are more productive in the absence of discrimination because they are more likely to be able to perform in accordance with their developed/undeveloped skills, rather than rely on race or gender as a criterion to offset their lack of skills, as for example in the building trades.
2   Non-discrimination encourages people with potential talents to develop them, for example becoming doctors or lawyers.
3   Discrimination can depress the wages and other standards that are applied to the majority group in various fields. For example, a hard-up group of discriminated blacks can bring down the wages of white workers and raise the price of white housing. Standards in criminal justice and voting rights for whites can also go down, especially for poor whites.
4   Discrimination leads to segregation, with wasteful duplication costs.
5   Discrimination leads to impoverished ghettos, with excessive costs for public aid, police protection, fire protection, juvenile delinquency and other slum-associated costs.
6   Discrimination hurts American influence in Africa, Asia and Latin America among non-whites.
7   Discrimination disrupts the American defense effort, especially when a

volunteer army tends disproportionately to mean members of minorities who join the army for economic opportunity. The Vietnam war was particularly disrupted by perceived discrimination at home and in the armed forces by black soldiers.

8　Discrimination gives whites a false sense of superiority, leading some of them to think they are doing better than they otherwise are, and thus adversely affecting their incentives to be productive citizens.

9　Discrimination can have an adverse effect on the guilt feelings of whites, especially those who have some ethical and religious sensitivity.

10　Discrimination leads to hatred and antagonism in those who are discriminated against, which can result in riots and other violent confrontations.

11　Societal discrimination lessens the freedom of those who do not want to discriminate, who might welcome anti-discrimination laws so that they will not be alone in their non-discriminatory behavior.

12　Anti-discrimination laws can help attract manufacturing and business to states and communities that would otherwise provide too unfriendly an atmosphere for many firms.

13　Discrimination decreases the consumer purchasing power of minorities, to the detriment of the total economy.

14　Discrimination divides whites among themselves, especially along international lines, thereby creating an additional form of antagonism and hostility.

Points disfavoring governmental anti-discrimination activities

1　It is better for people to refrain from discrimination voluntarily than to be ordered to do so.

2　It is argued that some minorities may be genetically different or inferior in terms of certain kinds of mental capabilities.

3　Prohibiting discrimination will lead to intermarriage, to the detriment of both races.

4　Prohibiting discrimination will mean increased economic competition for jobs and housing, and the loss of a cheap labor pool.

5　It is sometimes argued that God would not have made multiple races if He wanted them to mix.

6　It is sometimes argued that minorities are content the way things are, but this has been repeatedly refuted, especially in the 1960s, when blacks showed their discontent in highly intense ways.

7　Anti-discrimination is sometimes attacked on the grounds that it is associated with communist advocacy.

8   It costs money to enforce anti-discrimination laws, but budget appropriations have been extremely feeble.
9   One of the main arguments is that anti-discrimination can go too far and become reverse discrimination against whites and males under certain circumstances.

Preferential treatment

By preferential treatment is meant favoring a minority group member over someone in the dominant group, where both meet minimum qualifications but the dominant group member is somewhat, but not considerably, more qualified, as measured by some kind of test.

Arguments for letting near ties go to minorities

A near tie means where both the white applicant and a black applicant are approximately equally qualified.

1   They need the job more. The whites or males can find jobs elsewhere more easily.
2   Compensation for past discrimination, analogous to awarding damages.
3   In order to provide role models for minority people, such as police officers, lawyers and doctors.
4   Measurement involving subjective qualifications frequently tends to be biased toward the dominant group.
5   The need to break the vicious cycle of one generation after another being downtrodden.
6   The majority will benefit from preferential treatment in some ways, just as it benefits from prohibiting discrimination with regard to decreasing segregation costs, slums, psychological considerations, lessening antagonism, attracting manufacturing, consumer purchasing power, and so on.
7   There may be a better marginal rate of return from investing in someone who is showing improvement, as contrasted to someone who has always been operating at the maximum.
8   Minority members are needed to service the minority community.

Arguments for no preferential treatment

1   It is inefficient from the point of view of societal productivity to award jobs and admission to higher education programs not on the basis of merit.

2 Minorities will suffer as patients, clients or students of non-so-competent doctors, lawyers or teachers if the standards are lowered for minority professionals.

3 Preferential treatment requirements will drive away business firms from minority communities to avoid having to apply such rules.

4 Preferential treatment may disproportionately mean black preferences, to the detriment of Hispanic, Asian or other minorities.

5 Well-qualified minority members may not feel adequately appreciated because others will think they obtained their positions through preferences.

6 Preferences become a crutch that can lessen incentives to do well.

7 Preferences can spread to numerous categories of people, such as the aged, the handicapped, the young, women, the poor, veterans or relatives, until virtually everybody is getting preference and merit counts for relatively little, or substantially less than it should.

8 Applying preferences may not be so easy with regard to determining who fits into what racial categories.

9 Preferences are only justified as a temporary measure, implying that they are not capable of being defended in the long run.

10 It makes no sense to have preferences for voting or criminal justice, for example. Therefore why should it make special sense in employment and education?

11 It may antagonize whites and thereby generate friction.

Other points

1 A private employer can be allowed to go further under preferential hiring than a government agency can since private employers are not subject to the equal protection clause but only to civil rights statutes. If preferential hiring is bad, it is especially bad for the government to set a bad example.

2 A distinction should also be made between goals and quotas.

3 An important distinction is between facilitators that enable minorities to qualify and preferences that facilitate unqualified minorities getting jobs.

4 The distinction is also quite important between preference for qualified minorities who are being discriminated against and preference for unqualified ones.

5 Also important is the distinction between tie-breaking and preference where there is a substantial gap. Ties can be broadly defined.

6 A key object is to talk in terms of affirmative action, not preferential treatment, with the emphasis on facilitators and qualified minorities and doing so in order to equalize, not to unequalize in a reverse direction.

Cases that deal with preferential treatment

The *Bakke* case (University of California at Davis Medical School) says that unqualified preferential hiring is unconstitutional, but that it is permissible to consider race as a relevant criterion. The *Weber* case says that private employers can get away with preferential hiring when a government agency could not. A win–win or SOS Analysis of Anti-Discrimination Policy.

Table 2.1 applies a win–win or SOS analysis to anti-discrimination legislation especially in the context of employment. Conservatives want color blind hiring. Liberals want preferential hiring. Neutrals are willing to allow some forms of affirmative action such as (1) advertising in minority newspapers, (2) locating places of employment close to where minorities live, (3) removing irrelevant tests for employment which correlate with race, and (4) advertising that one is an equal opportunity employer. The win–win solution is to preserve the high merit standards of the conservatives but have affirmative action on the basis of economic deprivation rather than race, but the affirmative action is only for training to be able to meet the high merit standards.

Lessening discrimination across different rights

The first right concerns how to lessen discrimination against blacks in being nominated and elected to *political office* without interfering with majority rule. The conservative position is currently that black potential candidates should seek to be nominated and elected just like anyone else, without any affirmative action on the part of the politicians who decide who the candidates will be. The liberal position has not gone so far as to require any kind of ethnic balance in a list of candidates for offices that are being filled simultaneously, but that has been traditional as a matter of practical politics in multi-ethnic areas such as Chicago and New York, among many others. A more recent liberal position would be to say that, if a black candidate gets more votes than any of the white candidates in the initial election, there should be no runoff between the black candidate and the leading white candidate. The SOS position is to concentrate on making it easier to register and vote. Doing so would enable minority members who are poor to actively influence who gets elected. That in turn would influence what legislation gets passed designed to facilitate jobs and job-getting.

On the matter of *discrimination against black victims in criminal cases*, especially murder cases, the conservative position is to ignore the problem or ignore the statistics as not being relevant to individual cases. The liberal position is to abolish capital punishment given the discriminatory statistical

Table 2.1   Evaluating policies toward race relations

Criteria / Alternatives	C Goal Improve economy	N Goal Reduce tax costs	L Goal Equity	N Total (neutral weights)	L Total (liberal weights)	C Total (conservative weights)
C Alternative No affirmative action, but outlaw discrim. no pref. hiring	3.5	3	2	17	15.5	18.5
L Alternative Preferential hiring	3.5	3	2	17	15.5	18.5
N Alternative Affirmative action & temp. pref. hiring	4	3	2	18	16*	20*
SOS Alternative Upgrade skills in K-12, OJT & OIC	5	2	4	22	21**	23**

Notes:
1   Race relations is also an issue on which liberals and conservatives tend to make a more joint position rather than a more divisive position, unlike traditional economic controversies.
2   Discrimination in this context means requiring or allowing a white with a score of 40 to be preferred over a black with a score of 60, where 50 is the minimum score for one who is qualified, or where both are qualified but the white is preferred even though the black applicant is substantially more qualified.
3   Affirmative action in this context means only hiring blacks who are qualified, but actively seeking qualified blacks through (a) advertising, (b) locating one's physical plant, (c) removing requirements that are racially correlated, but not correlated with job performance, and (d) providing on-the-job training for all, but especially to overcome lack of training of blacks.
4   Preferential hiring means only hiring blacks who are qualified, but preferring qualified blacks over moderately less qualified whites, generally as a temporary measure to offset prior discrimination.
5   K-12 = Kindergarten through 12th grade; DJT = on-the-job training; OIC = Opportunities Industry Center which teaches such basic skills as how to fill out an employment application and participate in an employment interview.

patterns. The compromise position on capital punishment has been to make it more difficult, especially with regard to special procedures and when it can apply. The SOS position on the racial discrimination matter might be to have any state where the disparity is greater than ten percentage points suspend capital punishment until the disparity is reduced. That disparity is between the percentage of defendants who kill white victims who are executed and the percentage of defendants who kill black victims who are executed. The disparity can be reduced by imposing life imprisonment on some of the defendants who have been sentenced to die where white victims are involved. See the forthcoming section on 'Capital Punishment and Race Discrimination' for further details.

On the matter of *housing*, the present conservative position tolerates fair housing laws which prohibit discrimination but does not welcome any form of affirmative action in housing any more than it does in employment. The liberal position would provide for communities either removing their snob zoning laws or going further and requiring the adoption of zoning laws that affirmatively seek racial or economic class balance. The SOS position is to view the problem mainly as one of money discrimination rather than racial discrimination. As such, it can be partly remedied through rent supplements that are explicitly designed to bring about housing and school integration simultaneously. The broader problem is one of providing job opportunities so that blacks and other low-income minorities will have sufficient incomes to move into middle-income neighborhoods without rent supplements.

On the matter of *governmental services*, especially geographical misallocation, the conservative position is to ignore the problem. The liberal position largely ignores the problem too. Not many people are aware of the severity of the misallocation of police departments, fire departments and good parks, as well as good schools, to low-income as opposed to middle-income neighborhoods. There is much more awareness with regard to schools than to police and fire protection. The SOS would provide for the publication of statistics showing how much money per capita is spent for police protection and fire protection in particular by census tracts or neighborhoods for all cities with populations larger than about 50,000 or large enough to have more than one police station or more than one fire station. If the disparity in any city is greater than twice as much per capita in the middle-income neighborhoods as in the low-income neighborhoods, there should be an obligation under the equal protection clause of the constitution to upgrade the low-income neighborhoods – not necessarily to as high a level as the middle-income neighborhoods, but either up to some objective level of decency or more objectively up to at least half the per capita expenditure.

With regard to blacks as *consumers*, the conservative position is to be supportive of the public accommodation statutes of the 1960s, which specify that eating places and other public accommodations cannot discriminate against black consumers by refusing to serve them. Liberal organizations like the National Association for the Advancement of Colored People (NAACP) and the American Civil Liberties Union do not seem to show any concern for discrimination against minorities with regard to consumer matters. The pro-consumer organizations like the Ralph Nader organization are highly middle-class and not much concerned with minority consumers as such. Studies that have been made show heavy price and quality discrimination. The prices are substantially higher for the same goods in black neighborhoods than in white suburban neighborhoods. The quality of the products for the same name is substantially lower, with many stores deliberately moving shoddy merchandise from suburban stores to the black neighborhoods where there is less likely to be any protest. The laws that govern consumer fraud or product safety have no relevance. The SOS solution should be to stimulate competition in low-income neighborhoods. This could be combined with enterprise zone programs whereby stores would be subsidized to locate in low-income neighborhoods and thereby provide competitive pricing and quality as well as job opportunities. The businesses would still be making a profit but not near-monopolistic profits which go with being in a neighborhood where there is little competition and little mobility for shopping elsewhere.

Special situations

Dealing with layoffs and affirmative action simultaneously

The conservative position is to follow the usual rule in layoffs – that the last people hired should be the first people laid off or fired. That means no extra consideration is given to minorities who may be disproportionately represented among those most recently hired. The liberal position is to add some seniority to recently hired minority people. For example, each minority person hired could be given a few years' seniority on the grounds that, generally, minority people probably should have been hired at least a few years sooner than they were actually taken on. The neutral position might be to award some automatic seniority, but maybe only one year rather than a few years. Another neutral position might be to judge each case individually in terms of the age of the employee and other relevant characteristics in determining whether any additional seniority should be given.

The SOS alternative might be to handle layoffs only or mainly on the basis of merit qualifications, rather than seniority. Doing this should appeal to the conservative emphasis on merit. It would also allow some recently hired minorities to have a better chance of being retained than if only seniority is considered. The SOS alternative might also include a program for upgrading the skills of recently hired employees and other employees so that they can score higher on merit criteria.

Another modification might be to consider seniority among employees who are within the same merit range, or to consider merit within a broadly defined seniority range. Thus merit would determine who gets laid off among all employees who have less than 10 years seniority, 10–20 years seniority, and so on. See Table 2.2.

Table 2.2   Dealing with layoffs and affirmative action simultaneously

Criteria Alternatives	C Goal Merit hiring and firing	L Goal Do something for minorities	N Total (neutral weights)	L Total (liberal weights)	C Total (conservative weights)
C Alternative As is, no points	4	2	12	10	14*

L Alternative
  Preferential
  Non-layoffs,
  10 years
	2	4	12	14*	10

N Alternative One year	3	3	12	12	12

SOS Alternative
  Strict merit, no
  seniority
  Upgrade skills
  Seniority within
  a range
	5	5	20	20**	20**

Notes:
1   A preferential non-layoff means that when there is downsizing, some people do not get laid-off who otherwise would if the seniority principle is followed of 'last hired, first fired'. A 10-year preference means that a minority member hired in 1980 is considered as having been hired in 1970 on the theory that they would have been hired 10 years sooner if it were not for discrimination.
2   The win–win alternative says to throw out seniority completely since merely being hired long ago does not make one more qualified. Instead, pure merit or qualifications would be used for determining who gets laid-off. This would be better for recently hired blacks and women, than using seniority. A modification is that within a range of competence, such as being in the top 25 per cent on a test, then within that quartile, seniority would be considered.

SOS analysis relating capital punishment and race discrimination

The conservative position is to retain capital punishment even if it is discriminately administered. The liberal position is to abolish capital punishment because it tends to be discriminately administered, which means that defendants who kill white victims are much more likely to receive capital punishment than defendants who kill black victims. A neutral alternative is to allow capital punishment to be reduced to life imprisonment (or another sentence) on appeal. This is in contrast to the current system in which the severity of a legal sentence is almost never questioned by an appellate court, as opposed to reversing a sentence because of a procedural error or some other example of illegality.

The SOS alternative involves a national rule by the Supreme Court or Congress saying that, if there are more than ten percentage points separating the death sentences involving white murder victims and those involving black murder victims, then the death sentence shall be temporarily suspended until enough of the white victim cases are changed to life imprisonment so as to have a difference smaller than ten percentage points. See Table 2.3.

Table 2.3   SOS analysis relating capital punishment and racial discrimination

Criteria \ Alternative	C Goal Deter crime C=3 N=2 L=1	L Goal End discrimination C=1 N=2 L=3	N Total (neutral weights)	L Total (liberal weights)	C Total (conservative weights)
C Alternative Retain capital punishment	4	2	12	10	14*
L Alternative Abolish capital punishment	2	4	12	14*	10
N Alternative Modification by appeal	3	3	12	12	12
SOS Alternative 10% difference	>3.5	>3.5	>14	>14**	>14**

Voting rights in South Africa

Alternatives, goals and relations   The conservative *alternative* has been to deny blacks the right to vote. The extreme left-wing alternative of some of the Pan-Africans has been to deny whites the right to vote, or even to expel them from the country, meaning to deny that they have any right to even live in South Africa. The middling position is one person, one vote, although that could be considered a left-wing position since the blacks would dominate.

The black *goal* is basically for blacks to be better off. The white goal is not necessarily for whites to be better off than they are at present, but to at least not be much worse off.

The conservative position and the more extreme left-wing position would result in a kind of super-malimum position where both blacks and whites would be worse off. The only way the conservatives could succeed in keeping blacks from having the right to vote any longer would be through a system of repression even greater than they have attempted in the past. The country would be in a state of continuous guerrilla warfare with no protection from being bombed or assassinated. There would be no foreign business, or not much that would want to locate there. Much domestic business would leave.

If the extreme blacks had their way and all the whites were driven out, the results would be somewhat similar, in that there would be a lack of foreign investment. Much domestic business would leave voluntarily or involuntarily.

Developing an SOS   The *object* is to develop a system in which none of those bad things happen, meaning that (1) foreign investment does not shy away from South Africa, but substantially increases, (2) businesses within South Africa stay there and even expand to hire more people and make for more job opportunities, and (3) violence ends, as contrasted to merely being temporarily suspended as the situation is now, waiting to see what will happen.

The compromise position is not really one person, one vote since that is the left-wing position rather than the middle position. There are two left wing positions. One is extreme that says only blacks should vote. The more moderate left wing position says both blacks and whites should have equal voting rights. Likewise there are two conservative positions. One is extreme that says blacks should have no equal rights including voting, employment, education, criminal justice, and housing. The more moderate conservative position is that blacks should have equal rights on all those activities except voting.

The *compromise* position is one person, one vote but some kind of guarantee that the whites will not be outvoted in spite of the fact that they have so much fewer people. The proposed devices are, first, to partition the country into states like the original American 13 states. Every state, no matter how small, gets two senators. There would be basically four states in South Africa: the Cape provinces, Natal, Transvaal and the Orange Free State. The first two would be black, the last two could be dominated by Afrikaners. There could be more than eight senators. Maybe each state would have five senators so there would be 20 senators. But the blacks could not run the Senate any more than the north could run the US Senate. The white states would have the power to prevent even ordinary legislation from being passed, but especially any legislation that requires a two-thirds vote, such as the approval of treaties or appointments, and any amendment to the constitution would require three-quarters of the vote.

Everything that has been proposed is exactly what was adopted in the United States in the Constitution. There would be separation of powers, federalism and judicial review, everything designed to enable a minority of states to be able to prevent the majority from exercising the power that its numbers command. South Africa could have an electoral college in which the president would be chosen on the basis of how many senators each state has, which would have nothing to do with how many people they have, since every state would have the same number of senators. They would have a supreme court that would have the power to declare unconstitutional legislation that interferes with property rights or state's rights, all of which would be code words for white people's rights.

It is ironic that those who want to preserve white power in South Africa choose as their model the American Constitution, including the Bill of Rights. They are all of a sudden very much in favor of minority rights because they are the minority. Here the word 'minority' means numerical minority, not lacking in power.

A super-optimum solution would have to involve something that would be the equivalent of an internal economic union. It would have to involve a system whereby white business interests would have an environment in which they could prosper, and blacks would have job opportunities accompanied by merit criteria, affirmative action, with preferences for people who cannot satisfy a minimum competence level. It basically means going directly to what it is that each side wants to achieve by way of increased voting power and concentrating on how to more than guarantee that, regardless of the voting rights. It means elevating certain economic rights to a higher status than the status of federalism, separation of powers and the other constitutional issues.

Relevant SOS reasoning   The key way out is to emphasize both blacks and whites being much better off economically as a result of SOS thinking. That is, political power is directed toward economic well-being for each group. A crucial element is to get away from stability toward continuous economic growth. We can also expand governmental responsiveness to include being responsive to the people by helping them to upgrade their skills. Making meaningful those rights of continuous economic growth and the right to upgrade one's skills includes a right to sue, but also the establishment of appropriate institutions such as a ministry of international trade and industry.

There are a number of questions that can be asked of revolutionary South African blacks. First, what is going to happen to the whites? This is an implicitly racist question that shows rather biased sensitivity to what is going to happen to the whites, but not what is going to happen to the blacks, who may be in bad shape as a result of white flight, loss of investment and other socioeconomic disruptions. Second, how to get whites and blacks to make concessions, to reach the traditional compromise situation, which is better than civil war? The SOS question is how to enable both blacks and whites to be better off than their best expectations. See Table 2.4 for an SOS summarizing of these ideas.

RELIGIOUS GROUPS

Government interference

Why have religious freedom?

1   In a country that represents freedom and liberty, restrictions on religious freedom stir up strong resentment among minority groups because of emotional attachments; for example, many colonists left England to find religious freedom.
2   In a country with diverse religions, social conflict could be extremely harmful, bordering on civil war, as in the Thirty Years' War, Vietnam and Northern Ireland.
3   It is especially difficult to determine truth or effective policy with regard to matters of the supernatural. Let all points of view be heard and the truth will prevail.

When religious freedom should be limited

1   When there are immoral religious practices, as these would be intolerable, like polygamy.

Table 2.4   Voting rights in South Africa

Criteria ⟍⟍ Alternatives	C Goal Whites well off C=3 N=2 L=1	L Goal Blacks well off C=1 N=2 L=3	N Total (neutral weights)	L Total (liberal weights)	C Total (conservative weights)
C Alternative Only whites vote	4?	2	12	10	14*
L Alternative Only blacks vote or majority rule without minority safeguards	2	4?	12	14*	10
N Alternative (Bill of Rights) (see note 1)	3	3	12	12	12
N2 Alternative (US Const.) (see note 2)	3	3	12	12	12
SOS Alternative Economic rights (see note 3)	>3.5	>3.5	>14	>14	>14

Notes:

1   Neutral alternative 1 is minority safeguards such as free speech, equal treatment and due process.

2   Neutral alternative 2 is minority safeguards such as Senate, electoral college, and special majorities to pass, amend.

3   The SOS alternative includes economic growth, upgrade skills, combined with neutral alternative 1 and some neutral alternative 2.

4   The question mark in the first column emphasizes that whites may not be so well off if they prohibit blacks from voting, because blacks will rebel and make life unpleasant for whites to the detriment of the economy and the society. The question mark in the second column emphasizes that blacks may not be so well off if they prohibit whites from voting because whites will rebel and make life less pleasant for blacks to the detriment of the economy and society.

2   When they involve snakes or other dangerous practices in faith-proving ceremonies involving children.

3   In time of war, those with a religious objection can still participate as noncombatants or in other ways.

All regular free speech arguments

Freedom of religion, in the sense of seeking to convert other people, is a form of freedom of speech or communication. Thus all the usual pro-free speech arguments apply such as:

1   Truth will prevail in the marketplace of free circulating ideas.
2   Better policy will prevail with free circulation of ideas, including religious ideas.
3   Check on corrupt and inefficient leadership including religious leadership.
4   Raise standard of living including religious groups who tend to be poor partly for religious reasons.
5   Safety valve for disgruntled element including fundamentalist religious groups who feel left behind in changing times.
6   Individual dignity and happiness to influence one's destiny by being able to speak out, including preaching.

Government aid to religion

Points disfavoring aid even to the majority religion

1   Aid often leads to interference. The aid is unlikely to come without some strings attached to qualify for it. This is true regardless of whether we are talking about financial aid to parochial schools or stimulating prayers and bible readings in the public schools, or other forms of aid.
2   Aid leads to favoritism, real or perceived. It is extremely difficult, if not impossible, to allocate aid equally, since allocating equally on one criterion, such as population, would be unequal on another criterion, such as needs.
3   The majority religion in most places is a minority religion in other places, where members of the religion that is normally in the majority might find themselves subject to unfavorable treatment by the state or local government. All these points disfavoring aid should be points that can be accepted by religious people, including those in what is generally the majority religion.
4   It is expensive to aid religion, especially when giving monetary subsidies to parochial schools. Other forms of aid are currently considered constitutional but are still quite expensive; these include income tax exemption and property tax exemption.
5   Initiative may be impaired by outside aid. For example, prayers and

bible reading in the schools could decrease the incentive of outreach programs by the churches and the incentive to have religious activities within families.

6 Aid generates intense resentment and conflict. Example can be given of American communities that were riven by divisiveness over some aspect of aiding religion, more so than any other issue. The question of aid to religion has been highly divisive nationally in countries like France and Italy over the last hundred years, and even more so during the period of the Reformation and Renaissance.

Points favoring aid to religion

1 Not aiding religion creates an example or impression of the government being anti-religious.
2 If aid to religion could be obtained, that might promote more religious activity. For example, some religions would be benefitted by aid to their parochial schools, which is a form of religious activity.
3 The aid to parochial schools' position is also argued in terms of the parents of parochial school children having to pay double taxes to also support the public schools.
4 More people could be encouraged to become religious if the public schools were to do some indoctrinating by way of bible reading and prayers.
5 One can argue that religion aids societal productivity in a qualitative or ethical sense by increasing our concern for non-monetary considerations, as with, for example, a concern for the way benefits and costs are distributed.

Separation of church and state

A key defect in the government–religion analysis is that it is too broad over time and across places to be a controversial here-and-now policy analysis. The pro-religious position goes back to ideas associated with the Inquisition prior to the Renaissance, or with more recent events such as in Franco's Spain, which openly discriminated against minority religions. The anti-religion position goes back to the position of the French and Russian revolutionaries who felt intensely resentful towards the role that the church played in supporting the old regime, or to ideas associated with more recent examples, such as Communist China's attitude toward missionaries, who were viewed as capitalist agents. In the 1990s American context, it is more meaningful to talk about controversial relations between government and religion in the context of prayer or bible reading in the public schools. That kind of SOS table is shown as Table 2.5 on page 79.

Evaluating ways of handling relations between government and religion

Like free speech, separation of church and state is not an issue that divides liberals and conservatives the way economic issues do. A pro-religion position is illustrated by governments which have or are close to having a specific state religion, as in contemporary Iran (Islam), Israel (Judaism), Ireland (Christianity) and medieval governments. An anti-religion position is illustrated by governments which have sought to substantially decrease the influence of a dominant religion as part of a post-revolution activity, as in Turkey in the 1920s (Islam), the Soviet Union from 1920 to 1990 (Eastern Orthodoxy) and France and Italy after their revolutions (Catholic). The neutral position attempts to help religion in general but not one religion more than another. This includes aid such as tax exemption and grants, religious blessings at public ceremonies, and generic religious symbols on money or other government displays.

The super-optimum position allows virtually no aid to or interference with religious institutions. The concepts of aid and interference are difficult to deal with in the abstract. It is better to discuss aid in terms of something like organized prayers and bible reading in the public schools, or to discuss interference in terms of government interference with the refusal of Christian Scientists or Jehovah's Witnesses to allow emergency blood transfusions.

Whether the United States fits the SOS of religious institutions, it depends on what one means by virtually no aid or interference. The Supreme Court has clearly declared that aiding all religions is unconstitutional, yet it tolerates a great deal of aid on the grounds that the aid is to charitable activities rather than religious activities, or that the aid is too minor to be objectionable. See Table 2.5.

Public school prayers and bible reading

Organized payers and bible reading in public schools

Anybody can pray silently at any time in a public school, or read the bible at any time when other reading has not been assigned. The problem is one of organized prayers or bible reading which are conducted or encouraged by the school authorities, rather than just allowed on an individual basis.

The neutral position emphasizes the reading of religious literature from the major religions of the world as part of a social science course or a literature course (see Table 2.6). That kind of scholarly, non-indoctrination course is constitutionally acceptable and may be desirable for broadening

Table 2.5 Evaluating ways of handling relations between government and religion

Criteria / Alternatives	C Goal Avoid resentments	L Goal Increase creativity & diversity	N Goal Reduce tax costs	N Total (neutral weights)	L Total (liberal weights)	C Total (conservative weights)
C Alternative 'Pro' religion	1	1.5	2	9	9.5	8.5
L Alternative 'Anti' religion	1	1.5	2	9	9.5	8.5
N Alternative Some pro-aid, some anti-interference	3	3	3	18	18*	18*
SOS Alternative No aid, no interference	4.5	4	4	25	24.5**	25.5**

student backgrounds. Such a course, though, may be opposed by some conservative parents who do not want their children to learn about other religions. Such a course may also be opposed by some liberal parents who are afraid the course will be biased in a conservative direction.

The super-optimum solution emphasizes ethical training, rather than theological material. Such training could have a series of case studies for discussion purposes, such as how to deal with situations that involve being a good Samaritan and helping needy people in general. It could also deal with such values as freedom to disagree, fair procedures, judging people on the basis of individual merit and being a productive person.

Simplified SOS analysis of school prayers and bible reading

The conservative position is to allow organized prayers and bible reading in the public schools. The liberal position is to have no organized prayers or bible reading in the public schools. A compromise position might be to allow prayers when they are conducted by the students, not faculty or administrators, and then only on special occasions such as graduation ceremonies. The Supreme Court has not yet ruled on this position, although lower federal courts have held that, if the student-led prayers are during school hours and on school property, they are unconstitutional. The conservative goal is to stimulate religiosity and ethical behavior. The liberal

Table 2.6   Organized prayers/bible reading in public schools

Criteria / Alternatives	C Goal More ethical behavior	N Goal Less friction	N Goal Lower tax cost	L Goal More creativity	N Total (neutral weights)	L Total (liberal weights)	C Total (conservative weights)
C Alternative Prayer and bible reading	3	1	3	2	18	17	19
L Alternative No prayer or bibles	3	3	3	3	24	24	24
N Alternative Religious literature	4	2	3	4	26	26*	26*
SOS Alternative Ethical training	5	4	2	3	28	26*	30**

Note:
Given these calculations, the proposed SOS of ethical training is a clear winner on the conservative totals but not a clear winner on the liberal totals. The Clinton Administration has proposed a five-part SOS consisting of (1) ethical training, (2) allowing students to pray all they want on their own so long as they are not audibly disturbing others, (3) allowing students to meet in the school building after school hours to conduct a bible study club or related activities, (4) allowing students to meet at the flagpole before school hours to have a prayer session but without participation by teachers or school administrators, and (5) having elective courses that deal with history, sociology, literature or other scholarly aspects of religion.

goal is to stimulate diversity and creativity and to avoid dogma and divisiveness.

A super-optimum solution might be to include in the curriculum (at many levels) modules that emphasize ethical training. Such modules could be based on the Golden Rule and related concepts endorsed by both conservatives and liberals, without including the theological aspects.

The previous table dealing with prayer and bible reading (Table 2.6) has a set of ideas that are applicable to Table 2.7, which is an improvement because it has a simpler set of goals. There is also internal consistency, with the conservative alternative winning on the conservative totals and the liberal alternative winning on the liberal totals.

Table 2.7   Prayers and bible reading in the public schools

Criteria Alternatives	C Goal Ethical behavior C=3 L=1	L Goal Secular knowledge of social institutions C=1 L=3	N Total (neutral weights)	C Total (conservative weights)	L Total (liberal weights)
C Alternative Allow	4	2	12	14*	10
L Alternative Prohibit	2	4	12	10	14*
N Alternative Neutral prayer	3	3	12	12	12
SOS Alternative Ethical training and comparative religion	>3.5	>3.5	>14	>14**	>14**

Special situations

On the *use of peyote in religious ceremonies*, the restrictive position would be to prohibit it. The lenient position would be to allow peyote usage subject to no interference by government people. The position between these two might establish some conditions such as some kind of license that would be like a medical license, a prescription. On the matter of the use of peyote in Native American religious ceremonies, the conservative position is to arrest anybody that uses peyote just like cocaine or heroin. The liberal position would be to legalize all those drugs on the theory that prohibition like liquor prohibition does more harm than good. The compromise would be to make an exception for peyote. Such an exception though could be abused, and peyote usage could become widespread. A win–win solution would be to allow peyote and possibly other illegal substances to be used but only in religious ceremonies the way sacramental wine was given exemption from liquor prohibition. That should please conservatives because doing so promotes a form of religiosity. It should also please liberals because it does allow for more freedom than presently exists.

The restrictive position on *compulsory high school for Amish children* would be that, if they do not go to school until age 16, they or their parents will suffer penalties. The liberal position would be to let them drop out of school, but that is leniency bordering on permissiveness. The SOS position would be to provide a well-placed subsidy to the Amish community to provide a high school that is acceptable to secular authorities. The Amish people do not want to teach religion in their high schools. They do not want their children to come into contact with non-Amish children who will be a bad peer influence. If all the Amish children go to the same high school and it can have acceptable facilities, everybody should be happy, including conservatives who would like to see all children have at least a high school diploma so that they can be more productive citizens.

On the controversial issue of Sunday closing, the conservative position is all businesses should be closed on Sunday even if they are operated by Jews or Moslems. The liberal position is that nobody should have to close on Sunday since that is government support for the Christian Sabbath. A compromise position would be to let anybody stay open on Sunday who says they are not a Christian. Like the peyote exception, virtually all business people would suddenly become non-Christians like many non-American Indians would become peyote users. A win–win solution would be to allow Moslems, Jews, Seventh-Day Adventists and people who have a Sabbath other than Sunday to take off their Sabbath as a substitute for working on Sunday. This has worked well with Jewish stores being open on Sunday in Catholic Quebec to the pleasure of the store owners and their customers, all of whom are voluntary customers.

On the *refusal of medical treatment* for religious reasons, the restrictive position would not tolerate a religious exception where life-preserving medicine is needed. The lenient position would allow at least adults to jeopardize their lives for religious reasons, rather than force medicine or a blood transfusion on them. The compromise position is to require medication where children are involved. An SOS position is to talk in terms of allowing consenting adults to do what they want, but to say that anyone who wants to do what amounts to committing suicide is not a lucid, consenting adult. That SOS position argues that people who survive suicide attempts by pure chance tend to be glad they survived and that one could justify keeping them from committing suicide on the grounds that they will generally be pleased afterwards. It certainly sets a bad example, in terms of the sanctity and quality of life, for society to be allowing people to commit suicide. The counterargument is that people who refuse medical treatment for religious reasons think that God is going to save them and that they are not going to die. The situation is still life threatening since we know from previous experience that God does not save all such people. Even the person who deliberately tries to commit suicide may be hoping to be saved, not necessarily by God, but by relatives or friends.

In the case of *faith testing* that does not have anything to do with medication for life-threatening diseases or injuries, such as the use of strychnine and rattlesnakes, the restrictive position would invoke criminal penalties where someone is killed or injured, regardless of whether it is an adult or a child. The lenient position, which is definitely not necessarily the liberal position, would invoke penalties without considering the religious justification as a defense, although it might have some bearing on the sentencing, but not on the guilt. The compromise position with this kind of faith testing would be to distinguish between children and adults, as with compulsory medication. An SOS position would say that faith testing with rattlesnakes and the failure to get blood transfusions may be equally life-threatening and equally suicidal, and therefore equally subject to intervention. The intervention does not mean putting in prison the person who jeopardizes his own life. We do not imprison people who commit crimes while insane, and we are assuming that anybody who is suicidal is by definition insane, or at least mentally ill (although that is just a matter of semantics). However, a third party who encourages life-jeopardizing faith testing would be subject to prison penalties, regardless of whether children or adults are involved. We do not want third parties to be encouraging people to commit suicide; where a third party is involved, it is possibly not so much a matter of assisting a suicide as a variation on outright murder or manslaughter.

Resolving the troubles in Northern Ireland

Classifying the dispute

Northern Ireland is mainly (at least from an Irish point of view) an anti-colonial dispute. From the Protestant point of view (which is also an Irish point of view) this is mainly an ethnic dispute. If one says that the Northern

Ireland dispute is between Ireland and England, one is taking a pro-Irish Catholic position. If one says the dispute is between Irish Protestants in Northern Ireland and Irish Catholics, then one is taking a pro-Irish Protestant position. The Irish Catholics in Northern Ireland do not consider the Irish Protestants to be Irish at all, but a bunch of British carpetbaggers who do not belong there. The Northern Ireland Protestants to some extent consider the Irish Catholics to be terrorists and a bunch of disloyal people from the government of Ireland who do not belong in Northern Ireland.

Both views are wrong. The Irish Protestants have roots that go back about 450 years. It would be pretty hard to say they are some kind of foreigners. It is a bit like South Africa where blacks refer to Afrikaners as foreigners, even though they go back a few hundred years. The involvement of the Republic of Ireland is exaggerated by the Irish Protestants. In terms of international relations, it has had a 'hands-off' policy. It does not endorse the terrorism. Most of the Irish terrorists do have roots in Northern Ireland. They are not from Dublin, they are from Belfast.

Both are also wrong in the sense that it is not an anti-colonial war, and it is not an ethnic war. Ethnically, the Northern Irish Protestants and the Northern Irish Catholics all look alike and talk alike. One cannot tell from their culture that on Sunday one group goes to a Catholic church and the other group goes to a Protestant church. It is basically an old-fashioned class conflict, with the Protestants being the business people and the Catholics being the workers, and the workers resent how they are treated. The bomb throwing is a throwback to throwing bombs at the Czar or throwing bombs in the Haymarket riot.

Also it is a big exaggeration to use the word 'terrorists' when referring to the Irish Catholics when the Irish Protestants do a lot of killing in retaliation. Sometimes the retaliation is not triggered by any specific event but is just the nursing of long-term hatred. The Irish Protestants control the police. When the police kill Irish Catholics, that is a form of state terrorism like the old coal and steel police shooting down strikers in Pennsylvania or North Carolina or Colorado. It is possible for government people to terrorize their own populations.

As for what to do about the Northern Ireland situation, partition and an economic union are not meaningful. There is no easy line drawing. It is like the United States with blacks and whites mixed together. The Catholics do live in poorer neighborhoods, but they all live in the same city and the same small country. There is very little likelihood that the Protestants are going to leave and return to England, where they came from about 450 years ago. The solution does seem to require the kind of race relations legislation that the United States has had which recognizes that blacks are a low-income economic class and that whites have a relatively higher income. *There is need for legislation with regard to fair employment practices, fair housing and other forms of anti-discrimination in education, criminal justice and voting rights.* It has to be imposed by England, not be any legislature in Northern Ireland. Northern Ireland is part of the United Kingdom. The British Parliament does have the power to pass such legislation. Its failure to do so out of a kind of desire to be somewhat neutral is a sin of omission. This is also like the US case of some people blaming labor for the American economy declining relative to Japan and other countries. Other people blame manufacturing. The real blame is on the government for its sins of omission in not properly stimulating economic growth through well-placed subsidies and tax breaks. If we did a super-optimum solution analysis on the Irish problem, this would look like the American race relations problem, although we have said above that Northern Ireland is not an ethnic problem: *it is a class problem.* Likewise, American race relations is more of a class problem than a race problem, especially at the present time when more overt forms of racial discrimination have been outlawed.

SOS analysis

Alternatives   The conservative position on Northern Ireland is to repress the Irish Catholics, call them terrorists, or outlaw them, rather than outlaw the discrimination they are fighting (see Table 2.8). The conservatives want to retain the union with England. The liberal or leftist position on Northern Ireland is for union with Ireland. This is viewed as an independence movement seeking to overthrow a colonial authority as has occurred in former British colonies. A key difference is that this British colony is just a few miles away from England and has a higher percentage of English or British settlers than any other British colony. The neutral position, as in many of these disputes, would be to retain the formal union but grant more autonomy to Northern Ireland regarding its own legislature, executive, and courts.

Arguing by the left for union with Ireland seems unrealistic, since the Republic of Ireland is not pressing to have Northern Ireland become part of Southern Ireland. Southern Ireland would accept Northern Ireland if a referendum in Northern Ireland went in favor of joining Southern Ireland. That is not likely to occur, especially if the referendum requires approval by both groups. The Catholic Irish do constitute a numerical majority and could win in a referendum in which maybe 55 per cent of the population would vote in favor of joining Southern Ireland, with some intensity. And 45 per cent would vote even more vehemently against doing so. This would be a mildly democratic solution because the majority would rule. It would be undemocratic though because it may also be a slight majority with the big majority intensely opposed. The only legal authorities that could call a referendum are

Table 2.8   Applying SOS analysis to Northern Ireland

Criteria / Alternatives	C Goal Retain in UK and preserve business profits C=3 N=2 L=1	L Goal Closeness to Ireland & worker prosperity C=1 N=2 L=3	N Total (neutral weights)	L Total (liberal weights)	C Total (conservative weights)
C Alternative Outlaw the IRA	4	2	12	10	14*
L Alternative Union with Ireland	2	4	12	14*	10
N Alternative More autonomy	3	3	12	12	12
SOS Alternative Anti-discrimination legislation and increasing GNP	>3.5	>3.5		>14**	>14**

England or the Northern Ireland legislature. Neither is likely to do so. Both are dominated by pro-Protestant thinking that recognizes that Catholics do have the numerical majority.

If the conservative position is to outlaw the IRA as the solution to the situation, the liberal position would be union with the Republic of Ireland. (The term 'Ireland', on its own, is confusing: it is used to refer to the whole island, but in political science it is just used to refer to the nation of Ireland, which is only the southern part.) The neutral position would be perhaps to allow more autonomy. This is not an anti-colonial dispute, though, where the compromise is to let the colony have more autonomy but not complete independence. It is not a secession dispute. The idea of more autonomy is a neutral position for some other kinds of dispute, although it is sometimes seen in England as the equivalent of trying to force the people of Northern Ireland to solve their own problems and stop bothering London. The SOS would be to concentrate on anti-discrimination legislation and a program to increase the GNP of Northern Ireland.

Goals and relations   The conservative goals in this context are to retain Northern Ireland in the United Kingdom and to make Northern Ireland business profitable. The liberal goals are to move closer to Southern Ireland and to make economic life more pleasant for Irish Catholic workers.

Outlawing the IRA does keep Northern Ireland in the United Kingdom, but at a tremendous price. The price is not just the cost of putting down the violent disagreement with retaining the colonial status of Northern Ireland, but also the very adverse effect on the GNP and business profits. I cannot imagine that very many international businesses want to locate in Belfast these days, or have wanted to for the last ten years, or want to have their children go to school there. Union with Ireland is clearly contrary to the conservative goals and would not necessarily make businesses that much more profitable. Ireland is not such a prosperous place. It is basically a rural agricultural country that is still suffering from having been made to be a food supplier for England. It has never developed very much industry. Its main source of income, and this may be true of Northern Ireland too, may be checks sent by Americans to their families living in both Northern and Southern Ireland. Its main export is people to the United States.

On the side of the relation between outlawing the IRA and the liberal goals, of making life better for Irish workers, that is a negative. Union with Ireland would lessen discriminatory problems, but it does not result in increasing the gross national product. In fact, Northern Ireland's GNP may be higher per capita than Southern Ireland's at the present time. Belfast is a more industrial city than Dublin. Thus it looks as though we have a basic tradeoff, in that outlawing the IRA, at least relatively speaking, is conducive to conservative nationalist goals. And although it may not be so conducive to business profit, at least it is conducive to business preserving its management prerogatives. On the other side, union with Ireland may be more effective in lessening or wiping out discrimination than is outlawing the IRA.

The super-optimum solution

The SOS is capable of retaining Northern Ireland in the United Kingdom while at the same time making business more profitable, meaning making a higher GNP or a bigger economic pie, which also improves the condition of workers. Their conditions are improved in two ways: they are not subjected to discrimination because it is outlawed by Parliament, and the well-placed subsidies are likely to result in improved wages and job opportunities, especially if they include upgrading skills. As an aside, one might note that there may be a need for more vigorous anti-discrimination enforcement within England itself, not just Northern Ireland. In recent years, England has changed from a relatively homogenous ethnic country to one in which there are many complaints about discrimination against people from India, Pakistan, and the Caribbean. On the matter of well-placed subsidies to stimulate business and employment, one might also note that there may be a need for more such activity in England itself, not just Northern Ireland. The Thatcher government favored a laissez faire approach, at least in theory, with no government interference or subsidies. The Blair government and Laborites do not like the idea of giving subsidies to business. The solution may be indirect subsidies by way of tax breaks for adopting new technologies and improving worker training.

LANGUAGE OR CULTURAL GROUPS

Trilingualism in Philippine education

The *alternatives* are (1) only English in the schools, (2) only Filipino in the schools and (3) both English and Filipino. The SOS emphasis is not on what language is used, but on what the substance is that is covered. The emphasis is placed on substance that is relevant to national productivity.

All of these alternatives involve the local dialect as well. There is no way of avoiding that, which is where the third language comes in. As far as ideological orientation is concerned, speaking only English is associated with conservative elites, and speaking only Filipino has a left-wing nationalism to it. Retaining both is the neutral compromise. The SOS can be referred to as the 'language' of productivity, although with English in order to enable Filipinos to have access to the literature of the world that relates to productivity.

The *goals* were, first, access to the world's books, and second, national unity. The first goal is basically conservative. The second goal is basically liberal, although not necessarily so. This is where we developed three groups, A, B and C, at least with regard to the alternatives. Alternative D is a combination of A and B. The SOS alternative allows for both English and Filipino, but with an emphasis on increasing subject matter.

1   The A alternative is only English. This is endorsed by conservative business people who would like to have more access to international trade. It is also endorsed by liberal intellectuals who would like to receive more Fulbright grants and to contribute to the literature in their fields.
2   The B position of only Filipino appeals to cultural conservatives, but also to left-wing nationalists.
3   The bilingual position comes out neutral, regardless of whether the first and second positions are considered liberal or conservative.

As for *scoring the relations*, we need a third position which says 'only the local dialect'. If we call that position C, then it turns out to be a totally dominated position, since it provides the worst with regard to access to the world's books and the worst with regard to national unity.

In this context, combining English and Filipino (position D) should give the benefits of both. It does not, however, because it detracts from learning English in comparison with teaching only in English. It also detracts from national unity, since both English and Filipino are resented by people who speak only a local dialect, which is a very substantial percentage.

The big problem at the University of the Philippines was deciding how to *assign weights* if the alternatives were not clearly conservative or liberal.

1   The people who take the A position would give a high weight to access to the world's books, and maybe only a weight of 2 to national unity.
2   The people who advocate speaking only Filipino would give a low weight to access and a high weight to unity.
3   The people who advocate teaching in the local dialect would give a low weight to access and a low weight to unity, but a high weight to localism. That alternative may not have been used. It is one thing to say that there is no way of stamping out local dialects. It is another thing to say that the national educational system should encourage local dialects by arranging for books and teachers in every local dialect. We may eliminate that alternative as not being reasonable. What we may wind up with, though, is a fairly traditional analysis in terms of the liberal and conservative nature of the alternatives and goals.
4   We could say that the bilingual group is group D, and that it is placing a high weight on both access and unity. It could be referred to as the D group, rather than the neutral group.

With these weights, we can calculate four different *total columns*. The way things are now set up, we are operating independently of liberal and conservative concepts. This triangulation example serves the useful methodological purpose of how to handle policy controversies that are not strictly liberals versus conservatives but rather group 1 or A versus group 2 or B and possibly group 3 or C. Table 2.9 helps clarify and summarize the alternatives, goals, relations and weights.

Table 2.9 Trilingualism in Philippine education

Goals / Alternatives	Access to world's books	Unity	Totals A Access Wt=3 Unity Wt=2	Totals B Access Wt=1 Unity Wt=3	Totals C Access Wt=1 Unity Wt=1	Totals D Access Wt=3 Unity Wt=3
A Only English	5	4	23	17	9	27
B Only Filipino	2	4	14	14	6	18
C Only local dialect	1	1	5	4	2	6
D Both English and Filipino SOS	4	4	20	16	8	24
Both on productivity	5	5	25	20	10	30

90

SEXUAL GROUPS: GENDER AND PREFERENCE

Gender discrimination and multi-criteria pay equity

The problem

Comparable worth may imply the highly difficult problem of trying to say something about how much a janitor is worth compared with a nurse, independent of the marketplace: the marketplace gives a janitor twice the salary of a nurse, but the comparable worth people want to say that a nurse is worth more than a janitor because she has to have higher educational qualifications, the work is more dangerous, since she can contract diseases, and the work is harder – and even dirtier in a sense. But because she is a woman, she is paid less. See Table 2.10.

Table 2.10 An SOS approach to comparable worth

Criteria / Alternatives	C Goal Avoid overpayment C=3 L=1	L Goal Equitable wage C=1 L=3	N Total (neutral weights)	L Total (liberal weights)	C Total (conservative weights)
C Alternative Do nothing, i.e. leave to marketplace	4	2	12	10	14*
L Alternative Assigned comparable worth	2	4	12	14*	10
N Alternative In between	3	3	12	12	12
SOS Alternative MCDM comparable worth	>3.5	>3.5	14	>14**	>14**

The pay equity school does not try to determine how much a nurse is worth compared with a janitor; it simply says that it is inequitable that she be paid so much less. The situation is not solved, though, by just changing the words. The basic problem is there: how much more should she be paid than what she is currently getting? The solution is definitely not to decrease the pay that janitors get. That would not go over very well with janitors, or with unions in general. Raising her pay without lowering the janitor's pay does not go over very well with those in charge of the state budget. All of these points are almost totally irrelevant since they still do not answer the question of how much more a nurse should be paid.

The SOS approach is to determine what all the criteria are that should go into determining people's wages, to give the criteria relative weights, to score each job on each of the criteria and then to use the total scores to figure out by what percentage each person's salary should be increased. If nobody's salary is decreased, it is either increased or held constant. If there are 100 job classifications, all of them receive varying increases, except the one job classification that is the anchor. That gets the lowest total score. If that job classification is doing X work and X work is paid $4 per hour and winds up with a total score of 24, and nurses wind up with a total score of 48, the nurses should get $8 per hour.

Alternatives

The conservative approach is do nothing – literally to leave it to the market-place. If nurses are being paid $5 per hour and janitors $10 per hour, then that is what nurses and janitors are worth. The liberal approach is to say arbitrarily, without any systematic allocation analysis, a variety of arbitrary things. By definition, 'arbitrary' means that there is no rule that is consistent across states, across job classifications, across time periods, across any-thing. If janitors are chosen as the anchor point, and it is arbitrarily decided that nurses are twice as worthy as janitors, then nurses get paid $20 per hour. If whoever is making the decision decides that pilots are less worthy than nurses, or more specifically are about 75 per cent as worthy as nurses and janitors are only 50 per cent as worthy as nurses, then pilots get $15 per hour. The whole system is dependent on the arbitrariness of whoever is making the decisions. This arbitrariness is somewhat reduced by making it a collective decision of maybe five people representing different viewpoints. That makes it average arbitrariness rather than one-person arbitrariness. We would not call that the arbitrary approach, but rather the comparable worth approach. It might be called the assigned comparable worth, as contrasted to the multi-criteria decision making (MCDM) comparable worth.

The middling position is something in between the first two. If the mar-ketplace says janitors are worth $10 an hour and nurses $5 an hour, and the assigned comparable worth says janitors are worth $10 an hour since this does not lower their wages, but it says nurses are worth $20 an hour, then the neutral position likewise keeps janitors at $10 but nurses get between $5 and $20, meaning between the marketplace and the assigned comparable worth, which is $12.50. That is slightly less arbitrary because it does take the marketplace into consideration and the marketplace, one could argue, is not so arbitrary. It is based on supply and demand, although there is some argument that nurses are underpaid, in spite of the fact that there is a shortage of them, for sexist reasons.

The super-optimum solution is MCDM comparable worth. It is goal-oriented or criteria-oriented. It can include in the criteria what the marketplace wages are. Following the marketplace can be given a high weight as one of the criteria, but not the only criterion. It can also have as a criterion whatever some decision-making group assigns to each job classification as its 'worth'. In addition to those two criteria, one could have criteria that relate to the amount of education required, dangerousness or dirtiness. One would not have supply and demand since they are supposedly already included in the marketplace calculations. Nor would one include words like 'equity' because they supposedly are included in the decision making of the godlike people who are on the committee or the equitable people who are on the committee.

Goals

The conservative goal is basically not to overpay people, just like under minimum wage. No need to pay nurses $20/hour if an adequate supply can be obtained at $5/hour. Comparable worth is very much like minimum wage.

The liberals want a decent wage, but decent in the sense of equitable, rather than in the sense of providing for a minimum of food, shelter and clothing.

Relations

Doing nothing does well on avoiding overpayment. It keeps the wages down for everybody. Assigning comparable worth is bad for overpayment. It pays in the hypothetical situation $20 an hour to nurses who would otherwise be willing to work possibly for $5 an hour, or for something more than $5 but substantially less than $20. On the equitable wage side, doing nothing is inequitable. It is based strictly on the cold-blooded marketplace which is not concerned with how much people need, at least not directly, or how much people deserve in some sense other than a supply and demand sense. Trying to assign comparable worth, no matter how arbitrary it is, does attempt to be equitable and to recognize that at least part, if not all, of the reason for nurses being paid less than janitors is that janitors are males and nurses are females, or for porters being paid a lot less than conductors is that porters tend to be black and conductors white.

The SOS avoids overpayment, maybe not as well as doing nothing. Maybe it is only a little better than a 3, say 3.5. The SOS of MCDM comparable worth is more equitable than the marketplace, but perhaps it is not as equitable as a committee operating with something approaching divine guidance. The key thing is that, if MCDM comparable worth winds up with a 3.5 on both the conservative and the liberal goal, it is an overall SOS winner, even though it loses on each of the goals. This is a good example of clarifying that an SOS is not a dominating solution, meaning that it does not have to dominate on every single goal. That is unnecessarily too difficult a standard to meet.

Implications

If we were to use comparable worth as a case study, this could be a good example of a situation where the same subject matter can illustrate both choosing and allocating. Here we have used it to choose what approach should be used to determine wages. We would then use SOS allocation or at least P/G% allocation to implement the SOS choice. We could carry it further and talk about SOS allocation. It would mean that, for a few hundred job classifications, one would have to determine two sets of MCDM comparable worth wages. One would be a conservative set and the other would be a liberal set, depending on what weights one used for the criteria. That is not too difficult. One could then arrive at an SOS allocation by using the methods discussed in the allocation tutorial, Chapter 2 of S. Nagel and L. Bievenue, *Teach Yourself Decision-Aiding Software* (University Press of America, 1992). By doing so, one would raise the budget so as to cover both the conservative and the liberal allocations. What that would basically mean is that, since every job classification would get two allocations, one would simply choose the higher of the two, whichever one it was, and provide enough money to cover the higher of the two allocations. It would still be a form of SOS allocation if one just averaged the two, since that result would still be better than the previous conservative first choice, which was to do nothing, and better than the previous liberal choice which was to assign comparable worths arbitrarily.

However, this illustrates the importance of talking about initial expectations. The new average wage between the conservative and liberal may be better than both the original conservative and the original liberal, but not better than the new MCDM conservative and the new MCDM liberal. This occurs especially in allocation problems where, say, $100 needs to be allocated. The liberals say they should get $60 and the conservatives $40. The conservatives say they should get $70 and the liberals $30. The new SOS allocation is to find a way to get the budget up to $132 and then give the liberals $61 and the conservatives $71. Then the liberals might say that what they really want is not more than $60, but more than 60 per cent, and that they would now like to have more than 60 per cent of the new $132; and the conservatives might say that they would like to have more than 70 per cent of the new $132. This could go on forever. Each time a new budget is allocated, each side raises its estimate of what it would like to have. Therefore we have to specify better than the initial expectations, not better than some subsequent expectations after one sees that it is possible to satisfy the initial expectations.

Alleged biological basis for sexual preference discrimination and broader implications

The trial lawyers example

Male trial lawyers are reputed to have more testosterone than male lawyers who are not trial lawyers. This raises some interesting implications, one of which is that, if there are sex-related hormones that are responsible for job performance, one could argue that there is a biological basis for some forms of discrimination in terms of gender or sexual preference.

The counterargument is that, first of all, it may be totally irrelevant to note that trial lawyers have more testosterone than non-trial lawyers. To begin with, one needs to clarify the cause and effect relations a little. It may be that the trial lawyers start out with a very low testosterone level compared to other lawyers and that being a trial lawyer is so stressful that it somehow increases their testosterone level. The implication of the article may be, quite wrongly, that their testosterone level caused them to be successful trial lawyers. What we may need to do, if we want to resolve the causal relation issue, is, for example, to check the testosterone level of students entering law school and then look to see what they are doing ten years later. The implication in terms of the causal relation is that those with high testosterone levels may wind up 20 per cent trial lawyers, 90 per cent not or 80 per cent not, those with low testosterone levels may wind up only 5 per cent trial lawyers and 95 per cent not.

I believe that, in general, women have a zero testosterone level, but they may have some other hormone that distinguishes aggressive women from non-aggressive women. Thus, if we are going to talk about a hormonal basis for aggressiveness, we have got to take into consideration the female counterpart. Not all women are equally submissive or equally aggressive. If aggressiveness bears some relation to hormones, aggressive women must have more of some hormone than men do, even though it is not the same hormone. Much of this is pure nonsense because nobody is likely to have a hormone test for being hired by a trial lawyer firm. Much more relevant is a person's track record, including law school grades, writing for the law review and previous experience as a trial lawyer if this is applicable.

As in any discussion of discrimination, the odds are that there will be big overlapping normal curves. If the blue curve is the high testosterone curve and the red curve is a low testosterone curve, and the peak shows average trial lawyer ability, the blue curve has a higher level than the red curve. But there are plenty of people under the red curve at its right end who are much better trial lawyers than people under the blue curve at its left end, which means that each person has to be judged as an individual. That would not be the case if every high testosterone person was a great trial lawyer and every low testosterone person was a miserable trial lawyer; or if every black person was brilliant and every white person was dumb.

By normal curves we mean a distribution curve that is hill shaped. Intelligence is an example. The female normal curve involves many bright females and many not so bright females, but most are in the middle. Likewise, the male normal curve involves many bright males and many not so bright males, but many are also in the middle. The female middle may or may not be to the left of the male middle. The important aspect of normal curves on ability is that plenty of females, blacks, or other discriminated groups are smarter than plenty of males, whites, or other favored groups. Thus, normal curves argue in favor of merit selection rather than selection on the basis of gender, race, or other such characteristics. Biological characteristics or at least these kind with regard to qualitative characteristics tend to follow normal curves. Non-qualitative characteristics pretty much tend to follow discrete rectangles; for example, all females or virtually all females have uteruses and virtually no males have uteruses. There is no overlap on that. It is not a qualitative characteristic like intelligence or trial skill on which there is overlap across races, genders and sexual preferences.

Individual versus group characteristics

The more interesting implication for discrimination is not between males and females but between heterosexual males and gay males. The problem here is that the gay males are just as capable of having high testosterone scores as the heterosexual males. There is nothing biological that keeps them, unlike females, from having high testosterone scores. They have low testosterone scores biologically in the sense that they are born that way, but not because they are females. They are males. What it amounts to is that in future years, and perhaps this is already beginning, we may be talking about bona fide occupational qualifications that apply to heterosexuals as opposed to gays, just as a lot of case law has been developed with regard to males as opposed to females.

All of the literature, however, tends to be of very little value because all of the characteristic qualifications involved depend on the individual. For example, the average female is obviously shorter than the average male, and thus the average female is less qualified to play for the Chicago Bulls than the average male. Under the old law one could say that females could therefore be excluded from playing for the Chicago Bulls under the notion that height is a bona fide occupational qualification for playing for the Chicago Bulls. That is no longer the current law, partly determined by the marketplace. If a female comes along who is only two feet tall but has amazing accuracy that makes her commercially valuable to the Chicago Bulls, she is likely to be hired regardless of what the law says. Or if she is seven feet tall and can dunk like any other seven-footer, she may also be hired. It depends on her individual characteristics. That is what the courts are now saying, and that is what the owners of the teams are in effect saying too. They were willing to hire black baseball players before any legal rules required them to do so when it became obvious that they would otherwise be missing out on some rather good players: another plus for the competitive marketplace dealing with some of the problems of discrimination.

The high testosterone level may have nothing to do with performing well as a trial lawyer, but it may be a factor in self-selecting to become a trial lawyer if people who are highly aggressive think that being a trial lawyer is a way in which you can vent your aggression. Probably people who have high testosterone levels join police forces partly for that reason. Also it might be noted that one could have too high a testosterone level and become overly aggressive and thereby antagonize judges and juries, and interfere with out of court settlements that would be beneficial to one's clients and oneself on a one-third contingency basis.

Biological versus sociological characteristics

On the sociological level, discrimination can be handled, not necessarily more easily, but through different means, such as anti-discrimination legislation and skills upgrading. If people are biologically different, that is not so easy to change as contrasted to people's attitudes toward biological differences. Blacks are biologically different from whites. However, it is not their blackness that causes problems, it is the attitude of whites toward people who are black.

That is different from having a biological characteristic as an individual or as a group that is related to job performance. Very few jobs require white skin, except maybe playing Hans Christian Andersen in a movie. Even then make-up could handle the problem. Some jobs, though, do require intelligence or strength. The simple answer is that it does not make any difference if there are group differences of intelligence or strength: a group is not being hired, it is the individual. Presumably a rational employer would prefer to have a smart member of a dumb group than a dumb member of a smart group.

Suppose we have situation (situation A) where discrimination on the basis of merit would be quite justified, where everybody in Group 1 on IQ is lower than everybody in Group 2. The smartest person in Group 1 is dumber than the dumbest person in Group 2. A real-world example would be that an employer who is hiring people to go into a program for training computer programmers should not be required to hire retarded people regardless of whether they are black, white, male or female if they as individuals as well as a group cannot handle the work. That is not discrimination. Discrimination by definition means rejecting someone who is qualified because that person is a member of some ethnic, gender or age group, or any other group that is not liked.

The opposite extreme (section C) is where one has two normal curves. Group 2 has a higher average than Group 1 but about 40 per cent of the people in Group 1 are smarter than 70 per cent of the people in Group 2. In fact, one could even have the following situation. Group 2 consists of 10 people and Group 1 consists of 10 people. The people in Group 2 have an average IQ of 200. The people in Group 1 have an average IQ of 100. Yet one out of the 10 people or even all 10 out of the 10 people in Group 1 are smarter than everybody in Group 2 except one who is a super-genius bringing up the average. All you need in Group 2, which is the smarter average group, is one person with, say, a 300 IQ and nine retarded people with IQs of 10 apiece. The total is then 390. One problem with IQ, unlike money, is that you cannot have an IQ much higher than 200, whereas one could have fantastic wealth, thereby causing Group 2 to be richer than Group 1, and yet everybody in Group 1 is richer than everybody in Group 2 except the one person who brings the average up by being a billionnaire. The point is that, even with IQ as contrasted to income, the overlap between the two groups can be so great that it makes little sense to use the group characteristics, as contrasted to the individual characteristics, to make employment decisions.

The middle position (situation B) is where there is overlap but less than in the above examples. Suppose about 60 per cent of Group 1 is below the dumbest in Group 2 and about 60 per cent of Group 2 is above the smartest in Group 1. Each group has 40 per cent that are roughly tied: that is, the 40 per cent smartest of Group 1 and the 40 per cent dumbest of Group 2. The answer is that, so long as there is any substantial overlap, say 10 per cent and upwards, people have to be judged as individuals.

Criminal justice sentencing

If we have statistics that show that the average defendant, or even much higher than the average, say 90 per cent or 95 per cent, is guilty, we still demand individual proof. We do not say, 'Well, statistics show that 95 per cent of all people who are accused of this crime are guilty, therefore you are guilty', without a trial.

The reason is that it is so much worse to make the error of declaring someone to be guilty when they are innocent than it is to make the error of declaring someone to be innocent when they are guilty. One could argue that going to prison is much more serious than being hired or not hired for a job. And therefore the analogy does partly break down in that regard. A better reason is that it requires so little effort to judge a person on their individual characteristics in most hiring situations, whereas it may require a lot of effort to conduct a trial to determine guilt. A reasonably meaningful pencil-and-paper test could be given to a person who is applying to go onto a computer programming course. In fact, the pencil-and-paper test might have such questions as 'Have you graduated from elementary school?' If the answer is no, chances are they will not do so well on the course. In other words, the test does not even have to be an aptitude test: it can be a test of one's previous relevant experience and accomplishments. Therefore, if the incremental cost of judging people on the basis of their individual characteristics is very low, it should not be so important that going to prison is not at stake, but just being hired or not hired.

An additional point that is not sufficiently made in these situations is that we do not want to put innocent people in prison or fail to hire a good person just because it hurts innocent people and good potential employees. More importantly, it hurts society (or, in the employment context, it hurts the employer who is deprived of the good potential employee). In the case of convicting innocent people, it decreases respect for the legal system as well as wasting money confining people to prison who should not be there.

The SOS perspective comes into it because these problems are frequently treated as tradeoff problems, as suggested above, where we say that it is worse to make the error of convicting an innocent person than acquitting a guilty person. We should not be so concerned with which error is worse. We should be concerned with trying to decrease both kinds of errors – or both kinds of errors in the employment situation of failing to hire a good person and also mistakenly hiring a bad person.

An SOS analysis of discrimination against homosexuals

Doing nothing means leaving it up to the marketplace to determine job opportunities for homosexuals even if the marketplace results in discrimination. Anti-discrimination refers to prohibiting the non-hiring of a qualified homosexual because he or she is a homosexual. The neutral position involves a government pronouncement against discrimination, but without active enforcement. See Table 2.11.

The SOS alternative involves childhood socialization regarding the importance of judging people on the basis of merit, without explicitly mentioning homosexuals. At the teenage level, socialization and education should also include judging people on the basis of merit with an explicit mention of what groups have traditionally been discriminated against, including homosexuals.

The fourth goal of isolating and ostracizing homosexuals is held by some conservatives, but not all. Thus the conservative totals can be shown two ways, one with the fourth goal and one without it. The socialization approach wins over the conservative approach of doing nothing, unless one considers the fourth goal of ostracism. The socialization approach also wins over the liberal approach of anti-discrimination action by the government, at least in the long run.

We usually assume that conservatives give conservative goals a weight of 3 on a 1–3 scale, and that liberals give such goals a weight of 1, with the opposite weighting for liberal goals. That does not necessarily have to be so. On high national productivity, conservatives and liberals may be closer together, even in the context of discrimination against homosexuals.

PHYSICAL GROUPS: AGE AND DISABILITY

Greater than full employment

Optimum unemployment can be defined as having no more than 3 per cent of the labor force out of work. If the figure goes below 3 per cent, there may be insufficient movement upward from less to more appropriate jobs. The Humphrey–Hawkins legislation specifies 4 per cent as the target figure. One could, however, talk about unemployment that is below 0 per cent or better than 0 per cent.

For example, suppose there are 25 people in a society and 10 are in the labor force. Of the 10 in the labor force, two are unemployed, to give a 20 per cent unemployment figure. If a job is found for one of the two unemployed workers, then we have 10 per cent unemployment. If both formerly

Table 2.11 An SOS analysis of discrimination against homosexuals

Criteria / Alternatives	C Goal Entrepreneurial freedom	L Goal Equal opportunity	L Goal High national productivity	C Goal Isolate & ostracize homosexuals	N Total		L Total		C Total	
C Alternative Do nothing	4	2	2	4	24	16	20	16	28**	16**
L Alternative Anti-discrimination	2	4	4	2	24	20	28*	26*	20	14
N Alternative Pronouncement without enforcement	3	3	3	3	24	18	24	21	25	15
SOS Alternative Socialization[1]	5	5	5	1	32	30	36**	35**	26	25**

Note:
1 Teenage socialization regarding sexual preference; childhood socialization regarding equality and merit in general.

unemployed workers are employed and there is no new unemployment, we have 0 per cent unemployment.

Getting credit for adding to the labor force

If we expand the labor force, the unemployment figure is recalculated using a new base or denominator. Thus, if we improve the real or perceived job opportunities, so that four of the 15 people who were not in the labor force now become job seekers, then unemployment will go up to four out of 14, or 29 per cent. In other words, the unemployment figure as a social indicator in effect penalizes expanding the labor force. This may be an important defect in so important a social indicator.

Perhaps it might make more sense to say that putting to work someone who was formerly outside the labor force should be counted as partly offsetting one person who is already in the labor force but unemployed. Suppose we find jobs for all four of those new additions to the labor force. One could then say that unemployment has now dropped to two out of 14, or 14 per cent, from the figure of 20 per cent. Thus adding people to the labor force and finding jobs for them does reduce the unemployment figure, even if the previously unemployed people are not found jobs.

One could say that nought out of 14 in this context is better than nought out of 10, even if they both represent 0 per cent unemployment. Is two out of 14 worse than, equal to, or better than nought out of 10? The answer is 'equal to' if finding jobs for four people formerly outside the labor force is worth as much to society as finding jobs for two unemployed people who were already in the labor force. In other words, the answer to the question depends on the tradeoff between employing unemployed people 'out of' as opposed to 'in' the labor force. A two to one tradeoff seems reasonable.

A well-employed society should have a combination of a low percentage of unemployed people (as determined by the quantity of unemployed divided by the total labor force) and a high percentage of the total adult population in the labor force. Thus a society of 25 people is not doing so well on employment opportunities if it has 18 adults and only 10 are in the labor force, whereas another society of 25 people with 18 adults has 14 in the labor force. In other words, we need to place more emphasis on bringing more people into the labor force who are willing and capable of working. That includes older people, disabled people and single parents receiving public aid. Older people often have skills that could still be applied, especially in a white collar society. Disabled people and public aid parents can often be trained to qualify for profitable and satisfying jobs. The public aid parents may also need daycare services. Training and daycare involve tax expenditure, but the investment may be worthwhile if public aid expenses are reduced even more than the tax expenditure.

In the unemployment context, doing better than the optimum means seeking not only to get unemployment down to about 3 per cent or 4 per cent, but also to get the percentage of the labor force up to about 80 per cent or 90 per cent of the adult population. In an optimizing society, virtually every adult should be provided with sufficient job opportunities, job training and related services, so that virtually every adult will be constructively employed.

Getting credit for lessening underemployment

Doing better than the optimum in the employment context should also include having an expanding economy such that anyone who wants to take on a second job can do so. Thus we need to emphasize a third measure which gets at the extent to which employed people are fully employed. This really involves two measures. One relates to the percentage of employed people who work full-time. If only six of the 10 people in the labor force have at least full-time employment, we have a less well-employed society than if the figure were nine out of 10. Full-time employment can be defined as working 40 hours a week, although the standard as to what constitutes full-time employment has over the years involved a reduction in the number of hours. It is appropriate to reduce the number of years as society becomes more productive and people can produce more in fewer hours and thus earn more salary or wages for fewer hours of work.

The other measure of full employment could relate to the percentage of people who would like to have a second job who do have a second job. Suppose all 10 people are employed 40 hours a week, and four of them would like to work more, but there is no more work available for them. That means that 60 per cent of the labor force is happy with its jobs and 40 per cent are unhappy. It is, however, generally more important to employ unemployed people in the labor force than to provide more employment to those who already have a part-time, seasonal or full-time job. If the desirability tradeoff is two to one for unemployed in the labor force versus unemployed out of the labor force, the desirability tradeoff is probably about three to one for finding jobs for the *un*employed in the labor force versus the *under*employed. A more precise measure might consider the degree of underemployment for each worker.

A summary index

Thus we now have an expanded concept of doing better than the optimum of 3 per cent or 4 per cent unemployment. The expanded concept includes:

1   providing jobs for older people,
2   providing jobs for disabled people,
3   providing jobs for single parent public aid recipients,
4   providing jobs for others outside the labor force, including those who might otherwise be discouraged or depressed about finding jobs,
5   providing full-time jobs for those who are only working part-time or on seasonal jobs,
6   providing second jobs for those who want them, and
7   providing jobs for those who are already part of the labor force but are totally unemployed.

The category identified in (7) has traditionally been the only category of jobless people counted as unemployed. By obtaining jobs for the other six categories as well as category 7, we are doing better than the traditional optimum.

All these ideas can be incorporated into a new index of employment dance with the formula, $E = (F + P/3)/(L + A/2)$, where

E = employment index;
F = number of fully employed people in the economy (six people in our hypothetical economy);
P = number of people partly employed (two people in the theoretical economy);
L = number of people in the labor force (10 people);
A = number of able-bodied people who are not in the labor force; that is, who are not actively seeking jobs. That is an additional eight people.

This means the denominator of the index is $10 + 8/2$, or 14. The numerator is $6 + 2/3$, or 6.67. Thus the employment index is 6.67/14, or 48 per cent. This is in contrast to the traditional unemployment percentage which would be 2/10, or 20 per cent, with a complement of 100 per cent – 20 per cent, or 80 per cent.

The above formula has the following advantages over the traditional unemployment percentage:

1   it emphasizes the more positive goal of seeking high employment, rather than the more negative goal of seeking low unemployment;
2   the denominator considers both people in the labor force and able-bodied people outside the labor force at the two to one tradeoff mentioned above;
3   the numerator considers both people partly employed and those fully employed at the three to one tradeoff mentioned above; partly employed

could include those who are fully employed, but who are seeking additional work;
4   this index enables a society in effect to do better than 0 per cent unemployment or 100 per cent employment by fully employing people and by finding jobs for bodied people not counted in the labor force.

Both the employment index and the traditional unemployment percentage are incapable of going below 0 per cent or above 100 per cent. This is so under the employment index because one cannot employ more than all the people in the labor force plus all the able-bodied people not in the labor force. We could redefine the index in order to allow for improvements in the employment picture that would exceed 100 per cent. Doing so would mean using last year's labor force base or denominator, but this year's employed people or numerator. Thus suppose that, last year, or in the last time period, the denominator was 14 people and the numerator was 6.67. Suppose further that 10 more people were added to the labor force for whom jobs were found. That could cause the numerator to go up to 16.67, and the employment index to go up to 16.67/14, or 119 per cent. This is in contrast to adding the 10 newly employed people to both the numerator and the denominator. That would give an employment index of 16.67/24, or 70 per cent, which seems more meaningful.

Along related lines, one could subtract one unemployed person from the traditional unemployment percentage for every newly employed person who is brought into the labor force. With enough subtractions one could go below 0 per cent unemployment. That, however, would undesirably hide the fact that there are still some unemployed people in the labor force. One can, however, recognize that 0 per cent unemployment with more people brought into the labor force and less *under*employed people is better than 0 per cent unemployment with lots of discouraged people outside the active labor force and lots of underemployed people within it. Thus it is possible to do better than 0 per cent unemployment without getting into the conceptual problems of a negative percentage.

The Asian labor shortage

The problem

When I spoke before the Hong Kong government, they wanted to know about SOS with regard to a problem involving Hong Kong that they considered to be crucial, and that they were not able to resolve. The labor shortage was the problem, which they were approaching from a very traditional perspective.

On one hand, the solution was to import additional labor. In reality, the solution required no importing at all. All that was required was to stop arresting people who were seeking to cross the borders from every direction. These included the Vietnamese boat people, the people from the Chinese mainland, and the Filipinos. As of 1999 there is less of a labor shortage but there still is an immigration problem. Now that Hong Kong has become a province of China, one would think that people from other Chinese provinces could move to Hong Kong. That is what a Hong Kong court thought, but it was reversed in 1999 by the Beijing Central Government which does not want millions of people moving from other provinces to Hong Kong.

This leads to a dilemma that paralyzes decision making if the choice is one of retaining the labor shortage and thereby missing out on opportunities to make Hong Kong even more prosperous than it is, as opposed to allowing labor in and thereby diluting the population of Hong Kong. This is partly a racist thing but is also a legitimate concern regarding a lot of expense involved in education and welfare, although the immigrants may be especially ambitious people who in the long run will pay more than their share of taxes. This may be especially true of the Vietnamese boat people, although coming by boat from Vietnam to Hong Kong is not much more difficult than crossing the border from Mexico to Texas. They are, however, giving up whatever they had in Vietnam.

The SOS that seemed to be a kind of blind spot by virtue of the way the terms were defined is simply to redefine the labor force, so that suddenly there is a labor surplus. Redefining the labor force means recognizing all the potential labor there is, in the form of elderly people who are capable of working who are not doing so, disabled people, mothers of pre-school children, people with part-time or seasonal jobs, people who are looking for second jobs and, especially, people whose jobs and productivity could be upgraded.

The SOS table for conservatives and liberals

The *alternatives* are: (C1) import cheap labor, (C2) preserve national purity, (L1) preserve union wages, (L2) provide immigrant opportunities, (N) import some labor: less than either C1 or L2 would like, but more than C2 or L1 would like; (SOS) add to the labor force and increase labor productivity. This sounds rather ambiguous since one can add to the labor force by importing labor. In this context it means adding by drawing upon people who are already part of the society.

One key *goal* would be to increase the GNP, especially by filling orders that otherwise would not be filled. A second key goal is to minimize disruption to the existing society.

The *scoring* tends to involve the conservative alternative being mildly negative on the liberal goal and mildly positive on the conservative goal, and the opposite with the liberal alternative. The neutral alternative is in the middle on both goals, and the SOS alternative does especially well on both goals. Table 2.12 shows six alternatives, two goals, and twelve scores, as well as totals reflecting weights for nativism, unionism and an open door policy.

Table 2.12   The Asian labor shortage

Criteria / Alternatives	C1 L2 Goal Increase GNP	C2 L1 Goal Reduce disruption to society	N Total (neutral weights)	Total L1 & C2 weights (nativism & unionism)	Total L2 & C1 weights (open door policy)
C1 Alternative Import cheap labor	4	2	12	10	14*
C2 Alternative Preserve national purity	2	4	12	14*	10
L1 Alternative Preserve union wages	2	4	12	14*	10
L2 Alternative Provide immigrant opportunities	4	2	12	10	14*
N Alternative Import some labor	3	3	12	12	12
SOS Alternative Increase labor force and productivity	5	5	20	20**	20**

In this example there are two conservative alternatives and two liberal alternatives. It is not appropriate to say that one conservative alternative is more conservative than another, and that one liberal alternative is more liberal than another. They are just two different kinds of conservatism, and two different kinds of liberalism. One kind of conservatism is basically pro-business and is interested in maximizing business profits. The other is basically nationalist bordering on racist, and is more concerned with ethnic purity than it is with profits. One type of liberalism is pro-union: it is concerned with union wages – pocket-book liberalism. It is not concerned with civil liberties. The other liberalism focuses more on civil liberties.

Using labels, we could say that we are talking about business conservatives versus cultural conservatives, and hard-hat liberals versus civil libertarian liberals. These are reasonably neutral terms as contrasted to more derogatory or laudatory terms, such as mercenary conservatives versus racist conservatives, and pocket-book liberals versus intellectual liberals. 'Intellectual liberals' sounds laudatory, but Spiro Agnew called them 'effete', 'egghead' or 'pinhead liberals', which does not sound so laudatory.

There are other kinds of conservatives and liberals, but they are not all involved in the immigration issue. There are also religious conservatives who are very strong on issues that have to do with abortion, pornography, or prayer in the schools, who are not necessarily pro-business or racist, although there may be some overlap. Likewise, one can talk about a set of liberals who are particularly concerned with doing things for poor people. The hard-hat unionists are not very sympathetic to people on welfare. The civil libertarians may be concerned with the free speech rights and due process rights of people on welfare, but not necessarily advocates of bigger handouts. They may even be advocates of placing all kinds of strings on handouts, which would go contrary to the welfare liberals, just as the idea of strings goes contrary to the laissez-faire conservatives. At the present time, one can talk about two thirds of pro-business conservatives, those who want to do things for business but with strings attached, and those who want to do things for business but with no strings attached. Likewise, the liberals can be classified into those who want to do things for poor people with no strings attached, and those who recognize that strings may be good for poor people and society.

In terms of the initial or neutral totals, all the alternatives tend to wind up with total scores of 12 except the SOS alternative, because they all tend to do mildly well for a 4 on one goal and mildly poorly for a 2 on the second goal, or a 3 on both.

The liberal totals in this context favor alternatives C1 and L2, but it depends on what kind of liberal we are talking about. Maybe we have to say that both goals are ambivalent goals. An increased GNP is normally a liberal goal, but would be opposed by unionists in this context if it meant importing cheap competitive labor in order to achieve it. Therefore it would only be a liberal goal in the eyes of the L2 liberals. It is also a conservative goal in the eyes of the C1 conservatives. This could be a good example of a situation where it is not meaningful to refer to the goals as being conservative or liberal.

Each goal is strongly supported by both liberals and conservatives, but different kinds of liberals and conservatives. In the usual situation, all goals are supported by liberals and by conservatives, but the liberals like some goals relatively better than the conservatives do, and vice versa. Here it is not that the liberals like some goals relatively better than the conservatives do; it is that some liberals like some of the goals better than other liberals do. Likewise, some conservatives like some of the goals better than other conservatives do. In other words, there is a kind of conflict within conservatives on the goals as well as on the alternatives, and it might thus be meaningless to talk about a liberal total and a conservative total. One could talk about an L1 liberal total and an L2 liberal total and a C1 conservative total and a C2 conservative total. In that regard, increasing the GNP is a C1 goal and an L2 goal. Decreasing societal disruption is a C2 and an L1 goal.

This complicates the assigning of *weights* to a certain extent, but not very much. Table 2.12 shows how each group would weight the goals. Knowing that, we can calculate in our heads what the totals should look like. The subtotals could be put on the table. There are only two multipliers, namely 3 and 1. It is easy enough to show what each relation score becomes when multiplied by 3 and when multiplied by 1. We do not have to write anything down to show what each raw score becomes when multiplied by 1.

Calculating the four sets of new totals, we have the following outcomes.

1   For the L1 or unionist set, the winner is either preserving national purity or preserving union wages. They amount to the same thing in terms of whether external labor should be excluded or imported. Some might say that the racist conservatives and exclusionary unionists are strange bedfellows, but there is nothing very strange about this at all. It has occurred at many times in American history where otherwise economic–liberal union members would take sexist or racist positions.

2   The L2 or civil libertarian column or row has intellectuals and business people getting together because they share a willingness to allow for more open immigration, even though their reasons may be different.

3   On the C1 or business column or row, the results turn out to be the same as the L2 column because in the context of this subject matter and these goals, the business people who want to import cheap labor come out with the same totals as the intellectuals who want to provide more immigrant opportunities. We could get differences in these columns if we were to add a goal such as 'increasing individual firm profits', which would please the business types, but not necessarily the intellectual types. If we added a goal called 'rewarding ambitious immigrants', that would please the intellectual types, but not necessarily the business types. We would have to add two such goals in order to get a difference between the L2 column and the C1 column. We would then have to add two more goals to get a difference between the L1 and the C2 column.

4   The C2 or nativist column which reflects the goals of those who want to preserve national purity comes out the same as the L1 column, which reflects the goals of those who want to preserve union wages.

The reason we have four basic rows and two basic columns is because rows C1 and L2 are directed toward achieving the same goal of increasing the GNP. Likewise, rows C2 and L1 are directed toward the same goal of reducing disruption to society. We could force C2 and L1 to be separate in the United States by adding a goal like 'encouraging white Anglo-Saxon Protestantism'. That might please those who want to preserve national purity, but it would not please the average unionist, who tends to be Polish, Italian, Irish, Hispanic or otherwise Catholic. Likewise, we could add a goal that would please the unionists, but not please the ethnic purity people. All we have to do is just add a goal that is the opposite of encouraging white Anglo-Saxon Protestantism, such as encouraging diversity of religion and language in the United States. That is the opposite of preserving national purity, but it would be likely to please most unionists since they tend to be minority group people, at least in terms of religion, if not race.

All this can be expressed verbally, without cluttering up the table, which at present has seven columns, by adding four more goals. That would give it 11 columns which is not too horrendous, although the standard table only allows for nine. A main reason for not adding those goals is not that they would make the table too complicated, but that they are not as relevant to the immigration issue as the goals that we currently have. We could add just two more columns, since there is no reason why we have to add one column that talks in terms of promoting a single ethnic group (versus pluralism) and then another column that talks in terms of doing the opposite.

The best way to handle the problem is just to note that, although the L1 and C2 groups come out with the same bottom line, as also the L2 and C1 groups, they do so for different reasons. This table is not designed to indicate explicitly what those different reasons are. It is just designed to bring out which alternative is the best in light of the alternatives available and the goals to be achieved. The discussion can cover the possible motives for different groups placing the same high value or low value on a goal for different reasons. It can also explore why two groups have the same reasons but yet are different groups because they differ with regard to other matters.

The SOS alternative

Instead of concentrating on the diversity within conservatives and liberals, we could put more emphasis on the idea of solving the problem by raising goals above what is considered the best. That means raising the unemployment goal to be higher than just achieving zero unemployment in the traditional sense. That sense does not count large segments of the population as being unemployed. It simply defines them out of the labor force. Nor does it count large segments of the labor force as being underemployed. Instead, it defines being employed as simply having a job, regardless of how part-time or how beneath one's capabilities it is.

Doing better than what was formerly considered the best is now only one kind of SOS. It may be less interesting in at least some ways, because it may be simply a matter of definition, not a matter of actively pursuing well-placed subsidies, tax breaks or new policies. However, one does not solve the labor shortage problem simply by defining elderly people as being unemployed. One has to go further and talk about how to provide them with employment opportunities. But we may make a big difference if we start calling so-called 'retired' people unemployed. Just calling them unemployed may stimulate them to become more interested in finding jobs, and it could stimulate potential employers into doing more to seek them out. The concept of being retired creates an image of somebody who is practically dead, senile or decrepit in some sense. On the other hand, the concept of being unemployed (especially temporarily unemployed) creates an image of an able-bodied person who is willing and able to work if provided with appropriate opportunities.

In all the examples of doing better than the best by redefining 'best', we are talking about more than just definitions. How things are labeled does influence the behavior of the people who are so labeled, or the doers of the activities. It also influences the behavior and attitudes of other people toward those activities. In the Hong Kong labor context, the super-optimum alternative involves the means for achieving the super-optimum goal of doing better than zero unemployment. All the other alternatives focus on the tradeoff between importing labor and disrupting society and not importing labor and losing additional prosperity.

Broader implications

The Hong Kong labor problem illustrates labor problems throughout the world, not just Hong Kong. Every country has either a labor shortage or a labor surplus. No country considers its labor situation to be exactly in balance regarding supply and demand. The countries with a shortage, are Japan, Korea, Taiwan, Singapore, Hong Kong, Malaysia and, to some extent, the United States. The countries with a labor surplus consist of most of the underdeveloped countries that are willing to export labor, which include all of Central America, that exports labor to the United States, and northern South America, that does some exporting to Argentina and Chile, mainly in the area of unskilled labor. Unskilled labor has traditionally been the kind of labor that is exported from developing nations to industrial nations like the United States. That, however, is changing as the United States increasingly imports a skilled brain drain from throughout the world including China,

India, eastern Europe and western Europe. Those highly skilled people should not be referred to as a one-way benefit to the United States and a cost to their native countries. They do send back money, serve as role models, and they facilitate trade with their native countries. South Africa to a considerable extent operates as a strictly unskilled labor importer from the frontline states. It loses skilled labor to the rest of the world, including the United States and Canada. Israel is another example, importing lots of unskilled labor from the West Bank but losing its skilled labor at the top to the United States. The Hong Kong problem is primarily one of the need for more labor at the bottom, not the kind of unskilled labor that works in the mines of South Africa, but the semi-skilled labor that works in the assembly plants throughout Asia, or at least throughout the Asian countries that have that kind of labor shortage.

The problem illustrates the need for having international economic communities like the EU (European Union) or ASEAN (Association of Southeast Asian Nations). If such an international community functions properly, the countries that have labor surpluses export to the countries that have labor shortages and everybody is better off. There can also be interchange between economic communities, such as that involving the Philippines – not in the sense that the Philippines is exporting labor to western Europe, but in the sense that it is the largest source of labor in the Arab Middle East, and also sends a lot of people to Hong Kong, China and the United States.

On a more methodological level, the Hong Kong labor problem illustrates better than any other problem the idea of multiple liberal groups and multiple conservative groups that do not get along with each other. Another general principle which this example illustrates is the importance of how a policy problem is labeled. If the problem is referred to as the labor shortage problem of Hong Kong or Asia, this tends to lead to a solution of importing more labor. If the problem is referred to as an immigration problem or an ethnic relations problem, this tends to lead to a solution of avoiding the importing of more labor. The best way to refer to the problem is in such a way that one is pushed toward neither of these solutions but instead toward thinking in terms of a super-optimum solution in which all sides can come out ahead of their best expectations. That might mean referring to the problem as the underemployment problem of Hong Kong or Asia. Calling it that leads one to think about ways to make more effective use of willing and able people who are outside the labor force, and of people inside the labor force who are not working to their full potential.

3   Environmental Protection and Technology

SOURCES OF POLLUTION

Manufacturing

Super-optimizing refers to a new and useful form of public policy evaluation. It seeks to find solutions to policy problems whereby conservatives, liberals and other major viewpoints can all come out ahead of their best initial expectations simultaneously.[1] The problem of industrial policy can serve as an illustration, including the more specific problem of hand-crafted work versus assembly lines in India. One of the main arguments in favor of emphasizing hand-crafted work rather than assembly lines is that it is better for the environment, as well as better for the quality of the workplace. The super-optimum solution is thus one that will provide a manufacturing system that is even better for the environment and having a quality workplace than hand-crafted work is, while simultaneously more efficient than factory assembly lines.

Background and trends

India's textile policy and the informal sectors are almost an emotional topic in India because a part of Ghandiism has been considered to be the avoidance of industrialization and the factory system which caused so much upset in Europe in the 1800s. Gandhi is often pictured making things at a handloom in the informal sector in order to cast doubt on the necessity of people working in textile factories like the ones that exist in North Carolina. There are statistics on how well the handlooms are competing with mills in India. If one compares 1912 with 1939, production in the mills went up from about a million yards to four million yards. Handloom production went up from a million yards to a million and a half. However, if one looks at the

113

more recent figures, something has changed. In about 1990, the mills were producing less than they were in 1940, with 2.6 million yards, while production in the informal sector had shot up from 10.7 million yards. Yet the data show that in 1980 there were 452 power looms as against only 15 in 1942, and 944 in 1989. If there are so many more power looms, why are they not producing more cloth?

The conclusion is partly that Gandhiism is working psychologically. There has been a phenomenal expansion of informal handloom output, partly for ideological reasons. Probably no other developing nation has that kind of development. It does show that people can get satisfaction out of things that may not be so productive but are probably more enjoyable. Working on a textile mill assembly line in North Carolina is pictured in the movie, *Norma Rae*, as being very depressing, as contrasted to being one's own boss with the family loom.

This could be generalized a little. There is no question that highly mechanized collective farms in Russia are not as productive as a bunch of farmers working their own plots as their own bosses on into the night. Certain occupations or industries in certain cultures might be more productive if they tried to take into consideration individual psychology more, instead of treating people like machines. If the mills were capable of running solely by themselves, like Japanese mills where there is no dehumanizing because there are not many humans around, then one would have a kind of super-optimum solution of high productivity and no dehumanizing. The North Carolina mills which are like the India mills may give the worst of both possible worlds. Those may be super-maximum examples, where productivity is down for lack of incentive, and dehumanizing is up because of regimentation. The India handloom is very humanizing, but is not as productive as the Japanese automated factory.

This is relevant to African business development. At the 1991 Seychelles conference, this was one of the best debated subjects. Some people lauded the informal sector; others said that it was only justifiable as a means toward more efficient factories and should not be considered as an end in itself but just a stepping-stone.

The considerable increase in the total productivity of household looms in India as compared with factory looms at first seems rather strange. The explanation is that the household looms are not handlooms. They are machines, like sewing machines. They run on electricity. They constitute a compromise between home handicrafts and factory machines. They may seem like an ideal compromise, but they may sacrifice potential productivity that could come from more factory automation. They may also sacrifice some equity and quality of workplace that could come from home handicrafts, or more likely from a highly automated assembly plant.

Alternatives, goals and relations

Table 3.1 is a super-optimizing or SOS table. It shows goals to be achieved on the columns, alternatives available for achieving them on the rows, and indicators of relations between goals and alternatives in the cells. It also shows neutral, liberal and conservative totals in the columns on the right. Those totals reflect neutral, liberal and conservative weights for the goals. This is a simplified SOS table, only involving two goals and four alternatives. Other SOS tables may involve more goals and more alternatives.

Table 3.1   Handwork versus assembly lines in Indian clothmaking[2]

Criteria / Alternatives	C Goal Productivity C=3 N=2 L=1	L Goal Quality workplace L=3 N=2 C=1	N Total (neutral weights)	L Total (liberal weights)	C Total (conservative weights)
C Alternative Hand-crafted work	2	4	12	10	14*
L Alternative Assembly-line work	4	2	12	14*	10
N Alternative Cottage industry with small machines	3	3	12	12	12
SOS Alternative Highly automated assembly plant	>3.5 ~5	>3.5 ~5	>12	>14**	>14**

The Indian problem lends itself well to a simplified SOS. The conservative alternative is hand-crafted work by artisans, or just hand-crafted work. The liberal approach is a kind of Eli Whitney–Henry Ford assembly line that at one time was slightly considered such a technological advance. The compromise is the current Indian situation, which involves cottage industry using small machines.

We should say 'home industry' rather than 'cottage industry', although both could be interpreted as sweatshops. That is one of the drawbacks to this kind of compromise. It easily leads to people working at home, but they are not their own bosses. They may be more wage slaves than if they worked in a factory. They do piecework, and someone shows up every day or so to pick up what they have done. They are paid a pittance and work all hours. Just because they are at home does not mean that they have much quality of life or control over their hours. The problem is not solved by trying to find a new word for cottage industry or home industry. Whatever it is, it could become a sweatshop. The Indian data do not say anything about the quality of life of these people working at home. They just say that they are producing a lot of cloth, which may also have been true of the sweatshops in the New York garment industry in the early 1900s.

The conservative goal is productivity: turning out a lot of cloth at a relatively low price. The liberal goal is a quality workplace in terms of (1) safety, (2) a psychologically pleasant environment, (3) absence of pollution, and (4) work that is not drudgery. The hand-crafted work involves a quality workplace. It is not easy to do much polluting when one works with needle and thread. It is also pretty hard to get an arm chopped off by a power tool when one works with needle and thread. On the productivity side, though, needle and thread are not so effective.

One would expect assembly-line work to be more productive than cottage industry with small machines. However, if there are a lot of homes with a lot of small machines, they will outproduce a small quantity of assembly lines, even though one assembly line produces a lot more than one home. It depends on how we define productivity. If it is defined in terms of effectiveness or total output, then the Indian data shows that the home industry is doing better. If productivity means output divided by some kind of input of money and effort, then the assembly line probably does better.

A super-optimum solution

The super-optimum solution is to strive for the kind of factory that Japan has pioneered which is highly productive and not dehumanizing because it involves only highly skilled humans in the form of executives and engineers, and nobody on an assembly line except robots. Somebody may be on a console platform watching the robots. He or she may also be watching television – just like farmers in big harvesters having televisions in their cabs, very different from working with a scythe to harvest wheat.

We are referring here to highly automated assembly plants. Industrialists in Japan do not even like to use the word 'factory' because it implies something that is belching smoke. They call their car manufacturing plants assembly plants. General Motors frequently calls its car factories forges, which really suggests belching smoke. The word 'assembly' does evoke like assembly line, but you can have things being assembled without a line of people turning a bolt, like Charlie Chaplin in the movie on the dehumanizing Ford automobile company.

Such a plant achieves better than a 3.5 score on productivity, maybe even a 5. It is a quality workplace with very few injuries or unhappy employees. The energy source is likely to be reasonably clean rather than coal-burning. It may even be nuclear energy, although that raises safety issues, but the safety of nuclear energy is a separate matter. One could have a highly automated assembly plant that does not use nuclear energy or coal. It could even use solar energy, although that is not so likely with the current solar technology. It probably uses electricity and, if there are any chimneys belching, they are over at the power company, not in the assembly plant.

'Conservative' in this context does not mean pro-business. It means preserving traditions and old ways of doing things. Likewise, liberal does not mean pro-labor. It means pro-technology, industrialization, rather than non-industrial lifestyles.

This is different from African business development, although related. The African problem is basically large business versus small business, rather than factory versus home. A better way to put it that does bring out the distinction is that the Indian problem is handicrafts versus machines, while the African problem is small business (regardless of whether handicrafts or machines are involved) versus big business (regardless of whether handicrafts or machines are involved). One could conceivably have a big business that employs a lot of people who work with their hands.

There are two different SOS solutions. One involves a technological fix with machines that do not involve assembly-line workers; thus one has the productivity of machines without the dehumanizing of an assembly line. The other problem, the African problem, involves a sequential SOS where small business leads to big business and is not an end in itself. This requires consciously encouraging small businesses that are not dead-ends, but are likely to be capable of being expanded. It especially means small businesses that manufacture something, rather than small businesses that sell groceries.

Finding other super-optimum solutions

Finding SOS solutions is facilitated by the use of spreadsheet-based *decision-aiding software*, which allows one to work simultaneously with many goals, alternatives and relations. This includes being able to process data that has missing holes. It also includes goals that are measured in multiple ways. Such software also allows for 'what if' analysis to see how the tentative conclusions change as a result of changes in the inputs.

SOS solutions are also facilitated by having *checklists* based on generalizing from previous examples. Such checklists and examples can be found in the growing literature on super-optimizing. That literature includes win–win dispute resolution, growth economics and non-zero-sum games. (For further details, see the chapter on 'Super-Optimizing Analysis and Developmental Policy' in S.S. Nagel, *Global Policy Studies: International Interaction Toward Improving Public Policy* (St Martin's Press and Macmillan, 1991) and the chapter on 'Improving Public Policy Toward and Within Developing Countries' in S.S. Nagel, *Public Administration and Decision-Aiding Software: Improving Procedure and Substance* (Greenwood Press, 1990).)

Agriculture

Table 3.2 provides an SOS analysis of land reform in developing countries,[3] although it is based in particular on the author's experiences of working with people from the Department of Agrarian Reform in the Republic of the Philippines. The table is a classic SOS table, in that the rank order of the alternatives on the liberal totals are SOS, liberal, neutral and conservative. Likewise, the rank order of the alternatives on the conservative totals are SOS, conservative, neutral and liberal. One of the main arguments in favor of redistribution of large landed estates is that small farmers may be more likely to use natural methods of agriculture than large commercial farmers,

Table 3.2   Land reform in developing countries

Criteria Alternatives	C Goal Productivity	L Goal Equity	N Total (neutral weights)	L Total (liberal weights)	C Total (conservative weights)

C Alternative
  Retain land
  (0 units)
	4	1	10	7	13*

L Alternative
  Divide land
  (100 units)
	1	4	10	13*	7

N Alternative
  Compromise
  (50 units)
	2.5	2.5	10	10	10

SOS Alternative
  1 Buy the land
  2 Lots of land
  3 Coop. action
	4.5	4.5	18	18**	18**

and this would be better for the environment. The super-optimum solution is thus one that will distribute the land in such a way as to provide the environment with a high degree of productivity, equity and sensitivity.

The traditional inputs

More specifically, if we are talking about 100 units of land, the typical conservative approach tends to advocate retaining most of the ownership of the land in the hands of the traditional landed aristocracy. The typical liberal approach tends to advocate turning most of the ownership of the land over to landless peasants to farm. The typical neutral or compromise approach is something in between, although not necessarily exactly a 50–50 split of the 100 units.

The two key goals in the controversy tend to be agricultural productivity and a more equalitarian or equitable distribution of land ownership. The conservative alternative (by allowing for economies of scale that are associated with large land holdings) is more productive, but less equitable. The liberal alternative (of widespread land distribution) is less productive, but more equitable. The neutral compromise is somewhere between these relation scores, just as it is somewhere between the conservative and liberal distribution alternatives.

With these relation scores, we logically have the result mentioned above, where the conservative alternative wins with the conservative weights, and the liberal alternative wins with the liberal weights. We are also likely to get the classic compromise, which is everybody's second-best alternative, or worse. The 'or worse' means that sometimes liberals accept the compromise when the conservative alternative actually does better on the liberal weights, or the conservatives accept the compromise when the liberal alternative actually does better on the conservative weights. Each side may accept the compromise even though it is the third-best alternative to them, because they do not want to give in to the other side. That is not the case with Table 3.2, but it does sometimes occur in the psychology of public policy making.

The super-optimum alternative

The super-optimum alternative seems to involve three key elements. The first is that the land needs to be bought from the present landowners, rather than confiscated. If the owners are threatened with confiscation, one possible reaction is to establish death squads, to bring in American military power, or to do other especially nasty things that may easily cost more than the cost of buying the land. The United States probably could have saved a fortune in military and other expenditure on Nicaragua, El Salvador and

Guatemala over the last 10 or 20 years by simply using a fraction of the money spent to buy land from the owners to give to the peasants. The landowners would have saved the high cost of supporting death squads and other repressive measures to fight off the peasants who wanted to farm on their own land.

The second element is that lots of land needs to be involved. It cannot be a token program. The landless peasants in developing countries are no longer as passive as they once were. They cannot be easily bought off with trinkets, pie-in-the-sky religion, patronizing aristocrats and other relatively worthless bribes or distractions. They have demonstrated a willingness to fight and die for land in pre-communist China, in Central America and in other developing countries, including the Philippines.

The third element is the need to use modern technologies in a cooperative way to overcome the divisive effect of distributing the land in relatively small parcels to the landless peasants. Here is where the policy makers can learn from both capitalistic American farmers and communistic Russian farmers. American farmers are highly individualistic, but they recognize that it makes no sense for each of them to own their own grain elevators, combines and other big equipment which they can own collectively through producer cooperatives. In the Soviet Union, agricultural efficiency has been promoted through machine tractor stations where farmers can collectively share tractors which they cannot afford to own separately. This is true regardless of whether the individual farmers are associated with collective farms or private plots. Cooperative activities also involve the equivalent of county agents who help bring farmers together to learn about the latest seeds, herbicides, pesticides and fertilizers, and to gain other useful knowledge. Cooperative action can also include credit unions and drawing upon collective taxes for well-placed subsidies to encourage the diffusion of useful innovations.

With this combination of SOS elements, one can have agricultural productivity and equity simultaneously, which makes it a strong winner on both the liberal totals and the conservative totals. Appropriate timing may also be required, in the sense of moving fast to implement these kinds of ideas. The longer the delay, the more difficult such an SOS solution becomes. The reason is that the liberal left may acquire such a negative attitude toward the conservative right that the liberal left would consider buying the land to be a surrender to evil people. Likewise, the conservative right may acquire such a negative attitude toward the peasant guerrillas that they can see no respectable solution other than extermination of what they consider to be terrorists.

Learning experiences

One of the most interesting aspects of the Philippine land reform experience has been the many mistakes (or one might call them learning experiences) that have been made by well-intentioned agricultural experts who may have been overly focused in their expertise. This can be contrasted with the practice of policy analysts, who have a more generalist perspective. One should try to see how different policy problems and proposed solutions can be coordinated. Some alternatives have a 'domino effect', where the unintended consequences became devastating to what otherwise looks like a meaningful approach to increasing agricultural productivity.

Four examples were given by the people associated with agrarian reform in the Philippines. The first example involves telling farmers how they can double their crops by using better seeds, pesticides, herbicides, fertilizer and machinery, but not providing for any increased storage facilities for the doubled crop. The result was that much of the increased productivity rotted in the fields.

The second example involved telling farmers how they could arrange for as many as four crops per year, instead of one crop per year through the use of special seeds that have a three-month season: they go from being put into the ground to being ready to harvest every three months. The farmers, however, were not told how a one-person farm could plow, weed and harvest four times a year and still be able to attend fiestas.

The third example involved supplying the farmers with new pesticides that kill all the crop-damaging insects and weeds, but also the frogs and fish that live on the farms that the farmers like to eat. After the frogs and fish are killed, the pesticides and herbicides are withdrawn when it is realized that the farmers did not want to kill the frogs and fish. The result is that the farmers now have no frogs, no fish, and the insects are back. The thing to do might have been to continue with the pesticides, but give the farmers food stamps to buy frogs and fish from the local markets. The economy would then be better off because the increased farm productivity would more than offset the cost of the frog and fish stamps.

The fourth example involved showing the farmers how they can grow more efficiently with a tractor than with an ox. Such a demonstration may, however, fail to recognize that tractors do not make good fertilizer. The demonstration may also fail to recognize that, if you give one farmer and not other farmers in the area a tractor, the other farmers, especially his relatives, come to borrow that farmer's tractor. That farmer then has no tractor, no ox and no fertilizer. The correct solution might have been to give the tractor to the whole community collectively to share, the way American farmers share grain elevators or Russian farmers share tractors at machine tractor stations.

The idea of one tractor per Philippine farmer is American individualistic capitalism gone berserk, contrary to the realities of farming in the Philippines and other developing countries, or even developed countries. Every farmer in Champaign County, Illinois does not have a combine, and they do not feel deprived. They find it more efficient to hire a combine company, just as every American does not own a U-Haul trailer or a Greyhound bus, although they use them. Farmers want to use their own land, at least in most developing countries. There are many American farmers, however, who own no land, but who farm for landowners. They often make a lot of money getting paid to do it with their equipment. Wanting to own one's own land does not mean one wants to own a combine. The land is used almost all year long if you are a farmer. The combine gets used for one week, and it is recognized as wasteful to have to store it, have it depreciate, and make payments on it on a year-round basis. There is a need for combining individualistic land ownership with collectivistic sharing and renting.

Transport

Background

The Manila commuting problem is a good example of people in developed countries sometime having false stereotypes of policy problems in developing countries. Americans think that developing nations are simpler and even less urban than they actually are. There may be no country in the world that has a worse commuter problem than the Philippines. In comparison, commuting is relatively simple in New York, London, Paris, Berlin, Moscow, Tokyo and elsewhere.

It is more complicated in the Philippines for a number of reasons.

1   The Philippines has only one really big metropolitan city, to which people are flocking, whereas countries like the United States have many such cities – New York, Chicago, Los Angeles and so on.
2   Metropolitan Manila may be bigger in population and area than most other big cities where there is a lot of complaining about the difficulty of commuting. Metropolitan Manila consists of about five adjacent cities, including Quezon City which is a big city in itself.
3   Greatly complicating the commuting problem in Manila is that it is on mainly a peninsula where the Pacific Ocean is just waiting to flood any attempt to build a subway system. Further complicating matters is the lack of money for an expanded elevated or surface train system.
4   It has been proposed that there should be more vehicles that carry

numbers of people to and from work to ease the commuting problem. Washington, DC, for example, makes a big thing of providing special lanes for cars and buses that have numerous passengers, especially as part of a pooling arrangement. The Manila area probably has more small buses per capita than any city in the world. It has developed a mass transit system based on the extended jeep, carrying a dozen or more passengers crowded closely together.

5 Having more jeepneys, small buses and big buses would just further clog the highways and streets into and out of Manila. Jeepneys were originally jeeps left over from World War II that were converted into motor vehicles for carrying as many passengers as could fit inside or hang onto the sides. They would thus worsen the problem and make commuting even more time-consuming.

6 Having more bicycles would not handle the Manila commuter problem the way it helps in Beijing. Poor and middle-class people have too far to travel to do the journey by bicycle, and they can also ride the jeepney buses for only one peso, which is about one-twentieth of an American dollar. Thus it is not cost-effective to buy and ride a bicycle to work. Also the more influential car drivers would not tolerate giving up an auto lane on each side of the streets to be used by bicycles.

This commuting phenomenon is not peculiar to the Philippines as a developing country. Many developing countries have a capital city or central city to which rural people flock, looking for jobs. The people build whatever shanties they can. The city becomes highly overcrowded, not just relative to the jobs available, but in an absolute sense, given the limited space and the limited technological capabilities of moving people around in that space.

One of the main arguments in favor of a more streamlined system of commuting is that it is easier on the environment than a great number of small vehicles. Thus the super-optimum solution is one that can greatly reduce commuting time without overburdening the taxpayer and simultaneously improving urban environmental protection.

Alternatives

Table 3.3 shows the Manila commuter problem in the context of a decision analysis table or a super-optimizing framework. The conservative alternative (as is often the case) is to leave things as they are, or leave it to the marketplace to change things. Some conservatives like to talk about people 'buying cities' the way they buy products. In that sense, people supposedly vote with their feet by going to Manila. The invisible hand of Adam Smith may eventually cause them to change their votes and go back to the

Table 3.3   Manila's commuter problem

Criteria \ Alternatives	L Goal Less time commuting	C Goal Lower taxes	N Total (neutral weights)	L Total (liberal weights)	C Total (conservative weights)
C Alternative As is	1	4	10	7	13*
L Alternative Mass transit	4	2	12	14*	10
N Alternative Hodge-podge with/more jeepneys and buses	2	2.5	9	8.5	9.5
SOS Alternative Suburbs, regional cities, overseas & other empl. ctrs	4.5	4.5	18	18**	18**

countryside. That runs contrary to the saying that, once you have tasted the big city, it is hard to go back to the farm, especially if you are a landless peasant and have no farm to go back to. Maybe in the extremely long run, things get so bad in overcrowded cities that medieval diseases return periodically to decimate the population. That, fortunately or unfortunately, is not so likely given modern public health care.

The liberal solution tends to be spending big money, but often with no strings attached and with an unduly narrow focus on the immediate problem, rather than the bigger picture. Liberals also tend to project their middle-class New York or Chicago subway or elevated line, or Washington, DC car pooling. These alternatives were mentioned above as not so applicable to Manila and maybe not so applicable to most developing countries, for lack of capital. The available capital could probably be better spent on upgrading human skills and machinery for producing goods. It should also be noted that at least some developing countries may be in a good position to act fast, in time to prevent a good deal of urban congestion, rather than try to cure it or commute through it afterwards.

The neutral alternative, as in many situations, tends to involve splitting the difference between conservative expenditures or recommendations and those of the liberals. If the conservatives say spend nothing on mass transit (since it will overburden the taxpayer and may encourage people to move to

Manila), and if the liberals say spend many millions, the neutral compromisers try to find a figure in between. Doing so may result in half a train system and may be an example of where half a load is worse than none. A halfway system could be expensive without adequate incremental benefits. Neutrals also tend to emphasize trying a lot of things simultaneously. In this context, that would mean a few more jeepneys, small buses, big buses, bicycles and subsidized taxis. The result would probably be more congestion and more commuting time wasted, as mentioned above. Building wider highways for the additional vehicles is also unlikely to help. Many of the commuting roads in Manila are already much wider than Chicago's Outer Drive. The ultimate would be to clear out all the buildings, and have nothing but commuting roads.

Goals

As for goals, a key goal is to reduce the tremendous amount of time wasted getting to and from work. Only the richest of Filipinos, or the poorest who set up illegal shanties in whatever alley might be available, can afford to live near the central city. The people who live in those shanties frequently do not have jobs to commute to, and neither do the people who live in the rich villas. The working people tend to live considerable distances away, and they may spend two exhausting hours getting into central Manila and then getting out. Those hours are literally exhausting because the exhaust fumes are unbelievable owing to the stop-and-go operation of many diesel-fueled vehicles and propane buses. Many of the drivers and street vendors wear handkerchiefs over their faces.

Delays are also caused by numerous trucks going to and from factories that are in the central city, along with office buildings. Delay is caused by many beggars and street vendors who interfere with traffic at intersections. A further factor is having in the central city large military barracks that could be used for residential housing. Camp Aguinaldo, which is one of the main army camps in the Philippines, is in downtown Manila. Americans reading about soldiers from Camp Aguinaldo invading the Makati business district think they may have come as paratroopers. The soldiers simply walked down the block into the high-rise buildings. The hot climate further adds to the problem by making the commuting less bearable and causing a lot of overheated cars that stall and block traffic.

The second key goal is to keep the tax burden down. On the matter of tax burden, though, one has to distinguish between the short-run burden and the long-run burden. The long-run (if it is not too far away) is more important since it lasts longer. In this context, it may be necessary to spend a lot of money to do something about the problem in order to save a lot of commuter time later. More importantly, by enabling people in the Manila area to be more productive and healthy, the gross national product may benefit substantially, thereby increasing the tax base. If that happens then the percentage tax rate can be lowered subsequently and still bring in more money for other projects.

Saving commuting time for workers tends to be a relatively liberal goal, and saving tax money for taxpayers tends to be a relatively conservative goal. As with other SOS analyses, however, both liberals and conservatives endorse time saving and tax saving. It is just a matter of the relative emphasis they use.

Scoring and totals

In scoring the alternatives, leaving things as they are is terrible for saving commuting time, but it does have a positive relation with short-run tax saving. Spending a lot of money on a train system that would run through developed areas of Manila or on a median strip of widened highways could save commuting time, but it does have a negative relation with short-run tax saving. The neutral compromise is not much help on saving time, although it is not as bad as doing nothing. Likewise, it does have a short-run incremental tax burden, although not as bad as liberal mass-transit expenditures.

Looking at the totals, the conservative alternative comes in first using the conservative weights, with the liberal alternative in third place. Likewise, the liberal alternative comes in first using the liberal weights, with the conservative alternative in third place. The neutral alternative is everybody's second. It is possibly even the second or third choice of the neutrals, since the hodgepodge neutral alternative does poorly on both goals, although it is not the worse on both goals. In arriving at a super-optimum solution, the important thing is finding an alternative that exceeds both the liberal and conservative initial best expectations, not necessarily the neutral's.

The super-optimum solution

The super-optimum solution in this context has at least three parts. The first is to build up employment opportunities in the suburbs or outlying districts of Manila. The commuting is highly unbalanced. It is nearly all inward in the morning, starting at about 5 o'clock, and it is nearly all outward in the afternoon and evening, starting at about 3 o'clock. This is unlike the case of American cities, where there is an increasing growth in the suburbs as places for employment opportunities, not just bedrooms. Farmland northwest of Chicago in places like Schaumberg Township now has skyscraper office buildings and low-pollution factories.

As a concrete example, it is amazing that the University of the Philippines, which is located in Quezon City, outside Manila, does not have a high-tech area around it. That would take advantage of the fact that the university is the leading university in the Philippines and possibly the leading university in Southeast Asia. Most American universities that have engineering schools attract high-tech employment in their areas. The Philippine government could provide subsidies to create a high-tech employment area around the university. This would make a dent in the commuting problem and set a useful precedent for other subsidized suburban employment. Also important is that it would help subsidize technological innovation and diffusion. Doing this could have broader useful effects on the Philippine economy than just the Manila commuter problem.

The second part of a possible super-optimum solution is subsidizing the development of regional cities throughout the Philippines. Certain cities in the southern provinces of Mindinao and the middle provinces between Manila and Mindinao could be made more attractive to rural people from those provinces as places to migrate to, rather than go to Manila. They could even be made attractive enough possibly to get some people to move from Manila back to those regional cities in their home provinces. This is a kind of subsidization that has been done in the Soviet Union to encourage people to move west. It was also done by the United States to encourage people to move west, although more as a matter of providing people with land for farming in the west, rather than urban employment opportunities. The Rural Rehabilitation Administration during the 1930s, however, did provide low-interest loans to enable rural people from Oklahoma, Arkansas and elsewhere in the southwest to go to Los Angeles and establish gas stations and other small businesses or to become car mechanics, rather than go to Chicago, Detroit, Cleveland and New York, as was the case with poor southern blacks and whites.

The third part of the solution might be for the Philippine government to work more actively with a number of other governments that have labor shortages who could hire some of the excess labor in the Manila area and other parts of the Philippines. This might apply to Hong Kong, Singapore, Taiwan, Malaysia, Korea and even Japan. It might be worthwhile for the Philippine government to do more to upgrade labor skills to make that kind of guestworker program more attractive. Those guestworkers would also send back lots of money to help the Philippine economy, which might be even more important than relieving the Manila commuter problem. The Philippine government has developed labor-exporting relations with Arab countries on the Persian Gulf. As a result, the Philippines Airlines may fly into more Persian Gulf cities than almost any other non-Arab airline. This is another illustration of the need to elevate some of the policy problems of individual countries to a more international or global level.

With this kind of three-part super-optimum solution, commuting time could be substantially reduced, more so than doing nothing, having a mildly effective train system, or a hodgepodge of miscellaneous vehicles rivaling the evacuation of Dunkirk every morning and evening in Manila. Likewise, that kind of super-optimum solution could not only save taxes in the long run by increasing GNP and the tax base, but it could also help resolve many other policy problems besides the Manila commuter problem. Increased GNP through suburban employment, regional cities and overseas employment can do wonders with regard to reducing the problems of crime, poverty, discrimination and lack of money for education, health care, housing and other public policy expenditures. The SOS does show up in Table 3.3 as being a substantial winner on the liberal, conservative and neutral totals. That includes winning over the previous liberal and conservative alternatives or expectations even with liberal and conservative weights.

METHODS FOR DEALING WITH POLLUTION

Government structures

The purpose of this section is to discuss the relevance of federalism and separation of powers to environmental protection. The discussion is mainly in the context of American government, but what is said could apply to other countries since all countries have governmental levels and governmental branches which relate to environmental policy.

In a legally technical sense, there are three forms of government regarding how the *levels* relate to each other. The unitary form gives all power to the national government to delegate to the state governments as it sees fit. The confederate form gives all power to the state governments to delegate to the national government as they see fit. The federalism form involves a constitution that delegates some power to the national government and some power to the state governments, and they cannot constitutionally take away each other's powers. As a practical political matter, the concepts of centralized and decentralized are more meaningful. One can have a decentralized unitary government which may be more decentralized than a centralized confederate government. Thus this section is more concerned with the degree of centralization and decentralization in evaluating levels of government in the context of environmental protection.

In a legally technical sense, there are three forms of government with regard to the way the *branches* relate to each other. The parliamentary form involves a legislature which chooses the chief executive. The dictatorial form involves a chief executive who is capable of ignoring the legislature.

The presidential form involves a chief executive and a legislature who are both chosen independently by the people. One can also talk about the relation between the judicial branch of government vis-à-vis the executive and legislative branches. Under a system of judicial review, the courts can declare acts of the other two branches unconstitutional. Under a system of coordinate interpretation or legislative supremacy, the courts do not have such power. As a practical political matter, it is more meaningful to talk about what the division of labor should be among the three branches of government in dealing with a given policy problem, such as environmental policy.

To facilitate systematic evaluative comparisons among alternative types of decentralization of levels and separation of branches, this section makes use of multi-criteria decision making (*MCDM*) with a spreadsheet format. The essence of MCDM is processing a set of multiple goals to be achieved, multiple alternatives for achieving them, and relations between goals and alternatives in order to choose or explain the best alternative, combination, allocation or predictive decision rule. The spreadsheet format involves putting goals in the columns, alternatives in the rows, relations in the cells, and overall scores for each alternative on the far right, and the ability to do a 'what if' analysis that shows what it would take to bring a second-place or lower alternative up to first place.

Levels of government and environmental protection

More national authority There are various points favoring the allocation of relatively more authority to the national government in dealing with environmental protection. The national government is less subject to pressures from local business polluters. The states are competing with each other to attract business and are sometimes willing to relax their environmental standards in order to do so. The federal government is also less subject to pressures from local government polluters, including municipalities that do not like to be required to maintain better water filtration and sewerage plants and can ward off a state requirement more easily than a federal one.

The federal government can provide better coordination across states when they disagree as to what should be done. The federal government can promote uniform standards and enforcement, which may be desirable if they are of the appropriate quality. Business firms may like uniform standards in order to avoid having to comply with so many different standards. Federal competence tends to be a little higher, owing to the general prestige and funding associated with federal agencies.

More state authority   There are various points favoring the allocation of relatively more authority to the states or other sub-national units. The states are more aware and responsive to local needs and conditions. Even if Washington maintains dominant control, there should be decentralized field offices in order to provide useful information to Washington and in order to facilitate compliance with Washington policy.

States can sometimes handle the coordination problem through inter-state contacts and commissions, especially if Congress appropriates a subsidy to encourage that kind of coordination. There could be federal standard setting with state enforcement, using federal money, as with public aid. That way, the uniformity benefit is obtained while still having state and local enforcement.

Not all pollution is equally amenable to regulation at the federal level. Obviously, noise tends to be relatively local, and air pollution tends to know no state boundaries. Between these two are water, radiation and solid waste, each benefitting from different levels of control in the federal system. One could argue that the federal government is best when it comes to standards for new manufacturing facilities, but that old, already existing facilities should continue to be governed by the state and local areas as they have been. Otherwise, there is an element of unfair *ex post facto* retroactivity.

MCDM analysis   Many of these ideas are summarized in the Table 3.4, showing alternative roles for the national and state governments in dealing with pollution. The seven non-mutually exclusive alternatives (not including the SOS) are (1) virtually all power to the national government, (2) decentralized field offices, (3) inter-state compacts and commissions, (4) rule making by the federal government with enforcement by the states, (5) federal regulation of new facilities with state regulation of old facilities, (6) federal regulation for air pollution with state regulation for water pollution, and (7) virtually all power to the state and local governments.

Along with the seven alternatives are four goals or normative criteria: (1) being less subject to the influence of business, (2) reducing the undue influence of municipal governments, (3) allowing for coordination across the states, and (4) some sensitivity to local factors.

The first alternative of 'all power to the national government' should probably be ruled out as being politically unfeasible. Likewise, the last three alternatives (not including the SOS) are likely to be considered unacceptable because they do not meet minimum constraints in terms of pollution reduction. Thus the second, third and fourth alternatives are the ones most likely to be adopted as representing the optimal level or range on the continuum of alternative policies.

Table 3.4 Evaluating levels of government for dealing with pollution

Alternatives	L Goal Less business influence	N Goal Less municipal govt. infl	N Goal Coordination across states	C Goal Sensitivity to local factors	N Total (neutral weights)	L Total (liberal weights)	C Total (conservative weights)
L Alternative Only national Government	5	5	5	1	32*	36*	23
N Alternative. Decentralized field offices	4	4	4	4	32*	32	32*
N Alternative Inter-state compacts and commissions	4	4	4	4	32*	32	32*
N Alternative Rules for federal enforcement for state	3.5	3.5	3.5	4	29	28.5	29.5
N Alternative Federal for new facilities, state for old	2.5	2.5	2.5	4.5	24	22	26
N Alternative Federal for air pollution, state for water pollution	2.1	2.1	2.1	4.5	21.6	19.2	24
C Alternative Only state and local govt	2	2	2	5	22	19	25
SOS Alternative Combine All	>4	>4	>4	>4	>32*	>36*	>32*

Branches of government and environmental protection

More administrative authority　There are points favoring the allocation of relatively more authority to administrative agencies rather than to legislatures or courts. The administrative agencies have specialized expertise. They devote themselves full-time to environmental protection. They can take the initiative without waiting for cases to be brought to them. They can act more flexibly in light of changing conditions than legislatures can. They also have rather more independence from political pressures.

Administrative agencies are capable of providing due process in their adjudications and are capable of being subjected to judicial review. Due process in this context includes allowing the accused to present witnesses, cross-examine, have a neutral judge, appeal and be notified of the charges. Agencies are also capable of providing due process in their promulgation of regulations and of being subjected to legislative review. Due process in this context means holding hearings, or at least receiving recommendations and reporting whatever regulations are decided upon.

More judicial or legislative authority　There are points favoring the allocation of relatively less authority to administrative agencies over courts and legislatures. The courts provide even more due process, especially in criminal cases including conviction beyond a reasonable doubt, jury trial and right to counsel. A large business firm, however, would have no trouble hiring its own lawyer, and probably would not want a jury trial anyhow.

Legislatures do provide more opportunity for open hearings and the interplay of interest groups, which is more in conformity with democratic procedure. The influence of business interest groups, however, may not be so desirable from an environmental protection perspective. They may have plenty of influence over administrative agencies, too, depending on the ideology of the presidential administration, which is reflected in appointments to the agency at the top level.

Administrative agencies have become very slow in processing cases, bending over backwards to provide due process. In some ways they go further than the courts in allowing recesses for new evidence and in requiring elaborate opinions at the initial level. Administrative proceedings have added an additional level of delay, rather than substituting for court trials.

MCDM analysis　Many of these ideas are summarized in Table 3.5, which compares judicial, legislative and administrative emphases on nine different criteria: (1) specialized expertise, (2) full-time concern, (3) taking initiative, (4) acting flexibly, (5) adjudicative due process, (6) legislative due process,

(7) independence from political pressures, (8) responsiveness to public opinion, and (9) speed in processing.

The analysis shows that courts do especially well in comparison with legislatures on the criteria of full-time concern, adjudicative due process and independence from political pressures. Those criteria explain three of the most important subjects that are handled by the courts.

1 The courts are available on a full-time basis for resolving disputes among people that regularly occur with regard to contracts, property, personal injuries and domestic relations.
2 The sensitivity of the courts to adjudicative due process makes them especially appropriate for handling criminal cases.
3 Independence from political pressures makes the courts guardians of the first amendment and the equal protection clause of the constitution.

On all three criteria, administrative agencies do better than legislatures, and they even do better than courts when it comes to full-time devotion to a subject. The main reason for administrative agencies not handling common law, criminal law and civil liberties is that they have not been authorized to do so, and they are not likely to receive legislative authorization, given the acceptable work that the courts are doing in those areas.

On the matter of environmental protection, administrative agencies do score better overall than either courts or legislatures, as indicated by the combined raw scores in reading across how well the three branches of government do on a 1–3 ranking in environmental protection on the nine criteria. Administrative agencies do especially well on specialized expertise, initiative and flexibility, as well as full-time devotion to a single subject.

One might note that legislatures do especially well when it comes to being responsive to public opinion and legislative due process. They are thus the most appropriate government branch for majoritarian policy making.

Some conclusions on government structures

Conclusions to which this discussion leads on the matter of *levels* of government include the following:

1 centralization and decentralization are more meaningful predictors of effectiveness in environmental policy than more legalistic concepts like federalism;
2 a combination of centralization and decentralization produces more

Table 3.5 Evaluating branches of government for dealing with pollution

Criteria \\ Alternatives	L Goal Specialized expertise	L Goal Full-time concern	L Goal Take initiative	L Goal Act flexibly	C Goal Adjudicative due process	C Goal Legislative due process	N Goal Independent of political pressure	N Goal Responsive to public opinion	N Goal Speed in processing	N Total (neutral weights)	L Total (liberal weights)	C Total (conservative weights)
C Alternative Judicial emphasis	1	2	1	1	3	1	3	1	2	30	31	29
N Alternative Legislative emphasis	2	1	2	2	1	3	1	3	2	34	37	31
L Alternative Administrative emphasis	3	3	3	3	2	2	2	2	2	44**	52**	36
SOS Alternative Combine all										>44	>52	>36

134

effective environmental policy than emphasizing centralization or decentralization;

3   especially relevant are decentralized field offices, inter-state contacts and commissions and, to a lesser extent, rule making by the federal government with partial enforcement by the states.

Conclusions on the matter of *branches* of government include the following:

1   division of labor in terms of relatively specialized activities is a more meaningful way of analyzing relations among branches of government than using more legalistic concepts like separation of powers;
2   a combination of legislative, administrative and judicial emphasis produces more effective environmental policy than emphasizing one branch more than the others;
3   administrative agencies do especially well where there is a requirement for specialized expertise, initiative, flexibility and full-time devotion to a single subject. The courts do well where due process is especially needed, as in criminal prosecution. Legislatures do well where open hearings are needed to develop new legislation.

Some conclusions on the matter of *analytic methodology* are as follows:

1   systematic analysis is helped by thinking in terms of goals to be achieved, alternatives available for achieving them and relations between goals and alternatives in order to choose or explain the best alternative, combination, allocation or predictive decision rule;
2   systematic analysis is helped by analyzing what it would take to bring a second-place or lower alternative up to first place by changing the weights of the goals or the scores between the goals and alternatives.

It is hoped that this section will provide new and useful insights regarding levels and branches of government and especially how they relate to environmental protection. It is also hoped that the section will provide insights regarding the usefulness of multi-criteria decision analysis for analyzing various alternatives in the light of given goals.

Incentives[4]

The purpose of this section is to show how environmental protection can be facilitated by the substance of incentives theory and the methods of

multi-criteria decision making. The section emphasizes environmental protection, but the ideas are also applicable to other socioeconomic problems
and natural resources conservation.

The essence of incentives theory in a public policy context is that public
policy should seek to encourage socially desired behavior by (1) increasing the benefits of rightdoing, (2) decreasing the costs of rightdoing, (3)
decreasing the benefits of wrongdoing, (4) increasing the costs of wrongdoing, and (5) increasing the probability that the benefits and costs will
occur.

The essence of multi-criteria decision making in a public policy context is
the idea of systematically processing a set of (1) societal goals to be achieved,
(2) alternative public policies for achieving them, and (3) relations between
goals and alternative policies in order to choose or explain the best alternative, combination, allocation or predictive decision rule.

A simple model

Table 3.6 applies some of these basic ideas to a relatively simple example
involving only two goals and three alternative policies. One goal is pollution
reduction and the other is political feasibility. The three alternative policies
are relying on the marketplace, government regulation or pollution taxes.
Each alternative is scored on a 1–5 scale on each goal, where 4 means
conducive to the goal, 3 means neither conducive nor adverse, and 2 means
adverse to the goal.

The marketplace receives a 1 on pollution reduction because expenses go
up as a result of introducing pollution reduction devices, but income does
not go up since consumers are generally not influenced by the extent to
which a manufacturer pollutes the air, water or other aspects of the environment. At the opposite end of the scale, pollution taxes (if adopted) receive a
5 on pollution reduction. Pollution taxes are levied in proportion to the
amount of pollution which the firm causes. This potentially provides a

Table 3.6   Alternative ways of dealing with the problem of pollution

Policies \ Goals	Pollution reduction	Political feasibility	Sum
Marketplace	1	5	6
Regulation	3	3	6
Pollution taxes	5	1	6

strong incentive to reduce pollution. If it is less expensive to the firm to pay the taxes, its tax money can be used for clean-up or other anti-pollution activities. In the middle is regulation. It does better on pollution reduction than the marketplace, since regulation can involve fines and other negative sanctions. However, it does not do as well as pollution taxes, because regulation generally lacks strong enough negative sanctions and/or sanctions have a low probability of being administratively and judicially enforced.

On the matter of political feasibility, the scoring is in the opposite direction. The marketplace does well with a score of 5, at least when an anti-pollution program is first being proposed. This is so because the marketplace under those circumstances would be the prevailing system. If, however, we are talking about 1999, rather than 1970, reverting back to a marketplace approach might have virtually no political feasibility. Pollution taxes, on the other hand, have been successfully resisted in Congress and state legislatures by business firms and trade associations, who are understandably reluctant to bear the extra costs. They would prefer to have the pollution costs borne by the general taxpayer and those who breathe air, drink water or otherwise come into contact with pollution. Regulation has political feasibility since it is the prevailing system at different levels of government and for different types of pollution.

Looking at Table 3.6, one might conclude that there is a three-way tie between these alternative policies. One might then wonder why regulation became the prevailing policy. The answer is partly that there is not a three-way tie, since the marketplace falls outside the realm of feasible alternatives by generating virtually no pollution reduction, and possibly even encouraging pollution in order to save expenses. Likewise, pollution taxes fall outside the realm of feasible alternatives by being incapable of mustering sufficient support to overcome the strong opposition. Thus regulation is the winner, partly through the process of elimination.

A more realistic model

Table 3.6 is unduly simple in only presenting two kinds of incentive to reduce pollution, namely the negative incentives associated with regulation and the somewhat positive incentives associated with pollution tax reductions, and in presenting only two goals. Table 3.7 extends the MCDM analysis to include 19 policy alternatives and seven societal goals or criteria not including the SOS.

The alternatives are grouped in terms of increasing the benefits of rightdoing, reducing the costs of rightdoing, increasing the costs of wrongdoing, reducing the benefits of wrongdoing and increasing the probability of the benefits and costs occurring. This five-part list is useful for generating policy alternatives in a variety of different policy problems.

Goals   The goals can be grouped in terms of the three Es: effectiveness, efficiency and equity, and the three Ps: public participation, predictability and procedural due process. Pollution reduction is especially relevant to effectiveness. Clean-up funds are also relevant. In this context, an ounce of clean-up cure can be more meaningful than a pound of prevention if prevention is far more expensive. A water filtration plant to make the water drinkable, rather than having every factory on the river retool to generate only sterile water into the river, might be an example. Efficiency or monetary cost relates both to the general taxpayer and to consumers or workers. A third set of goals are the three Fs: constitutional feasibility, political feasibility and administrative feasibility. Political feasibility is especially important in this context. A fourth set of goals are the two Ss: liberal symbolism and conservative symbolism. Satisfying these goals is important for bipartisan support.

Alternatives   There are a number of ways of increasing the benefits of *rightdoing* in this context, such as providing reward subsidies to cities or businesses. These are subsidies that go beyond reducing the costs of pollution devices. They are bonuses for rightdoing, as in a cost-plus contract. Other benefits can include a reduction in the pollution tax rate, new government contracts and the income to business firms which can come from selling marketable pollution rights. Receiving a tax deduction to cover anti-pollution expenses reduces the cost of rightdoing. So does a cost subsidy to cities or businesses whereby the government pays part or all of the cost of anti-pollution devices. Cities are treated separately from businesses on alternatives 1–2 and 7–8 because the politics of passing a subsidy is quite different according to whether municipalities or business firms are involved. Cities are especially guilty of water pollution through bad sanitation systems or through the failure to adopt the latest anti-pollution methods and hardware.

The costs of *wrongdoing* can be increased by damage suits, publicizing wrongdoers, levying heavy pollution taxes, fines, jail and the loss of existing government contracts. Being in a position where one has to buy marketable pollution rights in order to satisfy an anti-pollution standard may put a business firm at the mercy of its competitors who have some extra rights to sell. The ultimate cost is a padlock injunction, which closes a business firm until it complies. The benefits of wrongdoing can also be reduced by confiscating profits which result from not complying with anti-pollution rules, analogous to the confiscation of profits from drug dealing and other forms of socially undesirable behavior.

Table 3.7 Evaluating incentives for reducing pollution

Criteria Alternatives	N Goal Political feasibility	L Goal Effective- ness in reducing pollution	L Goal Clean-up funds	N Goal Cost to general taxpayers	L Goal Cost to consumers or workers	N Goal Public participa- tion	N Goal Predicta- bility & due process	C Goal Stimulate business	N Total (neutral weights)	L Total (liberal weights)	C Total (conservative weights)
I Increase benefits of rightdoing											
C Alternative Reward subsidies to cities	2	5	3	1	3	3	4	3	48	56	40
C Alternative Reward subsidies to businesses	1	5	3	1	3	3	4	4	48	55	41
C Alternative Pollution tax reduction	1	4	4	3	2	3	4	3	48	55	41
C Alternative New govt. contracts	3.5	4	3	2.5	3	3	4	4	54	60	48
C Alternative Selling marketable pollution rights	3.5	4	3	3	2	3	4	4	53	58	48

Table 3.7 continued

Criteria / Alternatives	N Goal Political feasibility	L Goal Effectiveness in reducing pollution	L Goal Clean-up funds	N Goal Cost to general taxpayers	L Goal Cost to consumers or workers	N Goal Public participation	N Goal Predictability & due process	C Goal Stimulate business	N Total (neutral weights)	L Total (liberal weights)	C Total (conservative weights)
II Reduce costs of rightdoing											
C Alternative Tax deductions	4	3.5	3	2	3	3	4	4	53	58.5	47.5
C Alternative Cost subsidies to cities	4	3.5	3	2	3	3	4	3	51	57.5	44.5
C Alternative Cost subsidies to businesses	2	3.5	3	2	3	3	4	4	49	54.5	43.5
III Increase costs of wrongdoing											
L Alternative Damage suits	4	4	3	3	2	4	2	2	48	55	41
L Alternative Publicize wrongdoers	3.5	4	3	2.5	3	4	2	2	48	56	40
L Alternative Pollution tax	1	5	4	4	2	3	4	2	50	59	41
L Alternative Fines	4	3	3	3	2	3	2	2	44	50	38
L Alternative Jail	2	3	3	2	3	3	2	2	40	47	33
L Alternative Loss of govt. contracts	2.5	4	3	2.5	3	3	2.5	2	45	53	37

IV Reduce benefits of wrongdoing

L Alternative Buying marketable pollution rights	3.5	4	3	3	3	4	3	53	60	46
L Alternative Padlock injunction	2	4	3	2	3	3	2	1	40	48	32
L Alternative Confiscate profits	2	5	3.5	3	3	3	2	1	45	55.5	34.5

V Increase probability of benefits and costs

N Alternative Improve monitoring	4	4	3	2	3	3	2	3	48	55	41
N Alternative Bounties for reporting wrongdoing	4	4	3	3	4	2	3	52	59	45
SOS Alternative Combine all										

Policies to increase the *probability* of the benefits and costs occurring include improved monitoring systems and bounties for reporting of wrong-doing. An important aspect of increasing the probability of the benefits and costs occurring is arranging for the benefits and costs to be legislated and then effectively administered. Being legislated gets into the criterion of political feasibility, and being effectively administered leads to the second criterion in Table 3.7.

Relations   The relations in Table 3.7 are scored on a more sophisticated 1–5 scale, rather than a 0–2 scale. In a 1–5 scale, a 5 means highly conducive to the goal, a 4 means mildly conducive, a 3 means neither conducive nor adverse, a 2 means mildly adverse and a 1 means highly adverse. There are 19 alternatives times eight criteria in Table 3.7. That means 153 cells in the table, which is too many to discuss in detail. One might, however, look at the top row as an illustrative example.

Reward subsidies to cites are not very politically feasible. It is difficult enough to obtain subsidies that cover costs without an incentive bonus. It is especially difficult for a legislature to pass reward subsidies to businesses, rather than cities. On the other hand, reward subsidies are highly effective in reducing pollution. If a city or business firm can reduce pollution to zero for $100,000, and a legislature is willing to pay $120,000, both cities and businesses are likely to accept the offer. Doing so does nothing positively or negatively with regard to providing clean-up funds. The cost to the taxpayer is very high, but there is no cost to consumers of the firm's products or to the workers. Such a system does not involve any active public participation, unlike damage suits, publicity-related boycotts or bounties. Reward subsidies tend to have high predictability or objectivity as to who is going to receive them and to what extent. They are not likely to result in innocent firms being wrongfully accused, which is an important part of due process.

Results   The column at the far right sums the 1–5 scores in each of the eight criteria columns for each of the 19 policy alternatives. The alternatives that score relatively high (23 points or higher on a 1–2 scale) include (1) giving government contracts to business firms that satisfy or excel on meeting pollution requirements, (2) pollution taxes, although they may not be able to meet a minimum political feasibility level, (3) the buying and selling of marketable pollution rights as a cost to polluters and an income reward to non-polluters, and (4) bounties for reporting wrongdoing, whereby the general public shares in fines that are levied. The alternatives that score relatively low (meaning 20 or below on a 1–2 scale) include (1) reward subsidies to business which are opposed as being too expensive to the taxpayer, (2) fines which tend to be treated as petty business expenses to be passed on to the consumer, (3) jail sentences that are unlikely to be imposed and thus relatively ineffective, and (4) padlock injunctions that are opposed because they result in loss of employment and production.

Expanding the model

If the criteria are going to be weighted differently, political feasibility can be considered a constraint. Any alternative which scores only a 1 on political feasibility can be considered unfeasible. Of the other criteria, effectiveness in reducing pollution is probably the most important, followed by costs to the general taxpayer. The relation scores on these criteria could thus be doubled, thereby giving each of them twice the importance of the other criteria in determining the overall sum for each alternative.

In addition to these 19 forms of incentives, one can also analyze a variety of other policy alternatives. It might be interesting, for example, to analyze alternatives that relate to the division of labor between national, state and local government, and also between legislatures, administrative agencies and courts. One could also analyze structures that relate to the division of labor between the public and private sectors and between the government and the general public. One could also analyze alternative education programs to socialize people into considering certain forms of pollution as being unthinkable: they then never come to a point where they have to decide whether the benefits minus the costs of polluting outweigh the benefits minus the costs of not polluting.

The analysis can also be extended to other fields of public policy and for use in generating broader principles that relate to incentives and multi-criteria decision making. One broader incentives principle might be that rewards for rightdoing generate more socially desired behavior than penalties for wrongdoing. One broader MCDM principle might be that better conclusions are likely to be reached if one expands one's mind by thinking in terms of many alternatives and many criteria, while keeping the total quantity manageable and non-redundant.

The incentives approach can be contrasted with the unplanned marketplace, which may often be ineffective or adverse to encouraging socially desired behavior. It can also be contrasted with a regulation approach, which may overemphasize seeking to encourage desired behavior by fiat and penalties. The MCDM approach can be contrasted to traditional operations research and management science, which may overemphasize single objective functions and working with less important variables that happen to be measurable. The combination of incentives theory and multi-criteria decision making has virtually unlimited potential for facilitating environmental planning in a more systematic way, while, at the same time, the combination can be useful in processing important goals, alternatives and relations in order to arrive at better conclusions.

Privatization[5] or contracting out

The changes that are occurring in eastern Europe and in many other regions and nations of the world provide an excellent opportunity to apply systematic policy analysis to determining such basic matters as how to organize the economy, the government and other social institutions. Super-optimum solutions refer to public policy alternatives that can enable conservatives, liberals and other major viewpoints all to come out ahead of their best initial expectations simultaneously. The problems of privatization and inflation can illustrate what is involved in super-optimum solutions.

Alternatives

Table 3.8 analyzes the fundamental issue of *socialism versus capitalism* in the context of government versus private ownership and operation of the basic means of producing industrial and agricultural products. The essence of socialism in this context is government ownership and operation of factories and farms, or at least those larger than the handicraft or garden size, as in the Soviet Union of 1960. The essence of capitalism is private ownership and operation of both factories and farms, as in the United States of 1960. The neutral position or middle way is to have some government and some private ownership–operation, as in Sweden in 1960. The year 1960 is used because that is approximately when the Soviet Union began to change with the advent of Nikita Khrushchev. The United States also underwent big changes in the 1960s, with the advent of John F. Kennedy.

Table 3.9 refers to government ownership–operation as the liberal or left-wing alternative, as it is in the United States and in world history, at least since the time of Karl Marx. The table refers to private ownership–operation as the conservative or right-wing alternative, as it is in the United States and elsewhere, at least since the time of Adam Smith. In recent years in Russia and in China, those favoring privatization have been referred to as liberals, and those favoring retention of government ownership–operation have been referred to as conservatives. The *labels* make no difference in this context. The object of Table 3.9 is to find a super-optimum solution that more than satisfies the goals of both ideologies or groups, regardless of their labels.

Table 3.8   An SOS solution to socialistic versus capitalistic ownership

Criteria / Alternatives	C Goal Productive farms and property[1]	L Goal Equitable farms and property[2]	N Total (neutral weights)	L Total (liberal weights)	C Total (conservative weights)
C Alternative Land to the highest bidder	2+	2	>8	>8	>8
L Alternative Retain collective farming	2	2	8	8	8
N Alternative Collective farming with private plots	2–	2	<8	8	<8
SOS Alternative Govt ownership with contracting out to farming farmer[3]	4	4	16	16	16

Notes:
1 Productive farms and property refer to (a) producing a lot of goods and (b) at low cost.
2 Equitable farms and property mainly refers to (a) no exploiting of labor, (b) no despoiling the environment, and (c) no excessive holdings.
3 Farming farmers are farmers who actually farm whether they own farms or not, as contrasted to owners who do not do the actual farming but instead are lawyers, doctors, professors, etc.

Goals and relations

The key capitalistic *goal* is high productivity, in terms of income-producing goods substantially above what it costs to produce them. The key socialistic goal is equity, in terms of the sharing of ownership, operation, wealth and income. Other goals that tend to be more socialistic than capitalistic, but are less fundamental, consist of (1) workplace quality, including wages, hours, safety, hiring by merit, and worker input, (2) environmental protection, including reduction of air, water, radiation, noise and other forms of pollution, and (3) consumer protection, including low prices and goods that are durable, safe and high-quality.

Table 3.9 Government versus private ownership and operation

Criteria / Alternatives	C Goal High productivity C=3 L=1	L Goal Equity C=1 L=3	L Goal Workplace quality C=1 L=3	L Goal Environmental protection C=1 L=3	L Goal Consumer protection C=1 L=3	N Total (neutral weights)	L Total (liberal or socialistic weights)	C Total (conservative or capitalistic weights)
L Alternative Government ownership & operation (socialism)	2	4	2	2	2	24	32*	16
C Alternative Private ownerhip & operation (capitalism)	4	2	2	2	2	24	28	20*
N Alternative Some govt & some private	3	3	2	2	2	24	24	18
SOS Alternative 100% govt owned & 100% private operation	>3	>3	>3	>3	>3	>30	>39**	>21**

146

The *relations* between each alternative and each goal are shown on a 1–5 scale, where 5 means highly conducive to the goal, 4 means mildly conducive, 3 means neither conducive nor adverse, 2 means mildly adverse and 1 means highly adverse to the goal. We have here a classic tradeoff. Going down the *productivity* column, the liberal socialistic alternative does not score very high on productivity through lack of profit-making incentives and a surplus of bureaucratic interference, in comparison to the capitalistic alternative, assuming the level of technology is held constant. The empirical validity of this statement is at least partially confirmed by noting that the capitalistic countries of Japan and West Germany are more productive than their socialistic counterparts of East Germany and China, although they began at approximately the same level in 1945, at the end of World War II. Going down the *equity* column, the liberal socialistic alternative does score relatively high. By definition, it involves at least a nominal collective sharing in the ownership and operation of industry and agriculture, which generally leads to less inequality in wealth and income than capitalism does.

On the goals that relate to the workplace, the environment and consumers, the socialists traditionally argue that government ownership–operation is more sensitive to those matters because it is less profit-oriented. The capitalists traditionally argue that private ownership–operation is more sensitive in competitive marketplace in order to find quality workers and to increase the quantity of one's consumers. The reality (as contrasted to the theory) is that, without alternative incentives or regulations, both government managers and private managers of factories and farms are motivated toward high production at low cost. That kind of motivation leads to cutting back on the expenses of providing workplace quality, environmental protection and consumer protection. The government factory manager of the Polish steelworks may be just as abusive of labor as the private factory manager for the US steel company. Likewise, the government factory managers in the state factories of China may be just as insensitive to consumer safety and durability as their monopolistic counterparts in the American car industry.

A super-optimum solution

As for how the super-optimum solution operates, it involves government ownership, but all the factories and farms are rented to private entrepreneurs to develop productive and profitable manufacturing and farming. Each lease is renewable every year, or longer if necessary to get productive tenants. A renewal can be refused if the factory or farm is not being productively developed, or if the entrepreneur is not showing adequate sensitivity to workers, the environment and consumers.

As for some of the *advantages* of such an SOS system, it is easier not to renew a lease than it is to issue injunctions, fines, jail sentences or other negative sanctions. It is also much less expensive than subsidies. The money received for rent can be an important source of tax revenue for the government to provide productive subsidies elsewhere in the economy. Those subsidies can be used in particular for encouraging technological innovation diffusion, the upgrading of skills and stimulating competition for market share which can be so much more beneficial to society than either socialistic or capitalistic monopolies. The government can more easily demand sensitivity to workers, the environment and consumers from its renters of factories and farms than it can from itself. There is a conflict of interest in regulating oneself.

This SOS alternative is *only available to socialistic countries* such as the former USSR, China, Cuba and North Korea, since they already own the factories and land. It would not be economically or politically feasible for capitalistic countries to move from the conservative capitalistic alternative to the SOS solution by acquiring ownership through payment or confiscation. This is an example where socialistic countries are in a position to decide between socialism and capitalism by compromising and winding up with the worst of both possible worlds. That means the relative unproductivity of socialism and the relative inequity of capitalism. The socialistic countries are also in a position to decide between the two basic alternatives by winding up with the best of both possible worlds. That means retaining the equities and social sensitivities of government ownership, while having the high productivity that is associated with profit-seeking entrepreneurial capitalism. It would be difficult to find a better example of *compromising versus super-optimizing* than the current debate over socialism versus capitalism.

Technological fix

The Developmental Policy Studies Consortium was approached in the spring of 1992 to offer conceptual insights relevant to the Earth Summit Conference to be held in Brazil in June of that year. In response to the call for three levels of conceptual insights, we indicated that we would be pleased to contribute our insights regarding the relevance of super-optimizing policy analysis to the problems of economic development versus a clean environment in developing nations.

As for three levels of relevant insights, the first would be to communicate *what super-optimizing policy analysis is*. It is a new and exciting approach to dealing with public policy dilemmas whereby conservatives, liberals and other major viewpoints can all come out ahead of their best initial expecta-

Table 3.10 An SOS analysis of economic development versus a clean environment in developing nations

Criteria / Alternatives	C Goal Rapid economic development C=3 N=2 L=1	L Goal Clean environment C=1 N=2 L=3	N Total (neutral weights)	L Total (liberal weights)	C Total (conservative weights)
C Alternative Unregulated economic development	4	2	12	10	14*
L Alternative Anti-pollution regulations	2	4	12	14*	10
N Alternative Compromise regulations	3	3	12	12	12
SOS Alternative Improved manufacturing & agricultural processes	>4	>4	>16	>16**	>16**

tions simultaneously. See Table 3.10, which summarizes in table form some of the basic concepts. The basic alternatives are on the rows. The goals to be achieved are on the columns. Relations between alternatives and goals are shown in the cells tentatively using a 1–5 scale, where a 5 means highly conducive to the goal, a 4 means mildly conducive, a 3 means neither conducive nor adverse, a 2 means mildly adverse and a 1 means highly adverse.

Overall totals for each alternative are shown in the columns at the right. They include a neutral column where all the goals are given a middling weight of 2 on a 1–3 scale of importance. The second total column involves conservative totals where the conservative goals are given a weight or multiplier of 3, and the liberal goals are given a weight or multiplier of 1. The third set of totals are the liberal totals where the conservative goals are given a weight of 1, and the liberal goals a weight of 3. The conservative alternative wins on the conservative totals, and the liberal alternative wins on the liberal totals. The object is to develop an alternative that does even better on the conservative totals than the previous conservative alternative, and simultaneously does better on the liberal totals than the previous liberal alternative.

The second level of insight is to communicate *a recognition that such super-optimum solutions are realistically possible* and not just conceptually possible. A good example relates to the ozone problem and the use of fluorocarbons in hairsprays and other aerosol containers. In about 1985, such devices represented a serious threat in depleting the ozone layer and thereby causing a substantial increase in skin cancer throughout the world. The solution was *not* to rely on an unregulated marketplace, which normally provides almost no incentives to manufacturers to reduce their pollution. The solution was *not* regulation or prohibition, which tends to be evaded, expensive to enforce, and enforced with little enthusiasm given disruptions that might occur to the economy. The most exciting aspect of the solution (although the problem is not completely solved) was the development of new forms of spray propellant which are less expensive for manufacturers to use and simultaneously not harmful to the ozone layer.

That kind of solution tends to be self-adopting, since manufacturing firms, farmers and others who might otherwise be polluting the environment now have an important economic incentive to adopt the new low-polluting methods because they reduce the expenses of the business firm. This approach does require substantial research and substantial government subsidies for research and development, as contrasted to paying the polluters not to pollute, which is even more expensive and often not so effective, since they may take the money and pollute anyhow. The business firms generally do not have capital for that kind of research and development, or the foresight or forbearance which public policy and governmental decision making may be more capable of exercising. That includes international governmental decision makers, as well as those in developing nations.

The third level of insight is to communicate that *such solutions may be well worth pursuing to resolve the dilemma of economic development versus a clean environment* in developing nations. In the case of Brazil, for example, this may mean research and development to make better use of the rain forests as a source of low-polluting fuel for industries in Brazil and elsewhere. That is instead of wastefully burning off the rain forests and thereby having an adverse effect on global warming. The rain forests could conceivably be harvested as if they were a form of coal mine and possibly even analogous to the harvesting of crops. The carbohydrates could be economically converted into relatively clean fuel. This would be an expansion of the idea of ethanol as a source of fuel for running cars. Money invested in that kind of research could simultaneously aid Brazil in its economic development and lead to a cleaner environment for both Brazil and other parts of the world.

Other R&D subsidies could go into such ideas as developing ways of processing Brazilian crops to reduce simultaneously the pollution effect of the waste products and the processing costs. This is the kind of research activity that the United States Environment Protection Agency is encouraging in such fields as soybean processing in central Illinois by the ADM Manufacturing Company. It is the kind of research that seeks to find pesticides and herbicides that are even more effective than traditional ones in dealing with undesirable insects and weeds, but are at the same time less expensive than traditional ones. The University of Illinois Agricultural Engineering Department is at the forefront of this kind of research. The Materials Science and Engineering Department is also at the forefront of developing new polymers and other materials which are less expensive, more effective and less polluting in the manufacturing process than traditional metals. The department used to be called the Department of Mining and Metallurgy. Its work may be relevant to developing more effective, less expensive and less polluting ways of mining gold on the Amazon River than the current methods, which have the undesirable effect of adding to the mercury content of the river.

Research on the development of these improved manufacturing and agricultural processes is in need of a lot more money than it is receiving from such places as the Illinois state legislature. There is a need for the Big Seven countries and other international economic communities to devote more funding to this kind of SOS research. It does mean investing in ideas that may take longer to pay off than investing in a profitable but pollution-producing factory. The payoffs, though, are likely to be well worth the investment in terms of being able to achieve economic development and a clean environment simultaneously. This is in contrast to having to compromise or have tradeoffs which result in both less economic development and a less clean environment.

SOME CONCLUSIONS

On environmental policy, this is viewed as a form of business regulation by conservatives and resisted as much as any kind of business regulation. Liberals like environmental regulation partly because they traditionally do not especially like business and they like to see business regulated. These are not very good motivations. They are rather negative motivations on both sides. A more positive motivation would be for both sides to recognize how much better off everybody is with clean air and clean water, as the two main kinds of environmental protection. The same is true about a concern for toxic waste, acid rain, ozone problems, greenhouse effects, noise pollution, radiation pollution and conservation. The latest may be radon pollution which is now the first natural pollution (rather than manmade pollution) that has serious public health consequences. Regardless of the source (and radon pollution seems relatively unimportant compared to other forms of pollution), they are all subject to subsidies, tax breaks and other devices to encourage socially desired behaviour.

Desired behavior includes cutting back on the causes of pollution, or curing the pollution by cleaning up the water or the air after the pollution has occurred. That works well with water, but not so well with air. Although it could work also with air, by way of more innovative ideas that relate to seeding clouds in order to get the acid rain to fall over the ocean instead of over Canadian farmland. That may also require a big fan to blow the clouds where one wants to blow them, or require imaginative thinking regarding a microwave in the sky. It would take advantage of the electricity that is in clouds to get them to move where one wants them by electromagnetism instead of a big fan. It may be cheaper to allow the high smokestacks that put the acid content into the clouds, and then get rid of the clouds, than it is to get rid of the smokestacks. This is especially so since those high smokestacks are designed to prevent air pollution for people in the areas of the factories.

The super-optimum solutions in the environmental field are those where liberals and conservatives objectively recognize that everybody is better off in the sense of increased public health. We are not talking about the esthetics of wildlife or sunsets. Actually, the sunsets look better with polluted air. There is no sunset at all if the air is 100 per cent pure: the sunsets are being filtered through impurities in the air. What we are talking about is the fact that a high percentage of all cancers are due to environmental defects. This includes (1) lung cancer that is due to air pollution, (2) intestinal cancer that is due to water pollution, and (3) other cancers that are due to radiation that may be related to radon.

Environmental protection and conservation of nature are largely a governmental function. It is not profitable or equitable for private enterprise, including the maintenance of private parks, beaches and wilderness areas. Pollution reduction is a good example of the use of innovative marketplace incentives, such as marketable pollution permits. They allow business firms to pollute, but such permits are expensive to buy from one's competitors. The expense and a desire to avoid subsidizing one's competitors stimulate pollution reduction.

NOTES

1   For further material on super-optimum solutions where both liberals and conservatives come out ahead of their initial best expectations, see Lawrence Susskind and Jeffrey

Cruikshank, *Breaking the Impasse: Consensual Approaches to Resolving Disputes* (Basic Books, 1987); S. Nagel, *Decision-Aiding Software: Skills, Obstacles and Applications* (Macmillan, 1990); S. Nagel, 'Super-Optimum Solutions in Public Controversies', *World Futures Quarterly*, 53–70 (Spring, 1989).

2 For further details on the problem of hand-crafted work versus assembly lines in India, see Sanjiv Misra, 'India's Textile Policy and the Informal Sectors', in S. Nagel (ed.), *India Development and Public Policy* (Ashgate, 1999). Also see Deepak Mazumdar, 'The Issue of Small Versus Large in the India Textile Industry' (World Bank Staff Working Papers, 1984) and Sukhamoy Chakravarty, *Development Planning: The Indian Experience* (Oxford University Press, 1987).

3 On land reform and agricultural policy as it pertains to developing countries, see William Browne and Don Hadwiger (eds), *World Food Policies: Toward Agricultural Independence* (Lynne Reinner, 1986); John Mellor, 'Agriculture on the Road to Industrialization', in John Lewis and Laleriana Kallab (eds), *Development Strategies Reconsidered* (Transaction Books, 1986); Raid El-Ghonemy, *The Political Economy of Rural Poverty: The Case of Land Reform* (Routledge, Chapman and Hall, 1991).

4 For further details on incentives theory, see Barry Mitnick, *The Political Economy of Regulation* (Columbia University Press, 1980); Alfred Blumstein (ed.), *Deterrence and Incapacitation* (National Academy of Sciences, 1978); S. Nagel, 'Public Policy as Incentives for Encouraging Socially Desired Behavior', **3**, *Research in Public Policy Analysis and Management*, 131–40 (JAI Press, 1986).

5 On privatization in the Soviet Union and Eastern Europe, see Jan Prybyla (ed.), *Privatizing and Marketizing Socialism* (Annals of the American Academy of Political and Social Science, 1990); Richard Noyes (ed.), *Now the Synthesis: Capitalism, Socialism and the New Social Contract* (Holmes & Meier, 1991). The latter contains in an appendix an open letter to Mikhail Gorbachev advocating retention of title to collective farms while renting the land for entrepreneurial development. The open letter is signed by Nobel prizewinners Modigliani, Tobin and Solow, as well as leading economists from throughout the world. On privatization in general, see John Donahue, *The Privatization Decision: Public Ends, Private Means* (Basic Books, 1989); Randy Ross, *Government and the Private Sector: Who Should Do What* (Crane Russak, 1988).

PART II
INTERNATIONAL POLICY PROBLEMS

4   Promoting Democracy and Dispute Resolution as Foreign Policy

EXPORTING DEMOCRACY

We have plenty of Bill of Rights tables dealing with free speech, due process and equal treatment. The present object, though, is not to defend the Bill of Rights; it is to talk about how it is in the best interests of the United States to encourage other countries to adopt the Bill of Rights.

Conservatives like former President George Bush would never take the position that they are opposed to free speech. They just take the position that what is good for the United States may not be so good for Saudi Arabia. They may say such things as that these are people who only recently abolished slavery; you cannot expect them to move in just a couple of years from where the United States was in 1860 to where it is in the 1990s.

One good argument against this kind of nonsense is that in about the 1950s Saudis had perhaps never seen a car. They did not have to pass through all the ages and eras since the Stone Age before they could buy a car from General Motors. GM was glad to sell them one right away. One does not have to reinvent the Bill of Rights if it has already been invented. One can just buy it from whoever is selling it. It happens to be a free good that is available at no direct monetary cost.

Pro-US arguments

By supporting those feudalistic and dictatorial societies, all we are getting is some very short-run bootlicking. The monarchy has no lasting power. It will soon be replaced by young educated people. The monarchy, just like communist dictatorships, is providing education; it is not deliberately trying to keep people illiterate. If the people get educated, they will read about the Bill of Rights. They will read about what goes on in other countries and in no time at all they will want to change things. If we really want to keep the monarchy in power, we should advocate massive book burning. This should include the Koran, since it has a few subversive things to say about democracy. The feudalistic monarchy of Saudi Arabia would not tolerate burning the Koran. By being unwilling to burn the Koran, though, they are in effect undermining themselves. The Koran is one of the most equalitarian religious books.

By supporting free speech, we can gain some psychological benefits by feeling proud of ourselves instead of ashamed. People in the State Department, people who are tourists, people who are university people, do not have to apologize all the time for American foreign policy which runs so contrary to American ideals. By supporting free speech we facilitate the development of new ideas for improving those societies, which means making them more productive. This in the intermediate run, without even having to wait for the long run, means that they are likely to become better customers for the United States and better sellers to the United States. We do not make much money off feudalistic monarchies, as contrasted to dealing with countries such as Japan, which buys goods, and especially which sells low-priced, high-quality goods that add to our standard of living. They never would have become as productive as they are if they had not had open debate on how they should go about doing so.

Supporting free speech in places like Saudi Arabia provides for safety valves that allow people to let off steam and bring about social change through peaceful means. Otherwise, they take to guerrilla fighting, as in Central America. The United States in recent years has almost inevitably sided with the landlords, the feudalistic monarchies, the business people, against the guerrilla fighters, who tend to be workers and peasants. As a result, it gets drawn into a war like Vietnam or what could have been another Vietnam in Central America. A key reason for the Persian Gulf not becoming a Vietnam was that it was not workers and peasants against landlords, it was one country trying to take over another country.

Countries that lack free speech, and so bottle up discontent, tend to try to take the minds of their people off their problems by engaging in aggressive behavior toward other countries. This could partly explain Iraq's behavior toward Kuwait. As a result, we are drawn into a war due to the aggression that results from our not having facilitated free speech in the aggressor. We certainly did not encourage dissent in Iraq so long as Saddam Hussein was doing our bidding in the war with Iran, and as long as he was not giving Israel any trouble.

One could argue in favor of exporting free speech on altruistic grounds, in that it is good for other people just as it is good for us. That means bringing in all the arguments why free speech is good for people. We are not interested in doing that here. Here we are trying to argue that we are exporting free speech for selfish reasons, that it will help America's power in the world. This tends to go further than arguing in favor of socially desired behavior on altruistic grounds, although we could mention the do-gooder idea, too. More important, though, is arguing in favor of exporting free speech because it is good for the quality of life in the United States, regardless of what it does for other people.

Democracy compared to exporting other products

On exporting technologically innovative products, there is no disagreement. The former Bush administration would not say Saudi Arabia is not ready for US cars or computers. The problem here is how to sell the Saudis IBM computers when they can buy Japanese computers or, for that matter, Korean, Singaporean or Taiwanese computers that are just as good, or better, for less money.

Exporting technologically innovative products is quite different from exporting the Bill of Rights. There is no competition when it comes to exporting the Bill of Rights. No other country in the world can touch the United States with regard to what the US Supreme Court has done over the past 50 years regarding free speech, due process and equal treatment, partly with the help of Congress, administrative agencies, interest groups and state and local governments. In the case of technologically innovative products, though, the United States has some vigorous competition in the form of Japan, Germany and numerous other countries. The problem here is one of talking about well-placed subsidies and tax breaks. It deals with the business of incentives, competition, risk and positive thinking. All these ideas are much more oriented toward the technologically innovative productive side than the Bill of Rights side of the exporting.

Case studies of bad exporting

There is no need to concentrate too exclusively on Saudi Arabia, though that is a good example. We have had Bill of Rights problems with every developing region of the world. For *Asia*, we could mention the Vietnam War. We could mention losing China. We could mention present problems with the Philippines. All these problems can be attributed to failing to live up to our own principles expressed in the Bill of Rights. In *Latin America*, we could mention every Central American people; we could mention the dictatorships encouraged in Chile, Argentina and Brazil. In *Europe*, some of the blame for eastern Europe going communist is definitely attributable to the United States' failure to support democratic alternatives. The United States clearly blundered in Greece when the anti-fascist guerrillas wanted to have a democratic society after the end of World War II and throw out their monarchy. The Truman Plan came to the aid of the worst military junta, or one of the worst, that the world has ever known. The same mistake was made with Turkey. There was marked inconsistency, since Truman did support the democratic socialists in France and Italy, but not in Greece and Turkey. He and the conservatives would say that there were not enough democratic socialists to support, and likewise in China or in Vietnam; that it was support either the fascists or the communists, and the United States chose the fascists. That was untrue, though. All these countries had a sufficient core of democratic socialists that could have received American support. The United States could also have attached important conditions to the support that it did give to Chiang Kai-Chek, the Greek junta and the Turkish junta.

In *Africa*, the United States supported South Africa to the very end. In fact, some American conservatives have not yet caught up with the idea that the South African right wing now wants to dismantle apartheid. Some American conservatives have such a kneejerk reaction for supporting reactionaries that, even when the reactionaries change position, the American conservatives fail to show flexibility. This is illustrated by the attacks that many American conservatives made on Nelson Mandela, especially in Florida, calling him a communist dupe partly because he thanked Fidel Castro for the support that Castro gave to the anti-apartheid cause, at the same time that the conservative South African government was being supportive of Mandela. The United States have supported some of the most murderous killers in Mozambique and Angola who are not ideological fascists but are just roving, murderous bandits. But as long as they say they are anti-communist they get American arms, or at least they did when the Cold War was in a hotter state.

So much for the southern part of Africa. With regard to the northern part of Africa, to the very end the United States sided with the colonialists in Algeria, Tunisia and Morocco, just as it did in Vietnam. France caused US involvement in the Vietnam war, but not in the Algerian war. This was largely because the French, just like the government of South Africa, decided to be flexible, whereas the pro-American government in Vietnam never showed any flexibility. If France had continued the Algerian war, the United States might eventually have been drawn in. In the case of the British colonies in Africa, Britain gave all of them up without much bloodshed, as she did also in India and Asia. The major bloodshed in India was between Moslems and Hindus rather than between Britain and India.

Case studies of good exporting

We should give some examples where the United States has done some good and where exporting the Bill of Rights has paid off well. The best example would be the Marshall Plan, with its political rather than its economic aspects, in converting France and Italy to democracies when they were both run by fascists before the US intervention. If we go back over 100 years to find other examples, they include the Monroe doctrine cases where the French were ejected from Mexico and the Spaniards from Cuba; the United States supported Simon Bolivar in throwing off Spanish colonial domination in the early 1800s. That may be all there is with regard to America's record of supporting anti-colonialism, but these are good examples, because they show that at least in those instances we recognized that promoting the Bill of Rights could be in the best interests of the United States. Emperor Maximilian was quickly got rid of in Mexico during the civil war. There were good motives for getting rid of the Spanish from Cuba in the Spanish–American War, but the United States was at fault in the Philippines, becoming the colonial power there after getting rid of the Spanish.

Some presidents have supported democratic forces and have been admired by people in developing nations for doing so. These include President Carter, President Kennedy and President Roosevelt. All three were thought to be sincere, especially regarding Latin America, but also with regard to the world in general. FDR was strongly opposed to Nazi and Fascist dictatorships in Europe and Asia. Both Kennedy and Carter, though they never did much, were personally opposed to Franco in Spain and Salazar in Portugal. They did nothing to change those governments, but at least they did not invite them into the North Atlantic Treaty Organization or the European Economic Community, although France and England would not have Spain or Portugal either. Under Reagan or Bush, there might have been pressure placed on France and England to admit Spain and Portugal on grounds that they represent potential customers, regardless of their ideology, but fortunately they both became more democratic.

The handling of eastern Europe as of 1990 has not been so bad. That can be partly explained by saying that the democratic forces happen also to be in favor of a combination of free speech and free enterprise: glasnost and perestroika. If the reformers are only in favor of free speech, they might not get much American support. China is a good example of American support being available to a country that is in favor of free enterprise but not free speech. The Russian situation is currently unclear as to what the State Department's position is and whether it is desirable in terms of a Bill of Rights position. Gorbachev was the inventor of glasnost and perestroika, but was pushed out by more vigorous forces which may be operating too much in terms of a kind of naïveté as to how far Russia can currently be reformed, and also too much in terms of personalities.

Yeltsin said things that sounded more liberal, but he lacked the ability to pull them off. This is because he so antagonized conservatives and the military in Russia, whereas Gorbachev was not at first capable of appealing to both the left and right. Yeltsin could have played a kind of Mau-Mau role in order to push Gorbachev further toward democracy, and thereby make him more acceptable to the conservatives. Yeltsin, however, subsequently showed that he was not trying to make Gorbachev look like a moderate, but was really trying to push Gorbachev out and be his replacement.

As far as the United States' position was concerned, it did seem to be supportive of Gorbachev over Yeltsin. The United States would be reverting to its short-sighted worst if it were to come out in favor of the relatively small pro-czarist, pro-restoration of pre-1917 people. The Bush administration did not seem to offer them any support at all. And they do not seem to be of any great concern except to journalists who find them a bit quaint and crazy. The United States does not support people who are that far to the right. The people who were called conservatives in the Soviet Union were definitely not Bush Republicans. They were conservatives in the sense of not wanting to move in the direction of more free speech and free enterprise, and in wanting to preserve the Cold War. For the Bush administration it was a choice between Gorbachev or Yeltsin. Both were in favor of free speech, Yeltsin the more so, but he is less capable of bringing it about. Yeltsin took over, and Clinton embraced him both figuratively and literally.

EXCHANGE OF FREE SPEECH IDEAS

Trade and human rights

This analysis stems largely from the controversy over how far to go in withholding trade from China until human rights are given more recognition. The problem, however, applies to many countries that would like increased trade with the United States, but lacks a minimum level of domestic institutions.

The conservative position is to have trade without human rights conditions or prerequisites. The liberal position is to use trade to secure better human rights conditions, including the possibility of a pluralistic political system which allows two or more political parties that meaningfully compete for votes. A neutral position would think in terms of less substantial

Table 4.1 Exchange of free speech ideas

Issues	Conservative	Liberal	Neutral	Super-optimum solutions
1. Trade and Human Rights	1. Business profits.	1. Spread democracy.		1. Promoting trade and rights partly through education and communications.
	– 1. Trade without human rights conditions.	– 1. Trade with human rights conditions.	– 1. Trade with slight conditions.	
2. Copyright Piracy	1. Profits for copyright holders.	1. Circulate literature.		1. Government as an insurer. 2. Mutual access to courts. 3. Payment of royalties.
	– 1. Tariffs and sanctions for copyright piracy.	– 1. No raising of tariffs for copyright piracy.	– 1. Moderate raising.	

human rights such as visits by Red Cross workers to political prisoners, but not ending political prisoners.

The conservative position is oriented toward American business profits. The liberal position is oriented toward spreading democracy. Both sides endorse each other's goals, but not with equal weight.

The object of an SOS alternative would be to promote both trade and human rights, partly through education and communication. That means encouraging students from China and other such countries to come to the United States. Doing so means they are more likely to return with American values like democracy. That also means increasing the communication of democracy-related ideas by way of radio, TV, newspapers, books, and other forms of communication to China and other such countries.

The SOS alternative also recognizes that trade, even without human rights conditions, can promote human rights by promoting prosperity and internal education. Democratic institutions can also promote prosperity and trade. There is thus reciprocal causation, even without explicitly linking the two.

Trade when used to encourage human rights needs to be presented more as a reward or bribe, rather than as a threat or punishment. Trade has worked well to encourage democratic institutions in places like South Africa. It can backfire if trade is withdrawn to the point where extremists come to power (as in Russia), or to the point where the economy suffers long-term destruction (as could happen in Haiti).

Trade can also be used as a bargaining chip for other purposes besides human rights conditions, such as tariff reduction and the opening of investment opportunities, which conservatives would endorse, too.

International copyright piracy

The issue here is whether United States tariffs should be raised in retaliation against copyright piracy by other countries. Such piracy means reprinting books and other materials contrary to the monopoly rights and possibly the royalty rights of the United States copyright holders.

The issue is not the use of trade sanctions to promote peace, tariff reductions, or democracy on the part of other countries. Those uses of trade sanctions seem more acceptable to liberals and conservatives, as contrasted to the use of trade sanctions to stop the free circulation of literature.

The issue is also not the use of trade sanctions to retaliate against patent piracy such as making clones of IBM computers without permission or royalties. That may be less of a problem because IBM and other manufacturers should be able to compete well by having effectively low prices and high quality products without needing a legal monopoly. They can also more easily sue large manufacturers, as contrasted to basement printing or VCR operations.

Those who advocate raising tariffs are seeking higher profits for copyright holders such as book publishers and movie companies. They argue that people will not write or publish books unless they can make big profits. However, the only books that are subject to copyright piracy tend to be books on which big profits are already being made.

Those who advocate not raising tariffs are interested in seeing the circulation of American books, music, movies, and related materials to the rest of the world. They tend to believe that such circulation generally promotes the kinds of values the United States endorses, including democracy, prosperity, and peace.

An SOS solution that could enable both sides to come out ahead would be for the government to act as an insurer to copyright holders. The government would pay for part of their losses to copyright piracy in terms of the difference between the profits they are making and some reasonably high profit level, which may be lower or higher than the profits they are currently making. Such a level might be expressed as a 100 per cent return on one's investment although possibly a different level for different types of copyrights in terms of books, movies, music, or software.

The SOS solution might also include mutual access to the courts of all countries to be able to bring lawsuits against pirating companies in order to collect reasonable royalties. Perhaps there could be an international court dealing with copyrights, patents, and trademarks. The problems are largely between private sector business firms than government manufacturing, but the government could assume a responsibility for providing appropriate dispute resolution institutions and for paying non-prohibitive royalties.

SOME LESSONS FROM THE PEACE CORPS

It may be said that it is not very good for a government agency to get off to a terrific start. One can argue that, subsequently, the only direction they can go is downhill, even if it is doing so well to begin with. However, that does sound rather silly: every activity should try to get off to as good a start as possible, in anticipation of its being able to build on whatever its start is. Also, if it starts at 95 on a 0–100 scale and slips down to 60, it may still be much better off than if it starts at 10 and rises to 50.

There is something to be said for hard-nosed realism. The Peace Corps took pride in how naively idealistic it was. It emphasized a kind of incompetent volunteerism rather than competent volunteerism. There is a big difference between competency and incompetency which is not the same thing as being highly paid versus being a volunteer. The beltway bandits or aggressive commercial firms that provide consulting services for foreign agencies are extremely highly paid and extremely incompetent. The lawyers who work as volunteers or near volunteers for Legal Services Corp., the American Civil Liberties Union (ACLU) the National Association for the Advancement of Colored People (NAACP) and other public interest organizations are paid virtually nothing and are extremely competent. The Peace Corps seemed to operate under the assumption that, if you want volunteers, you have to have incompetent people, and never tried to change that fundamentally wrong idea.

The right thing is to do as the Policy Studies Organization does: it pays nobody anything to write book chapters or articles, or to edit or write books; it has the top experts writing volumes for Greenwood and Macmillan, and previously Sage and Lexington. The answer is to make the work highly worthwhile for non-monetary reasons. Then people will work well without asking for money. We are experiencing the same thing now with the Developmental Policy Studies Consortium, where worldwide experts are volunteering to participate in writing research papers or doing training activities for no money at all, because they consider it to be a good cause which has prestige in the academic world and in the world of international interaction.

Competent people are almost embarrassed to volunteer for the Peace Corps. A top political scientist might be embarrassed to say that he or she is doing volunteer work for the Peace Corps because the image would be that they are digging wells or putting fertilizer on rice, not that they are teaching political science. They are paid maybe $50,000–$100,000 a year to teach political science, which they would be pleased to teach in Africa, Asia or South America. People are paid a few thousand a year to dig wells, and maybe less than that for shoveling fertilizers. Thus, to use political science experts in the Peace Corps is almost like Mao Tse-Tung's program to humiliate political scientists by making them pick rice, or, worse, the Khmer Rouge program to take Cambodian professors and not only have them pick rice, but have them physically abused at the same time. At least the Peace Corps does not physically abuse its volunteers.

What went wrong with the Peace Corps is not that the Reagan administration ruined its idealism or youthfulness, or ruined its neutrality in partisan matters. It was ruined before Reagan got there. He did not do anything to improve it, although he actually tried. The idea of bringing in retired doctors and lawyers was a step in the direction of improving the quality of volunteers. He was attacked for his efforts to improve this on the grounds that he was trying to replace the idealistic 20-year-old Democrats. That may have been part of his motivation, but he was still on the right track in saying that there might be some people willing to volunteer who could do more than be redundant to the local people. The key thing that he failed to do is to have a program that would perhaps call upon the American Political Science Association, the American Bar Association, the American Plumbers Association, maybe 300 different professional associations to round up volunteers to work in the Plumbers for Developing Nations, or Lawyers for Developing Nations, or doctors and so on. It would have created an adult, meaningful version of the Peace Corps in different occupations, or of Volunteers in Service to America (VISTA). Maybe the next administration might try something like that. The Clinton administration has not done it, possibly because it sounds too much like George Bush's emphasis on adult volunteerism which was all talk and no action. The Republicans would not do it because they basically do not like volunteers. They like people who want to make money. They do not trust volunteers. Thus, if the Democrats are not going to do it and the Republicans do not want to do it, it is probably not going to get done, since the associations probably will not take the initiative themselves.

Volunteerism in technical assistance

Some principles

The Peace Corps has not failed because it came under the sway of right-wing zealots. We suggested above that liberals accuse Reagan of having ruined the Peace Corps by infesting it with right-wing types. That is not so. I would say that perhaps Kennedy ruined the Peace Corps long before Reagan by infesting it with small thinkers, regardless of whether they are left- or right-wing.

There are some principles that relate to better use of potential outside personnel in the regular government agencies, like the Agency for International Development (AID), United States Information Agency (USIA) and the State Department, rather than the Peace Corps. For example, if a government agency wants expert volunteers, especially from the academic community, it should totally forget the idea if it is going to have any kind of *loyalty test* with reference to the Republican Party, or the Democratic Party, or to any organization or body. The concept of questioning people's loyalty may go over well with corporate people whose philosophy below the CEO level is basically a boot-licking philosophy of 'my boss right or wrong'. Academics, whether they are conservative or liberal, are very independent people. The only thing they would say they are loyal to is determining truth, beauty and goodness, and even then they would not use words like loyalty.

Some of the points made with regard to the Peace Corps could apply to volunteerism in these other agencies. For instance, they should work through professional agencies in different disciplines and different occupations, rather than trying to work directly with individuals. That includes independent organizations like the Policy Studies Organization (PSO) as well as bigger ones like American Political Science Association (APSA). The people who do the coordinating or serve as liaison should be well-regarded academics themselves, or well-regarded plumbers, if they are working with the American Plumbers' Association. Volunteers are much more likely to come forth if they are asked by people like themselves, not people whom they view as politicians or bureaucrats regardless of whether they are liberal or conservative politicians or bureaucrats.

There must be provision for short-term involvement. Academics cannot sign up for more than a few weeks, let alone a whole semester or year. The philosophy Ralph Nader operates under should apply, namely that it is better to get world-class people who change over every week than tenth-rate people who stay on forever. The Fulbright program, which some people think is a success, is really not very good. It is not doing any great harm, though it may be wasting a substantial amount of money. It does not attract good academics. It requires too long a commitment. A good academic who is really active cannot afford to go and teach in Afghanistan for a year, meaning 52 weeks. But 26 great academics might be willing to show up for two weeks at a time and cover the whole 52 weeks, or 12 good ones close to a month at a time, or a few weeks. There is no such program that I am aware of in any of the agencies that are concerned with developing countries. PSO sends people out for a week or two at a time, but all with money from the Ford Foundation, the Asia Foundation, the Midwest University Consortium for International Affairs (MUCIA), the University of Illinois, or PSO internal funds – not money from AID, although USIA does have an AmParts program which allows for short-term involvement.

The AmParts program has special problems, in that it is such a perversion of what developing nations need. It does provide for short-term changeover, but mainly of basketball players, saxophonists, bongo drum players – just what they need in starving Bangladesh. The USIA has done a miserable job providing people with information, which is what the 'I' stands for; that is, information that they can use to improve their quality of life.

One thing that has really damaged these agencies in the past 35 years but which may be over is the Cold War, which meant sending people guns rather than hybrid seed, or sending them military experts rather than experts on how to develop small manufacturing operations than can grow big enough to have something to export. The Cold War foreign aid was literally murderous. It did not lengthen lives in developing nations, it shortened them. It was responsible for the killing fields of Cambodia, Mozambique, Angola, Guatemala, El Salvador, Nicaragua, Chile and Afghanistan. Everywhere in the world where there was any kind of left-wing reform going on was met with guns for training mercenaries to run death squads. That was not just inefficiency, it was evil at its worst. Supposedly, there are no more death squads being trained or financed by those agencies, including the CIA.

It is important on the positive-thinking side to view developing nations help not as some kind of charity, but instead as a way of making nations into better consumers of American products, better suppliers to American industry and American consumers and better citizens of the world community. These pro-American motives are very conducive to improving the gross national products of developing nations, which cannot buy American products if they are impoverished. They cannot manufacture much of anything Americans would want if they are impoverished. They are a drain on the world community and possibly a potential place for the insurgency that leads to civil wars or worse.

Some negative reactions

Some of the above might provoke negative reactions from various people for various reasons. For example, some would say that it is naively idealistic to think that there is any kind of system of volunteers that could work. People always need to be paid; people are basically mercenary. The idea of free services could be rejected on the grounds that it sounds like something that might come from Mother Theresa or Jane Adams.

Others might say that it sounds too academic, not in the sense that it is highly technical but in the sense that it smacks of the ivory tower, which is a little different from being idealistic. The second criticism means inexperienced. Not worldly-wise.

It might also be rejected because it rubs the wrong way those who have to decide whether it should be published, because they might take some of the arguments personally. This might be especially true of those people who are in the government agencies which are being criticized, but also of those who have operated in the system which does include big money-oriented academics.

It is also very verbal. It would have to be dressed up with some tables. It would be more likely to be published if we were to develop a couple of super-optimizing tables in which we say that the conservative approach is to buy the services of academics, the liberal approach is to wait for them to show up as volunteers and the middling approach is to at least to establish some kind of agency like the Peace Corps or some kind of unit within AID. The super-optimizing solution emphasizes working through their associations. That is the most constructive idea above. The same remedy might apply to both the Peace Corps and AID, even though the Peace Corps' causes for lack of success are different from AID's causes.

An SOS analysis

Alternatives

The conservative alternative is to buy technical assistance (see Table 4.2). During the cold war conservatives also put a lot of emphasis on buying military power and on buying highly visible but not necessarily highly useful projects like dams and factories. Technical assistance is actually a relatively liberal idea with regard to the way it is attained, and it is to the Peace Corps' credit that they emphasize technical assistance. Unfortunately, it is assistance with relatively trivial things such as how to dig a well, rather than how to do policy analysis. The key element, though, when it comes to conservatives, is buying it.

The liberal type going back to the days of socialist medals in the early USSR involves getting people to do things by giving them such medals. It is

Table 4.2   Volunteerism in technical assistance

Criteria Alternatives	C Goal Effective- ness	L Goal Cost saving and efficiency	N Total (neutral weights)	L Total (liberal weights)	C Total (conservative weights)

C Alternative
    Buy technical
    assistance
	4	2	12	10	14*

L Alternative
    Rely on do
    gooders
	2	4	12	14*	10

N Alternative
    Volunteerism
    agencies, e.g.
    Peace Corps
	3	3	12	12	12

SOS Alternative
    Work through
    professional
    associations
	5	5	20	20**	20**

the idea that people can be made to do wonderful things out of dedication to doing good. It is the do-gooder liberal philosophy. We could put it down as 'rely on do-gooders'.

The neutral compromise is to try to facilitate the do-gooders through establishing government agencies that specialize in do-gooders, of which the Peace Corps is a splendid example. It is hard to find any other examples, let alone better examples. No agency relies more on do-good motivation than the Peace Corps, and what it gets is a lot of 20-year-old volunteers who are not especially competent to do anything particularly worthwhile. They do not do any harm, though, except in the sense that they give the United States a false sense that it is doing a lot of good.

The super-optimum solution is to work through academic disciplinary associations and occupational associations so that it becomes a matter of occupational prestige. This is a little bit like the National Recovery Administration in the Depression. There it was trade associations working to bring the country out of depression. Here we are talking about professional associations, not furniture manufacturers, and the purpose is to bring developing nations out of a long-term depression, meaning hundreds of years, not just 1929–39.

Goals

The key goal is effectiveness in improving the quality of life in developing nations. A second goal is to keep the costs down. With both these goals the super-optimum solution scores well, but that is true of SOS's in general – there is nothing unusual about that.

Relations

This becomes a tradeoff, in that one should be able to obtain greater effectiveness with a lot of money than by relying on volunteers. Thus, the conservative approach maybe deserves a 4, the liberal a 2 and the neutral a 3 on effectiveness.

On efficiency or cost-saving, volunteers are obviously cheaper than paid people, so we give them a 4, and paying people a 2. The neutral is in the middle. The SOS is the best if we change cost-saving to efficiency because then we are talking, not just about getting the cost down to zero, but about getting the cost/benefit ratio down as low as possible, meaning the amount of dollars that have to be paid for so many units of improvement in the quality of life. Volunteers in that sense are inefficient even though they cost nothing. They are inefficient in that they are not doing any good. The professional associations also cost nothing. This is especially true of the government, although it could give some money to the professional associa-tions to coordinate a clearinghouse system. The important point is that, even if the professional association approach costs a little more than the volun-teers showing up without being recruited, the benefits are so much greater as to produce a very good cost/benefit ratio. If the pure volunteers cost only a penny but are producing nothing, they are infinitely expensive. If the professional association volunteers cost twice as much, meaning two cents, but they give four cents in benefits, that is the equivalent of a 50 per cent rate of return, which is not bad interest on a savings account. This is true even though they cost twice as much as the pure volunteers.

Three sample technical assistance providers

The sample

I wrote to the *International Foundation for Electoral Systems* (IFES) in the 1990s with regard to diverting some AID money for a symposium book of experts on electoral policy in developing nations. A better way to put it is diverting the travel expenses of one person monitoring one election from the total funding that may allow for as many as 100 people to monitor 10 elections. In other words, we are not asking for any elections to cease being monitored. What we basically are asking for would never be missed in terms of decreasing any impact, but could greatly increase the improvement of political reform more so than not canceling all 100 people. No need to say that doing this one symposium is worth more than 100 people spending a day or two taking notes. We can do both. Either side would feel a bit disturbed if they were told that they are perhaps not making the best possi-ble use of the taxpayers' money.

The second provider is the *Carter Center*, which is a non-profit policy institute and not a commercial firm or funding source. The third provider is the *National Endowment for Democracy*, which has been dragging around longer than any of the others. The last correspondence with them was a letter from David Petersen on 13 November which has still not been an-swered. These are three very different institutions in the developmental technical assistance field and could represent an interesting analysis about how to stimulate high-quality, low-cost technical assistance.

Example of types

A *highly ideological think tank* may do more harm than good with regard to American foreign policy, although it may be achieving some new objectivity as a result of the end of the Cold War. It demonstrates how to ruin useful technical assistance, just as the CIA used to make life so miserable for legitimate ministers, journalists and scholars by having CIA people pose as ministers, journalists and scholars, so that nobody would trust any American ministers, journalists or scholars who really could be doing some useful things on behalf of American policy. In fact, CIA policy was that the more trusted and more efficient some occupational category was, the better the reason to disguise CIA people as people in that category – which does logically follow if the only purpose of the CIA is to deceive for the sake of deceiving or to infiltrate for the sake of infiltrating, rather than having a purpose that has to do with promoting American national interest.

A second example is a *policy institute* that may be trying too hard to impress people who read the *New York Times* rather than people who read more scholarly literature or, worse, people who read *Time* magazine. A third example is an aggressive commercial firm schmoozing with a government agency for their mutual monetary gain. The government agency justifies its existence because it has aggressive commercial firms to fund, and aggressive commercial firms justify their existence because they have government agencies funding them. This is a kind of political symbiotic relationship to the detriment of whatever the real purpose is behind the funding, which in this case is to promote political reform. The result is a lot of wasted money that could be better spent elsewhere.

Favorable perspectives

Viewing these three providers in the best light, one could say that either the National Endowment for Democracy has learned, from its past experience in generating negative reactions, to be less ideological, or the end of the Cold War has made its Cold War philosophy obsolete – in other words, it never really learned anything. It would continue in the same manner now, except that the evil empire stimulus is no longer there to stir up the natives in Africa, Latin America and Asia, although they could perhaps tell the people in Africa, Asia and Latin America that Japan is their new enemy, trying to sell them all these low-priced, high-quality products to their detriment. This is a key part of the new CIA mandate, to engage in industrial espionage, and they will probably soon be involved in destabilization of Nissan, Toyota and so on, as they used to be in Chile.

Jimmy Carter and his people deserve credit for seeking to establish relations with Emory University, in recognition that university experts on foreign policy might have something to contribute. That certainly is better than Nixon's isolation from potential sources of useful information and ideas, and better than President Ford's being a total dropout who never says anything anymore. And Reagan was moving in that direction too. Some say Bush was already there, in the sense that he had retired before his term was up with regard to taking any kind of aggressive action against anything except Saddam Hussein, who, interestingly enough, is now being blamed for the recession. The reasoning is that so much money was spent fighting Saddam Hussein that it damaged the economy. That is a total lie, for a number of reasons. One is that the war was highly profitable. Germany and Japan put up more money than it cost the United States. From the point of view of making money in the international balance of payments, we should have more such wars and maybe charge Japan and Germany even more next time. It is also a lie because the recession began before the Gulf War and the Gulf War did nothing in either direction to change the trend lines. The recession actually began the day Reagan took office by incurring such a monstrous national debt which has handicapped the kind of spending by the federal government that could not only end the recession but get the United States back onto a more productive track, instead of so much money going to pay interest on the national debt and obsolete defense spending that still goes on out of inertia.

In the case of the International Foundation for Electoral Systems, this is a slight notch above the typical aggressive commercial firm. The foundation does have on its board of directors some people with relevant credentials, although not enough to be considered respectable among experts on electoral politics and developing nations. In fact, I recognize only one name out of nine, namely Richard Scammon, who had been a Cold War idealogue who at one time was compiling a lot of raw data on electoral statistics, but has never written anything other than things that read like the World Almanac. I think they managed to get on their board of directors some former activists in the Democratic National Committee, and a Republican like Scammon to provide some bipartisanship, but there is nothing that could qualify as expertise on developmental electoral policy.

Some criteria of quality technical assistance

With regard to what could be done in terms of quality work, many questions may be asked. Is anybody interested in reading the reports describing what the technical assistance providers have done? Is there a book publisher that is interested in publishing their material? Are there journals that are interested in at least publishing article-length versions that describe their experiences and their ideas?

Do their ideas or whatever are the results of their expenditures have applicability across other places or basically just to the one place that they focused on? Do these products have applicability over time, or are they of no value even the next day, like a typical newspaper article, or like the notes taken at the Zambian elections. Do the ideas cut across other policy problems, or do they have applicability only to a very specific policy problem, not even a specific category?

Are the products presented orally at conferences or conventions or anywhere else where someone is interested in hearing about them? So is their work funded by peer review funding sources like National Science Foundation (NSF), or only by the awarding of contracts in the same way that paperclips are bought? Are their materials used in teaching? Does anybody who teaches foreign policy, international relations, policy studies or whatever subject matter they are in use their material to instruct students on how to do something?

Who do they get letters from, asking them for copies of their materials? Do they come from people in developing nations who want to make use of their ideas? People who teach about developing nations? People who do research and writing about developing nations? Or basically none of the above?

What are the credentials of the staff? Do they have PhD degrees? Do they write articles and books? Do they have professorial appointments? Are they invited to be consultants by developing nations? Or do they basically sit and takes notes in Lusaka on election day? Or perhaps they consider going to the library and finding a list of all the books that have been written on Zambia to be scholarly research? This, of course, can now be done by a machine, with no particular need for a human being.

Cost criteria

The cost criteria might include certain questions. To what extent do these bodies get experts who might normally be paid as much as $25,000 for a report or $500 or more a day, to work for nothing? What do they charge for honoraria when they have been asked to speak at the equivalent of a Lectureship at the University of Illinois? This is a silly question, because generally they are not asked. But we want criteria that do apply to some recipients of government contracts that are asked. Not all the recipients are like the three we discussed above. Some are much worse. An example of better ones would be Ed Kolodziej's highly impressive Arms Control Institute, which has an unbelievable number of world-class speakers every week who come to the University of Illinois to speak on his program for relatively little money, for the prestige of doing it.

They do charge consulting fees. How much do they charge per hour, versus how much does Ed Kolodziej charge per hour? The point being made is that Ed Kolodziej should be invited to give his reactions because he is very familiar with government contracting in the defense field, especially arms control, and may have a lot of insights on how it can be done more effectively and efficiently, with effectiveness getting at the quality or benefits, and efficiency deals with the costs. There are other academic policy institutes, and non-academic ones, that could also be used as excellent models. Brookings is an excellent non-academic model, although it is highly academic in the sense that virtually everybody associated with them has a PhD and a professorial rank. It is non-academic in the sense that it is not associated with a university. If we were going to do some in-depth case studies, which is not very likely, Brookings would be a good example of the non-academic contract recipient, although I think Brookings has a policy of never accepting government money; it only accepts foundation money. In its original charter, which it has never changed, it says that accepting government money inevitably leads to biased reports designed to please people in government, and that it will never bid on a government contract or accept one that is awarded to it without even bidding. If we need a non-academic institute that does accept government money, then we come to the conservatively ideological ones like the American Enterprise Institute and the Heritage Foundation. These may illustrate the Brookings principle that accepting government money does either deliberately or unconsciously change one to look like one's master.

The academic institutes that accept government money are also somewhat notorious for prostituting themselves. Some of them argue like the CIA, which stands for Center for International Affairs, at Harvard that they were biased and unobjective before they started accepting government money. That is unusual. Most deny that they were biased and unobjective before or after, but the Harvard CIA seems to delight in antagonizing liberals, just as Aaron Wildavsky used to delight in the same thing during the Vietnam War, from the opposite end of the country.

Trying to come up with a cost criterion is not the same as coming up with a quality criterion. The cost criterion is very simple. One looks at somewhat similar projects and sees how much is charged by the aggressive commercial firms as opposed to the academic institutes. One can compare different aggressive commercial firms with regard to how expensive they are and different academic institutes with regard to how expensive they are. The point is not that we are trying to rate each institute, as an insurance company might rate cities for fire insurance. We are trying to talk about broad categories such as (1) commercial institutes like the IFES, (2) non-university academic institutes like Brookings and (3) academic institutes that are departmentally based like the institute Ed Kolodziej, versus academic institutes that happen to be on the same campus but are not departmentally based, like Harvard CIA or the Hoover Institute at Stanford. I do not think there would be much disagreement as to which of these are the most costly. The disagreement is more likely to be on the quality side, with the defenders of the commercial bodies saying that their people have hard-nosed realism and meet time deadlines better and stay narrowly within the subject matter specifications. There is some question as to whether that is true or not and some question as to how important it is to come up with junk on time rather than something useful late. Or how important it is to come up with a report that answers the question as to whether X causes Y, as contrasted to a report that deviates from that question and says yes, X causes Y but it also causes Y2 which may be an undesirable side-effect, and that X2 may cause Y even more than X causes Y. The latter kind of answer is more likely to come from academic research than from commercial research. In other words, even using the criteria of commercial types of on-time and in-focus, one can say they are not doing a very good job because we do not want narrowly focused research. At the same time, we do not want a contract to be awarded to investigate fusion energy and then have the money used to study the sex life of eels, assuming that that has nothing to do with fusion energy. Likewise, it is good to allow a little extra time to do the job better, but not to go into infinity and never turn in any report.

THE PRO-DEMOCRACY MOVEMENT: THE UPRISING IN THAILAND

Causes

Long term

1 Industrialization causing education which causes resistance to being ordered by a dictatorial government.
2 History.
   a 1932. Threw off absolute monarchy. Replaced with military control-led government.
   b 1973. Successful student revolt with much loss of life, 50 to 1,000.
   c 1976. Restored military until 1988.
   d 1988. Civilian.
   e 1991. February Suchinda coup.

Immediate causes

1 For the Coup.

    a   Choice of deputy defense minister.
    b   Choice of army commander-in-chief.
    c   Choice of investigator of assassination plot.
2 For the Pro-Democracy Demonstration.
    a   Recent election in March. First prime minister was in drugs.
    b   Promise of Suchinda not to be prime minister.
    c   Wipe out corruption, but appointed leading crooks.
    d   Refusal to call special election.
    e   Refusal to allow constitutional amendment with grandfather clause.
3 For the Killings.
    a   Virtually no use of water cannon, tear gas, or rubber bullets, instead automatic weapons, long clubs, and few shields.
    b   Alleges students shoot first, communist takeover, disrupt the monarchy.
    c   Isolated head, given middle class involvement, the provinces, and some segments of the military.
    d   A cornered madman concerned about face.

Remedies

Immediate

1 Pressure from Abroad.
    a   Total embargo.
    b   Boycott all Thailand products.
    c   Like South Africa.
2 Pressure from Within.
    a   Business buy-off. Business support for opposition Chaulit or Chamlong.
    b   University support for resignation. Restraint is not enough.
    c   More demonstrations, not less.
    d   Military opposition.
    e   Provincial opposition.
    f   Middle class professionals.
    g   Monarchy including king, crown princess, and crown prince.
    h   Mass media.

Long term

1 Withdrawal of United States support for the military.
2 Legal.

a Constitutional amendment that no prime minister, civil service, or government position while still military.
b No prime minister who is not elected.
c No military for crowd control.
3 Socialization into democratic principles of freedom to disagree with government and to be allowed to convert others.

Predictions

Short term

1 Military may refuse to step down. They may stall for time thinking that will lead to loss of interest by demonstrators.
2 Demonstrators and opposition parties will become impatient and again take to the streets. This time possibly with more anger inspired by perceived support from many or even all major segments of Thai society including some military.
3 Stubborn vicious military like Suchinda, Kaset, and Issaprong may order troops to stop angry demonstrators. Then killing and maybe counter-killing could be worse than before.
4 Alternative is face-saving departure with big money to go overseas as in the past.

Long term

1 Parties along conservative and liberal lines instead of personalized groups.
2 Maybe judicial enforcement of the constitution.
3 More international, more American, and thus more regard for free speech, due process, and treatment on merit.
4 Contracting out as SOS between private and government ownership and operation.

Implications from the Thailand crisis case study

1 The problem of civilian versus military government. The SOS is to (a) phase out military rule to establish civilian rule, (b) no military person should be in a policy job while in the military, and (c) only the police should be used for crowd control, not the army.
2 The problem of stability versus modernization. Requires well-placed subsidies and tax breaks to bring quality modernization. That means

upgrading the skills of workers mainly through on-the-job training, including workers who are displaced by new technologies. It also means facilitating the adoption of new technologies that create jobs, improve productivity, and increase exports. Emphasizing quality refers to (a) workplace safety and quality, (b) environmental quality, and (c) quality consumer products.

3   The causal analysis problem of explaining the success of the pro-democracy demonstrations in Thailand versus their failure in Tiananmen Square.

4   The inconsistencies on the part of American foreign policy that relate to interfering with foreign governments in the Cold War or the drug war, but not even offering non-interfering assistance on behalf of pro-democracy forces.

5   The role of middle class people in bringing about social change, which is a key factor that we have emphasized before as essential to having a stable democracy.

6   The much greater respect for intellectual input in developing countries or, for that matter, almost any countries compared to the United States. That illustrates or relates to saving one of the newspaper headlines which came out I think on Thursday, 21 May, and indicated the high regard that people in Thailand have for what people in the universities are advocating. It may have been in Friday morning's paper in the Bangkok Post. The heading is, 'Academics Demand a New Government'. Behind that is some of the explanation for why Japan is doing so much better than the United States, namely the high regard that Japanese business people, like Thai businesspeople, have for university professors, especially American university professors.

7   As a kind of quaint aspect of the Thai crisis, that might have some interest to the Serbian royal family. They should observe how the Thai King handled the situation, which is nicely covered in the headline on Thursday's *Bangkok Post*, that the King tells the factions to work on compromise. Immediately that was the end of the whole violence, demonstrations, and everything immediately resorted back to a peaceful state. It is not because the Thai people are monarchists. It is because the Thai royal family is, to a considerable extent, responsible for the high respect for higher education. Every higher education degree is personally handed to the recipient by a member of the royal family at graduation time. The family has a family tree filled with PhD's, MD's. The person who is probably most in line for the throne also has a PhD degree.

8   The role of legalistic action is also important in the Thai example in that there is a strong consensus that the situation at its height could be

defused through a constitutional amendment, and even now the consti-tutional amendment idea is important. In other countries, like Latin America, amending the constitution would be considered close to a farce with not much enforcement. In Thailand, they take seriously what the constitution provides and want it to specify that no one can be prime minister unless the person is an elected member of Parliament, regardless of how many or what percentage of Parliament chooses a non-elected member to be prime minister.

9   The situation also illustrates how being stubborn and nonfunctional with regard to face-saving, can be self-destructive and interfere with an SOS. The military prime minister could have easily arranged for a special election to get elected and thereby remove the key objection, but refused to do so on the grounds that it would be an admission of wrongdoing. Instead, he lost the whole job and may lose his life as well. Even if he does not lose his life, he is in total disgrace.

10   There may be other implications from that case study which we need to write up. One is the importance of economic boycotts by the United States as bringing about favorable governmental changes. We saw that to some extent already in South Africa and the refusal to do that in China. A big factor that turned the business community against the military prime minister was the boycott that was already in effect contrary to the Bush administration, with numerous American import-ers canceling orders. Not because they were so sympathetic to the pro-democracy movement (though that may have been part of it), but because they explicitly said or implied they did not want to deal with some kind of banana republic military dictatorship. They wanted re-sponsible, businesslike people. The important thing is that kind of economic pressure can definitely change governmental decision-making. It was ridiculous for the Bush administration to say it would have no effect in China, South Africa, or elsewhere. It simply reflects that the Bush administration did not place a very high priority on changing overseas governmental decisions to a more pro-democracy direction and that selling a few more widgets is more important.

11   It also has international implications by virtue of setting an important precedent and role model for other developing nations that military dictatorships are not the way to go. That can be the eleventh implication. Thailand is highly regarded in the developing world. It is a newly indus-trialized country, although the other newly industrialized countries are also getting rid of or lessening their military dictators or civilian dicta-tors, such as South Korea, Taiwan, and Singapore to some extent.

12   An especially exciting implication of the Thailand crisis case-study is that it generated the concept of an International Dispute Resolution

workshop or IDR workshop. Such a workshop builds on the concept of an SOS workshop which the Policy Studies Organization has been conducting since our China workshops of 1989, 1991, and 1992. An SOS workshop is a gathering of professors, practitioners, graduate students, and others to learn about methods for arriving at super-optimum solutions to public policy. Such solution can enable conservatives, liberals, and other major viewpoints to all come out ahead of their best initial expectations simultaneously. An IDR workshop involves the same subject matter as an SOS workshop. It differs from the usual SOS workshop in that at least some of the participants are invited to attend because they are associated with nations, provinces, ethnic groups, or other groups that are in violent conflict with each other. The workshops can last anywhere from a full day (or less) to a week (or longer). The idea is that during that time, the people whose groups are normally in conflict will be stimulated to think more about how all sides or viewpoints can come out ahead of their best initial expectations simultaneously.

The IDR workshop that was conducted at Chulalongkorn University during the Thailand crisis was not premeditated. It was supposed to be an SOS workshop. It turned into an IDR workshop because during the conducting of the SOS workshop, the Thailand crisis occurred. Partly by coincidence, the participants in the Thailand SOS-IDR workshop included such people as a colonel in the Bangkok police force and a pro-democracy former Communist guerrilla teaching in the Public Administration Department. Some of the emotional interaction was defused by virtue of face-to-face contact. Some of it was also defused by virtue of the nature of the subject matter that was being discussed. The subject refers to how all sides to highly emotional disputes can come out ahead of their best initial expectations simultaneously. The Thailand crisis was resolved before anybody participating in the IDR-SOS workshop had an opportunity to communicate any of the ideas to their colleagues in the police system or among the demonstrators. Future IDR-SOS workshops are, however, now being planned that will include people simultaneously from India and Pakistan, and a separate workshop that will include people simultaneously from mainland China and Taiwan.

Differences and similarities between China and Thailand

1   China worse. Beijing had a 90-year-old dictator that people were waiting to die. This caused a restraint on pro-democracy demonstrations. Thailand has or had a 55-year-old military dictator who was in very

good health. Nobody suggested waiting for him to die. Many people suggested ways to accelerate his death.

2 Thailand worse. Beijing was actually more restrained in some ways than Thailand. It is a civilian dictatorship, not a military dictatorship. Civilian police were largely used to deal with the students including unarmed police officers with clubs and some tear gas. They could not use water cannons because Beijing does not have a water system that can get up enough pressure to do any blasting of water at people. The Thailand crowd control consisted of heavily-booted paratroopers with assault weapons including high-powered machine guns and tanks.

3 Both same. A key difference is that Thailand sought to exercise some constraint out of sensitivity to world opinion and the export-import business. Beijing has also been sensitive to that. That is not the key difference.

4 Thailand better. The key difference is that in the past two years the Cold War has ended. Many parts of the world have moved greatly toward democratization including Eastern Europe, Africa, Asia, and Latin America. We could give some concrete examples. Thus, world opinion and student opinion is less tolerant of dictatorships.

5 The main thing that needs explaining is why the pro-democracy demonstrators succeeded in Thailand and failed in Beijing. The timing may be more important than the place. A further proof of that is that the students failed in 1976 in the same place because the world was not so ready for democracy as it is now including Thailand.

Examples of the world moving toward greater democracy

1 In Eastern Europe as of about 1989 at the time of Tiananmen Square, virtually every country had a one-party Communist dictatorship. They now have multi-party systems with more choices for the voters than can be found in the United States.

2 In Africa every founding father is either out or in big trouble. That includes Kenneth Kwanda in Zambia who was voted out, Mr Mbuto in Zaire and Mr Moy in Kenya. None of the democracies are in any trouble in Africa. Nigeria is also in trouble. It is run by a military junta. The people in Africa are becoming increasingly educated and unwilling to be told what to do by military or non-military dictators.

3 The military dictators have been thrown out of Argentina, Chile, Brazil, Uruguay, Paraguay, Panama, Nicaragua. There is no place that is an exception with the possibility of Peru. Even Peru represents a move toward greater democracy in the sense of the last presidential election

resulting in the first time since the Incas maybe that somebody who was not part of the Spanish elite was elected. In this case it was somebody who wasn't even Hispanic but was Japanese. Although maybe it is possible to be Hispanic Japanese if he is a Peruvian citizen and speaks Spanish.

4   The fourth continent or region is Asia. This is a place where progress is not being made so well, although Thailand is an example of progress in the sense that the military has been thrown out and they are likely to have a civilian government on into the future. In Burma, the military has more explicitly taken over than in the past. Japan represents a one-party state as much as ever and sets a bad example. Afghanistan has moved from a Communist dictatorship to what may be a Moslem extremist dictatorship like Iran. That is not quite true. Iran has moved away to a considerable extent from its Moslem extremism. Afghanistan has moved from Communism to more democracy given differences among different Moslem groups than was previously the case. There are rumblings at democracy in Saudi Arabia and Kuwait, although moving very slowly. The Philippines just completed a reasonably democratic election which is a big improvement over the previous Marcos non-elections. Taiwan has become more democratic. Mainland China has also become more democratic than it was under Mao and the Cultural Revolution. The Tiananmen Square incident was partly a manifestation of pro-democracy desires even though they did not succeed.

5   What it adds up to is the world as a whole is becoming better educated as a result of industrialization and less willing to accept medieval or military dictatorships.

HUMANITARIAN VERSUS NATIONAL INTEREST CRITERIA IN MAKING FOREIGN POLICY DECISIONS

People differ on foreign policy, but the differences are not that liberals are in favor of a kind of soft or pacifist or humanitarian foreign policy and the conservatives are in favor of a hard, tough foreign policy. That is absolute myth. It all depends on who the enemy is. It is amazing how soft and lovable conservatives can be when the enemy is Nazi Germany in the 1930s, but how tough they can be when the enemy is Communist Russia in the 1960s or 1970s.

Also the distinction between national interest and humanitarian criteria should not be considered the same thing as hard-line and pacifist. One can advocate a humanitarian approach for highly mercenary, hard-nosed reasons. Humanitarian foreign policy is good business. We do much better business with democratic governments than with dictatorial ones. We can defend encouraging democracy on do-gooder grounds, but that is normally not very effective. If it can be defended on money-in-the-pocket grounds, it gets more support, as long as it is not made too crass.

Also, from a purely military perspective, promoting democracy is good. We have better allies among democratic countries than among dictatorial countries. France and England are more likely to be allies of the United States in any world conflict than whatever dictatorships are left in the world, or past ones like Franco's Spain. By definition, nationalistic dictators are not very cooperative. One thing that keeps fascists from taking over the world is they are so nationalistic they cannot work well with each other, whereas democracies can.

If one talks about the issue as being national interest versus humanitarian interest, then we really have a tradeoff.

1 The national interest people sound like some kind of hard-hearted group that wants to be friends with any dictator that is pro-American.

2 The humanitarian interest people sound like a bunch of softies that perhaps want to go to war on behalf of anybody that claims to be in favor of democracy, although the usual humanitarian types just endorse democratic governments; are not willing to fight for them. They still come out as being naive, regardless of whether they are pacifists or aggressive humanitarians.

3 When the issue is stated in these terms, it is hard to find a compromise. The national interest people sound like they are giving up the national interest, and the humanitarian people sound like they are being inhumane. One way to decrease the possibility of a compromise or an SOS solution is to label one side Total Righteousness I and the other side Total Righteousness II.

The point made here is not so much that talking in terms of national interest versus humanitarian interest leads to an inherent tradeoff conflict. One point is that the people who claim to be advocating the national interest are usually advocating their own ideological interest, in the sense that both liberals and conservatives tend to take a hard-line, hawkish position depending on who the external enemy is. Likewise, the so-called humanitarians are highly flexible according to who the external enemy is. Conservatives show great humanitarian concern for what is going to happen to blacks in South Africa if there is a boycott. They do not, however, show such interest in blacks in the United States.

Different distinctions may be made:

1   truly hawkish people and truly pacifist people that are hawkish no matter who the enemy is and that are pacifist no matter who the enemy is;
2   hawks that change their stance according to who the enemy is, and likewise with pacifists;
3   those who advocate a national interest who support dictators, and those who advocate a national interest who support democratic governments;
4   pacifists who support democratic governments but not dictators, although they will support either democratic socialistic or democratic capitalistic governments. In other words, in determining where the volte-face occurs, one may need to think in terms of capitalism versus socialism and democracy versus dictatorship.

A superpacifist would support *not* going to war against Hitler. Likewise, a superhawk would support going to war against Canada if Canada says something nasty, regardless of the effect that going to war has on America's economic interest or whether the other country is capitalistic or socialistic, or dictatorial or democratic. The superhawk overreacts to insults wherever they come from. The usual hawk only overreacts to insults if they come from, say, a communist government, but it is all right for the pro-American Turkish government to torture American prisoners as long as they stay pro-American with regard to allowing American airbases. That is one reason for the cold-war hawks not liking Amnesty International, because AI finds fault with pro-American governments sometimes, and even with the United States government.

This chapter is meant to show how supporting democracy in dispute resolution and foreign policy is an SOS. It simultaneously promotes both the national interest and humanitarian considerations.

5 Global Policy Studies and Economic Communities

GLOBAL POLICY STUDIES

What the field includes

The field of global policy studies can be defined as the study of international interactions designed to deal with shared public policy problems. Such policy problems can include:

1 trans-boundary problems, such as people, pollution or goods literally going across international boundaries;
2 common property problems, such as the oceans, Antarctica or the atmosphere, which nobody owns but are a kind of common good that need to be regulated, or else (like the tragedy of the commons) they will be devoured, to the mutual detriment of the nations of the world;
3 simultaneous problems like health, education and welfare, about which all countries can learn from each other.

How the field differs from related fields

Global policy studies is related to international relations, comparative government and public policy studies. None of these three political science fields, however, is studying the subject of global policy studies adequately. International relations concentrates on relations among countries that relate to diplomacy, alliances and the resolution of disputes that might otherwise result in war. There are international institutions concerned with public policy studies, such as the specialized agencies of the United Nations, but they are not part of the mainstream of the study of international relations. One might also note that important international interactions associated with global policy studies, such as the economic summit meetings, or other less formal meetings among government officials of various countries designed to deal with shared policy problems, may not be institutionalized.

The field of comparative public policy is cross-national in the sense of dealing with a multiplicity of countries. The analysis, however, tends to treat one country at a time. Sometimes comparisons are made across countries, with an attempt to explain and evaluate differences and similarities, but the element of international interaction, which is essential to global policy studies, is missing. 'Global' does not mean that all countries of the world interact simultaneously, but rather that all countries of the world share the policy problems under consideration, or at least potentially share them.

The field of policy studies tends to concentrate on the single country of the political or social scientist who is working in the field. Some policy studies scholars do look to other countries, but mainly for the purpose of getting ideas that have predictive or prescriptive power within their own countries. They seldom look to international interaction, although they may look at the interaction that occurs between states, provinces, cities or other sub-national units within their own countries. If each country seeks to maximize its own quality of life without cooperative interaction, the countries in general may suffer important opportunity costs, as in other sub-optimizing situations. The classical example is each country trying to produce whatever goods it produces best, so that, as a result, the world winds up with surpluses and shortages on all goods. It should be noted, however, that in the absence of world government it will be necessary for individual countries working together by formal or informal agreement to make use of the positive and negative incentives which they have available for encouraging internationally desired behavior.

Multiple dimensions

The field provides good balance on a number of dimensions, including the theoretical, geographical, purposive, disciplinary, ideological and methodological.

1   There is balance between cross-cutting theoretical matters and those that are not specific in nature. The theoretical orientation, however, is not overly abstract, and the discussion of the specific policy problems does not emphasize anecdotal case studies.
2   Balance among various parts of the world is represented by the researchers in the field, including political and social scientists from England, Germany, Poland, India, Spain, the Philippines and the United States.

There is even better balance in terms of the countries that are referred to by the researchers which include all major parts of the world.

3 Balance between prescriptive or evaluative analysis and predictive or explanatory analysis means that the field is concerned with both explaining variations in the occurrence of international interaction for dealing with shared policy problems and prescribing how such international interaction can be made more effective, efficient and equitable in achieving its goals.

4 With regard to balance across disciplinary perspectives, the researchers in the field are primarily political scientists, but they recognize that one cannot deal adequately with policy problems without bringing in the perspectives of other social sciences and other fields of knowledge, such as economics, sociology, psychology and natural science.

5 Balance across ideological perspectives: here the researchers in the field come from a variety of ideological backgrounds in terms of how government should relate to the economy or to the people, and how government should be organized. There may, however, be an underlying pragmatism that is especially associated with policy studies, as contrasted to political theory, and a searching for solutions to global policy problems that will be recognized as desirable regardless of ideology. There may also be an underlying virtual unanimity in favor of an expansion of the elements of democracy that are conducive to academic creativity and interaction, as contrasted to balancing democracy and dictatorship.

6 Balance across methodology orientations includes studies that emphasize verbal analysis or quantitative analysis. However, there may be a tendency to get away from unstructured verbal description and to make more use of systematic analytic frameworks such as talking in terms of multi-criteria decision making. Doing so involves analyzing a set of goals to be achieved, alternatives available for achieving them, and relations between goals and alternatives in order to choose or explain the best alternative, combination, allocation or predictive decision rule. There may also be a tendency to get away from unthinking cross-national quantitative description that involves correlating policy-irrelevant or policy-relevant variables against other variables or each other for 160 members of the United Nations.

Current developments

It is difficult to say when the study of international interaction to deal with shared policy problems first began. One landmark book in the field is

Marvin Soroos, *Beyond Sovereignty: The Challenge of Global Sovereignty* (University of South Carolina Press, 1986). Before that, there have been studies of specialized agencies within the United Nations and the League of Nations, including the International Labor Organization, the World Health Organization, and other international agencies concerned with specific policy problems. The earlier literature tended to focus on these semi-governmental institutions rather than on more informal types of interaction. A key volume in the earlier literature is Robert Keohane and Joseph Nye, *Power and Interdependence: World Politics in Transition* (Little, Brown, 1977).

A key event since publication of the Soroos book is the establishment of a Research Group on Global Policy Studies within the International Political Science Association. That group arose as a result of the enthusiasm shown at the 1988 IPSA triannual meeting in Washington, DC at the global policy studies panels. The group flourished in subsequent triannual meetings in Buenos Aires in 1991, Berlin in 1994, and Seoul in 1997 with activities planned for Quebec City in the year 2000.

ECONOMIC COMMUNITIES*

Systematic policy analysis

What I am going to present is a way of somehow bringing together national independence and international entities. The area of political science I specialize in is not international relations, which is becoming increasingly appealing to me; rather, my specialization is public policy analysis, related to a variety of analyses of public policies.

The elements for this type of analysis are some goals to achieve, generally and to begin with, some alternatives provided by those goals, and an awareness of the relationship between the alternatives and the goals to be achieved. There are two key solutions. (1) tentative solutions, only tentative and subject to change, and (2) 'what if' analysis: that is, what would happen if the alternatives or the relations were to change; how the tentative solutions would change; if there were to be changes in what is being incorporated, how this would affect tentative conclusions. That is, basically, public policy analysis.

Recently this analysis has emphasized arriving at tentative solutions, which are compromises in which, in a dispute, for example, we must have

* This section is taken from a presentation entitled 'International Economic Communities: Super-Optimum Solutions' by the author at the International Political Science Association XV Pre-Congress Symposium at the University of Belgrano Graduate School in Buenos Aires, 19–20 July 1991.

100 dollars or we will go to court and the defendant says that he is only going to pay 20 dollars. A compromise is reached at 60 dollars, the middle point between 20 and 100. The same type of solution applies to international relations: compromise. Both parties try to make themselves feel good, saying that they could have done worse. There are no winners. Both sides are losers: if one side says that they have to have 100 dollars but they only receive 60, they have lost 40; if the other side says that it cannot pay more than 20, and pays 60, it has also lost 40. Compromise is better than facing liability charges, going on strike or going to war, but compromise is not as good as super-optimum solutions.

Super-optimizing in general

Super-optimum solutions mean that both sides come out better than their initial best expectations; that is, in the liability suit, one side would pay more than 100 and the other less than 20. This happens in trials in the United States, in Argentina, and all over the world. It is what is called 'structured settlement'. In other words, it is part of the new movement for the resolution of alternative disputes. The defendant and the plaintiff reach an agreement by which both sides come out ahead. Sometimes it can be a win–win situation.

In the real world of liability litigation where high sums of money are paid, an American insurance company litigated with a Japanese company for 1,000,000 dollars last year (author is also a lawyer and informal judge in the Federal Court System of the USA). In this case, the insurance company asked for one million dollars, saying that, if this was not paid, they would take the other party to court; the Japanese company said they could not give more than 300,000 dollars because to give more would be to admit that they were negligent and that they made faulty audio equipment that caused a fire. The Japanese company said they would give 300,000 dollars because this was what proving their case would cost them if they had to go to court. Through the settlement arrived at, the insurance company made more than one million dollars and the Japanese company paid less than 300,000 dollars. The Japanese gave the insurance company many computers for their offices, as well as TV sets as prizes for the agents that sold the most policies, and they also gave the insurance company claims against American defendants that the Japanese company could not collect. All this amounted to more than one million dollars, but it cost the Japanese less than 300,000 dollars. (The policy claims had been taken at a loss and meant nothing to the Japanese.)

In this case in particular, we want to show how this analysis can be applied to the issue of national independence and international entities. Also our purpose is to examine not only the substance but also the methodology. If you give a person a fish, he can eat for one day, but if you teach him how to fish, he can eat for the rest of his life. If you give people an answer to their question about national independence versus international entities, they will probably know only part of the problem. But if you teach them or tell them about the way to analyze it, they will be able to apply it to many other problems. In other words, super-optimizing analysis implies thinking in terms of alternative policies and political goals.

National–international alternatives

The conservative approach to the problem of national independence and international entities emphasizes nationalism and separatism. There are many different types of nationalism. We are going to bring them all together. Now here we have two examples of separatism: one is very negative, the separatism of Quebec, in Canada. This separatism is so negative that, not long ago, the last time I was there, I went into a tunnel and at the entrance there was a sign in French that said 'Do not enter this tunnel if carrying the following objects, including explosives'. It was not in English, because separatism in Quebec is so extreme that English is not allowed, not even on signs that warn against carrying dangerous objects in a tunnel. The best separatist, I believe, would not support a ban on certain languages which are not Basque, so that no one can speak Castilian Spanish or French, because it is recognized that there are many people in the Basque Provinces who speak French and Spanish and they would be harming the education of their children if they banned those languages.

The Basque example while Franco ruled Spain is an anti-colonial type of separatism moving in this case from a dictatorship to democracy. In the case of Quebec in Canada, they are not moving away from a dictatorial government to establish their own democracy; they are moving away from a national democratic government to establish a system like the Vichy French government. There are many types of separatism and nationalism. What they all have in common is they support the goal of sovereignty and national identity.

To national identity we could also add moral stature, which many citizens want for their country. Liberals, on the other hand, reject nationalism and talk about world government. Then again, when they talk about world government there are many different positions. In its most extreme form is the unique government (there are no countries); countries become provinces or counties, as for example in England. The least extreme form is probably what we have in the United Nations, which is a very loose type of confederation but is also a form of world government. It has a legislature, a judicial structure and executive branch, three governing branches, many officials, many government organizations, different groups, and it represents a government. It includes almost the entire world. It is made up of something like 185 nations as of 1999, and 185 out of a total of under 200 world nations are members of the United Nations.

The neutral position tends to emphasize a regional government, talking about governments in terms of institutions, legislatures, courts, chief executives, high ranking officials and so on. This means something like the authority of the Tennessee Valley, something that divides states. In the present case we are talking about the divisions between several nations. One type of regionalism is to have a dam on a river that involves more than one country. An example is the Rhine hydroelectric project, which borders Germany and France. For example, a regional government is where a series of nation-states get together and create some sort of rather loose regional government, which is a union of other subregional element.

The government of the United States can be called a federalist regional government and the former Soviet Union was legally a federalist regional government because it called itself a form of federation or confederation. The idea was to try to bring together some nation-states which were a part of a greater entity. Some groups would be better off if they were separate and each was a nation-state. But when one creates a nation-state and makes them be part of a confederation, there could be greater or lesser friction because now there will be tension insofar as a province thinks that another province is favored. Then they fight over who should receive more resources from the central government. If they were separate countries they could not complain of favoritism on the part of the central government because there would be no central government. On the other hand, when one is trying to unite nation-states in one confederation, one soon faces the possibility of violence as a result of secession. There will be no secessionism if there are no united nation-states.

Goals and relations

Does this mean that the world should simply be left to dissolve into ten thousand nation-states or ten thousand separate political entities? There is a super-optimum solution that tells us that we are better off with the conservative goal of national identity and not that of separatism, and we also have the liberal goals of creating labor, consumer goods and peace.

One can say that nationalism and separatism, at least moderately, lead to national identity, but in some cases nationalism goes so far as to rule national identity. Then a belligerent nation-state enters the scene, like Nazi Germany, that ends up losing its identity and losing a war. The same can be partly said about the nationalism of West Germany under Mr Kohl. Germany included East Germany, quite poor, and West Germany, quite rich. Unified Germany is now less of a world power. Another good example of this can be seen elsewhere. South Korea has announced that it will indefinitely postpone its plans of reunification with North Korea, which it had recently promoted under the notion of nationalism. They said 'We are all Koreans', as Mr Kohl said 'We are all German', but South Korea did not want the burden of the poor North Koreans. It is enough to say that one can affect one's identity and position through excessive nationalism or in case or war, one can lose a war.

Now we move on to the liberal goal of quality of life. Nationalism and separatism are negative as far as quality of life is concerned. As regards nationalism, we talked about economic nationalism and high tariff taxes. It will adversely affect consumers, and it will adversely affect most labor because if the consumers have to pay higher prices to buy appliances, they will have less money available for the multiplier effect and the invest effect. On the other hand, if nationalism implies keeping out advanced technology from other countries, this is going to affect the job market and if one plays with goods and products other countries are going to prosper. This in turn will affect peace because then jealousy will be manifested and people will perhaps want to take things from others.

SOS

We assume that the government is going to be efficient. This can lead to work and peace if investment is promoted and jobs are created. It is possible to create a better division of labor, a key point in the philosophy of both Adam Smith and Karl Marx. Each country should create its own domestic market, creating a lot of monopolist countries. The new key term is not 'free market', but 'competitive market' (a free market can easily degenerate into a monopolist market if this means that the companies have the freedom to conspire over agreements that will allow them to quickly get rid of the competition), but this refers to competition between countries. There are many countries that can produce cars and they can greatly contribute to the development of automobile technology and to the reduction of prices and the increase in productivity. Very often this expertise is related to exclusivity and monopoly, and there may be some truth in the idea that competition can be expensive, although this is not very likely. It is worth paying the price of duplication if one obtains the advantages of competition. MITI in Japan does not allow monopolies. It subsidizes several electronics companies and its theory is that it does not want any company to gain 100 per cent of the world market share; it does not want one company to become a monopoly and then stop its progress.

There is nothing dramatic here. Many people think that a super-optimum solution is a magic potion, but it has served as an approximate model for the entire world. It is difficult to imagine an economic community like ABC (Argentina, Brazil, Chile) or a Latin American community that would possibly go all the way to Mexico from Argentina. Then an economic community of the western hemisphere. Then one can think of a world economic community that would consist of separate economic communities. The key idea is that of an international economic community, where one does not have to give up sovereignty.

France is still France although it is part of the European Economic Community. It is now a prouder France. Former president Mitterrand loved to brag at the meetings of the EEC, because this gives France a special position. Now France is a large bearing in a large wheel, where previously it might have been a small bearing in a small wheel. France has individual authority; and as part of the EEC, it has collective authority. Member countries improve their positions and preserve their national identity as long as the key element of this community is free exchange, free trade, free migration of workers that are allowed to go wherever work is, and freedom to deal with environmental issues. All these problems are resolved across borders, and this strengthens the economies of the members. Then this makes one think that if we fix the economy of the countries, then the recipient will generally improve.

Totals

The main reason for discrimination is lack of sufficient funds to make everybody happy. If the pie of the gross national product grows by a small percentage, then one will improve. If the gross national product does grow in eight years (two presidential terms) by over 6 per cent, it will double the American or other gross national product. Let us say that a small investment allows the accumulation of interest on interest, the compound effect that is higher than the multiplying effect. This raises economic status and all that is related to it: the quality of life. The international community can certainly create more jobs, better products, more peace than a world government. Here we add another criterion: feasibility. If political feasibility is not necessary, we do not care how well things are being done. It can be said that we have a world government in the United Nations. Yes, but it is not coming up with economic plans to reduce world tariffs through multilateral or unilateral agreements. The United Nations is not involved in this.

Questions

How can we make each side of the controversy accept a common rating and evaluation of their criteria? Can computation be applied to your model? Is it necessary to apply computation to your model?

The question is, how does one arrive at super-optimum solutions to solve controversies with a high emotional content? Well, I am going to make a comment about our workshops. It has to do with super-optimizing workshops which contrasts with passive observation. In the future we are going to have 'hands on' workshops in which we will use computers, although it can be done without computers. The mathematical computation is simple, but the computers can be useful, especially if there are alternatives to explore, they can be useful for the 'what if' analysis, or if we want to make several changes to evaluate the effects. What we should obtain is an alternative that will increase the conservative goal and the liberal goal simultaneously. That means a 5 in a scale of 1–5, at least. This is pretty easy to do if we think about it.

The world is too used to talking in terms of compromises and what we have here is a typical compensation, where the conservative alternative works well for one goal but not so well for the other. The same thing happens with the liberal alternative. As a result, everybody arrives at compromise solutions, thinking that this is God's will, practically, that this is inherent to the nature of the world, but there are practically no political science issues that have been studied with our method. In Tuesday's workshop we will distribute a checklist with ten ways of arriving at super-optimum solutions. One way is very general – let us say thinking of things which are positive concerning both conservative and liberal goals. Other approaches will have to do with liability suits where there are some litigants who are people rather than political issues. Then we try to create something where one side gives up something that is not very valuable for them, but that is very valuable for the other side. This is how this worked with the electronics company and the insurance company mentioned earlier. The Japanese electronic company defendant (Sanyo) gave up old computers of very low market value and it also gave up monitors of big-screen TVs. Its insurance company gave up claims of no value to them, but of great value to the other side. This is called big benefit for one side and small cost for the other. Here we have a very simple example that is part of many policies carried out under the Reagan and subsequent administrations. It is related to wage supplements, bonuses, coupons and vouchers to bring two sides together like management and labour.

Recently in the Philippines, for example, there was a dispute with management about minimum wages. The management said that they could not pay more than 90 pesos a day for minimum wages. The workers said that they would have to make at least 100 pesos or they would starve. The company said that, if they paid more than 90 pesos, they were going to have to lay people off and could not hire new workers, and then people were going to starve anyway. In this case a compromise solution would have been 95 pesos a day. An agreement was reached by which the company would pay 89 pesos a day (less than 90). The workers would receive 101 pesos a day (more than 100). The difference of 12 pesos a day would be a supplement provided by the government – let us say a conditional subsidy whereby the company agrees to hire unemployed, disabled, old and young people who might not be active in the workforce and whom the company must train to make the 101 pesos a day worth it. On the other side, the workers must accept these jobs and enter the training programs and, if in this case they do not pass their exams, they will be fired. This is not a free bonus. The workers must update their skills to earn what they are being paid. This approach is known as the benefactor approach, where a third party is willing to bridge the gap between the management and the workers.

This worked very well in China, where the government was not the third party, but students were. In a dispute between professors and the government, the faculty demanded 300 monetary units, arguing that the door-to-door lemonade vendor made more than 300; the government offered only 200 units, so the compromise was 250 units. The super-optimum solution consists of the government paying the faculty 190 monetary units, but the faculty receiving 310 monetary units. The difference comes from establishing a low-tuition system to replace the current no-tuition system. The low tuition system would provide for scholarships and other forms of student aid for those who could not afford the tuition. The SOS would also allow for larger student enrollment without lowering admission standards.

6 International Dispute Resolution

The material which follows deals with international peace. The previous chapters dealt with international democracy and international prosperity. In order to discuss peace, prosperity, and democracy in a win–win or super-optimizing context, one needs to look to historical examples partly because the present time is fortunately short on international wars. There has been no war between national armies since the Persian Gulf War of 1992. NATO bombed Serbia in 1999 but there was no fighting between Serbian soldiers and NATO soldiers and thus there were no NATO deaths or casualties. That was an unusual war even though it is called a war. In order to provide a meaningful case study of a global or even an international dispute between sovereign nations, we need to go back to the Cold War interaction between the United States and the Soviet Union.

Likewise, we no longer have wars between colonies and mother countries since the last major colony to fight for independence was probably Namibia seeking its freedom from South Africa which was obtained in 1989. Instead, we need to talk about controlling countries and quasi-colonies or client-states such as the example of the control the United States formerly exercised over the Philippines.

When it comes to wars or violent disputes between central governments and secessionist provinces, we can find some examples in the 1990s although they are lessening. All 16 conquered republics of the Soviet Union were allowed to go free without any substantial violence. Likewise five of the six republics have parted from Yugoslavia with relatively little violence compared to the American Civil War or Moslem India seeking to secede from Hindu India. A good example of a recent war of secession was Chechnya seeking to secede from Russia but even that is a historical example. It is not likely to be repeated elsewhere in view of the bad experiences on both sides.

The fourth category of wars that were used in this chapter on International Dispute Resolution consists of disputes between conflicting nations within a country. That is a type of dispute that seems to have increased in recent years rather than decreased. As of 1997–8 according to statistics from the Jimmy Carter Center in Atlanta, Georgia, there were five places involving inter-group disputes within a country in which there are more than 10,000 deaths. That includes Afghanistan, Algeria, Congo, Rwanda, and Sudan. As of a few years earlier we could also count Bosnia, and as of 1999, we could count Kosovo. The case study used here is the situation of former Yugoslavia in the early days which emphasizes Slovenia, Croatia, and Serbia, although the problems and possible win–win solutions are similar to Serbian Bosnia, Croatian Bosnia, Moslem Bosnia, and Kosovo.

DISPUTES BETWEEN SOVEREIGN NATIONS

Bilateral arms reduction stemming from the USA–USSR agreements exceeds the liberals' best expectations since liberals had been pushing for a freeze as a radical left-wing alternative to increased arms build-up. The idea of a drastic reduction clearly goes beyond a mere freeze. Bilateral arms reduction exceeds the conservatives' best expectations since it has been accompanied by a reduction in the threat of the Soviet Union, rather than an increase. The reduced threat could mean a substantial increase in funds available for improving the American economy, which both conservatives and liberals should welcome.

A joint perspective

That kind of win–win analysis is shown in Table 6.1. The alternatives in about 1985 were (1) a conservative alternative of a nuclear arms build-up and the Strategic Defense Initiative (SDI) or Star Wars, (2) a liberal alternative of a unilateral freeze or disarmament, (3) a neutral alternative of conventional arms development, and (4) an SOS alternative of bilateral arms reduction.

The goals of both the United States and the Soviet Union were (1) the conservative or nationalistic goal of avoiding being conquered, and preferably conquering the other side, (2) the liberal or pacifist goal of avoiding nuclear war, (3) the neutral goal of reducing the burden of the economy, and (4) a second neutral goal of being politically feasible.

The relations between the alternatives and the goals are shown on a 1–5 scale. A 5 means highly conducive to the goal. A 4 means mildly conducive, a 3 means neither conducive nor adverse, a 2 means mildly adverse and a 1 means highly adverse. The neutral totals involve giving each goal a mid-

Table 6.1 Evaluating policies toward arms control

Criteria / Alternatives	C Goal Avoid being conquered C=3 L=1	L Goal Avoid nuclear war C=1 L=3	N Goal Reduce burden on economy C=2 L=2	N Goal Politically feasible C=2 L=2	N Total (neutral weights)	L Total (liberal weights)	C Total (conservative weights)
C Alternative Nuclear arms build-up and SDI	4.5	1	3	1	22	15	22.5*
L Alternative Unilateral freeze or disarmament	2	4	3	3	24	26*	22
N Alternative Conventional arms development	3	3	2	3	22	22	19
SOS Alternative Bilateral arms reduction	5	5	5	4	38	38**	38**

dling weight or multiplier of 2 on a 1–3 scale. Thus the neutral totals simply involve adding the relation scores and doubling the sum.

The liberal totals involve giving the neutral goals a middling weight of 2. The liberal totals give the conservative goal a low weight or multiplier of 1 on a 1–3 scale. They give the liberal goal a high weight of 3 on the 1–3 scale. Thus the liberal alternative wins on the liberal totals before we look at the SOS alternative. The conservative totals also involve giving the neutral goals a weight of 2. The conservative totals, however, give the conservative goal a high weight or multiplier of 3, and the liberal goal a low weight or multiplier of 1. Thus the conservative alternative wins on the conservative totals before we look at the SOS alternative.

The SOS alternative of bilateral arms reduction does so well on all four goals that it exceeds the best that the conservatives previously offered using the conservative goals and weights. It also exceeds the best that the liberals previously offered using the liberal goals and weights. Exceeding the best expectations of both conservatives and liberals is the essence of a super-optimum solution.

Two separate perspectives

Table 6.2 shows how the US–USSR arms control negotiations might be viewed as of 1990. Eight alternative positions are shown: four for the United States and four for the USSR. Each side is faced with basically the same four alternatives:

1 Keep the arms situation as it is. This is the most conservative reasonable alternative in 1990. It is no longer being actively proposed that the arms race should be increased.
2 Have a big reduction in arms. This is the new liberal alternative. It is interesting to note that liberals were formerly advocating a freeze, which is now in effect the conservative alternative. This is a good example of yesterday's liberal sometimes becoming today's conservative.
3 Have a small reduction between (1) keeping things as they are and (2) a big reduction. This is logically the neutral or compromise position. It typically involves no innovative ideas, but merely splitting the difference between the conservative and liberal positions.
4 A super-optimum solution which could consist of a combination of a big reduction and various international trade agreements between the United States and the Soviet Union, or even more broadly between the United States plus western Europe and the Soviet Union plus eastern Europe.

Table 6.2   A super-optimizing perspective on USA–USSR negotiations as of 1990

USA perspective		National security (C)	GNP (L)	Neutral totals	Liberal totals	Conservative totals
C	As is	3	3	13	12	12*
L	Big reductions	2	4	12	14*	10
N	Little reductions	2.5	3.5	12	13	11
SOS	Big reductions & trade	4	5	18	19**	17**

USSR perspective		National security (C)	GNP (L)	Neutral totals	Liberal totals	Conservative totals
C	As is	3	3	12	12	12*
L	Big reductions	2	4	12	14*	10
N	Little reductions	2.5	3.5	12	13	11
SOS	Big reductions & trade	4	5	18	19**	17**

Notes:
1   The symbols for the alternatives stand for relatively conservative (C), liberal (L), neutral (N) and super-optimum solution (SOS).
2   The conservative totals involve giving national security a multiplier weight of 3 and GNP a weight of 1. The liberal totals involve giving GNP a weight of 3 and national security a weight of 1. The neutral totals involve giving both national security and GNP a middling weight of 2.
3   The conservative alternative wins on the conservative total before considering the SOS. Likewise, the liberal alternative wins on the liberal total, and the neutral alternative on the neutral total.
4   The SOS alternative wins decisively on all three alternatives for both the USA and the USSR.

203

The four alternatives which the Soviet Union is considering are virtually identical to those of the United States. It is often the case in bilateral dispute resolution that the two sides are faced with the same alternatives. They differ mainly regarding their goals. Inspection is no longer such a big issue as a result of increased openness on the part of the Soviet Union and improved surveillance technology. Afghanistan is no longer such a controversy in view of the Soviet withdrawal. Likewise, the United States has stopped giving military aid to the Nicaraguan rebels, and it looks as if there will be a reasonably meaningful electoral process in both Nicaragua and Afghanistan.

On the matter of goals, there are basically only two, although they could be subdivided, and other lesser goals could be added. Since there are two goals on the part of the United States and two goals on the part of the Soviet Union, there are four goals altogether.

1   Promoting the national security of the United States. This is a relatively conservative goal. It is also endorsed by liberals, especially if the external threat is from a right-wing source, as in World War II, or even a dictatorial left-wing source, as during much of the cold war.
2   Promoting the gross national product of the United States, including the idea of full employment and increased international competitiveness. This is a relatively liberal goal, especially if full employment is emphasized, but also strongly endorsed by conservatives, especially if the emphasis is on international competitiveness and reduced inflation.
3   Promoting the national security of the Soviet Union. This is definitely an important goal of the Soviet military and also the civilian government. Too often the American State Department takes the position that the Soviet Union has nothing to worry about from the United States. What is more important is not whether they have anything to worry about, but whether they perceive that they have something to worry about.
4   Promoting the gross national product of the Soviet Union. This is also definitely an important goal of the Soviet Union, especially the civilian government and the civilian population. Too often the CIA and people in the State Department take the position that the Soviet Union does not care about consumer goods and raising living standards. It is obvious at least since 1988 (if not before) that people in the Soviet Union and eastern Europe do want a better quality of life in terms of both economic goods and political accountability.

Table 6.2 shows how US negotiators are likely to perceive the relations between each alternative and each goal. The relations are expressed on a 1–5 scale. A 5 means that, if the alternative increases, the goal is likely to increase greatly; a 4 means that the goal is likely to increase slightly; a 3 means that the goal is not likely to increase or decrease; a 2 means that the goal is likely to decrease slightly; and a 1 means that, if the alternative increases, the goal is likely to decrease greatly. If the first alternative is to keep things as they are, that is likely to have no effect on either national security or the gross national product. Therefore, a 3 is inserted into the two cells in the top row for both the United States and the USSR. If the second alternative is to have a big reduction in arms, that is likely to be perceived as causing at least a slight decrease in national security by the United States and by the USSR. The funds that might be released from such a reduction, however, are likely to be perceived as being capable of increasing the GNP of the United States and the GNP of the USSR by using those funds to develop and diffuse new technologies that will increase each country's economic capabilities.

The third alternative of a small reduction scores a 2.5 on national security, between the 3 of doing nothing and the 2 of a big arms reduction. Likewise, a small reduction scores 3.5 on GNP between the 3 of doing nothing and the 4 of a big arms reduction. Like a typical compromise, it achieves the worst and the best of both of the other alternatives. As a result, it generates about the same total score. All three of the traditional alternatives generate total scores of 6 for both the United States and the Soviet Union. That means they are all about equally undesirable or equally desirable. The compromise alternative, however, is more likely to be adopted because it scores higher on the unshown goal of political feasibility. It is more politically feasible because both conservatives and liberals will vote for it as a second choice. They will then console themselves by saying that things could have been worse if the other side had won.

Under a super-optimum solution, both sides do win, and they can do even better than their initial best expectations. At first glance, one might question how a big reduction plus trade can result in more national security than a big reduction alone. That implies that national security is only dependent on how well armed each country is. A country that has a lower GNP than it could have may be weakening itself regarding arms capability and the ability to fight a war. More importantly, trade between two countries who might otherwise be hostile can create a mutually beneficial interdependence that decreases the likelihood of hostile interaction. Good examples include the unwillingness of the Reagan administration to punish the Soviet Union for its invasion of Afghanistan by prohibiting grain shipments, or the unwillingness of the Bush administration to punish China for its suppression of the pro-democracy movement by invoking trade sanctions. In both cases, the supposedly less anti-Communist liberals were more likely to favor the grain embargo and trade sanctions partly because they are less sensitive to the value of international business transactions. In other words, active trading between the United States and the Soviet Union can do more to decrease the likelihood of their going to war and thus to increase their national security than either an arms increase or an arms decrease. This explains the 4 in the SOS row of the national security column.

The 5 in the SOS row of the GNP column reflects the fact that a big reduction alone generates a relation score of a 4 by a virtue of the funds that are released from arms development to be available for supply-side economics, industrial policy and the development of new technologies. It is no coincidence that, among the top industrialized countries of the world, Japan and West Germany now score the highest in productivity increases and the lowest in arms expenditure per capita. The United States and the Soviet Union score the highest in arms expenditures per capita, while they score the lowest in recent productivity increases. In addition to the effect on GNP of the big arms reduction, the SOS also produces a positive effect by virtue of the trade agreements between the West and the East. One might say that the United States does not need the Soviet Union as a trading partner. For that matter, one could say that the United States could survive with no outside trading partners, and maybe the Soviet Union could too. If both countries want to improve substantially their living standards, however, they should take advantage of their potential abilities to buy and sell each other's products. The Soviet Union is one of the leading grain buyers in the world and could be a leading buyer in almost any field, given the size of its population. It is also one of the leading producers of oil and gold, and it could become a leading producer in other fields if it concentrated its resources on what it can do relatively well, the way Japan has. The United States could sell grain and other products to the Soviet Union in return for gold, oil and other products, thereby easing the international deficit, which can be paid in gold, and the US energy problems.

Everything that is shown in Table 6.2 can be subjected to a computerized 'what if' analysis. Such an analysis enables one to determine what it would take to bring any of those alternatives that are tied for second place up to first place. It also enables one to determine the effects of adding additional goals, changing the alternatives or changing any of the inputs. Gauging that kind of 'what if' capability may be the most important purpose that is served by working with decision-aiding software. Some of the benefits can also be obtained by working with a spreadsheet matrix (like that of Table 6.2, with alternatives, goals, relations and total scores) even if the matrix is not computerized. One type of sensitivity analysis that is often especially helpful is asking what would be the winning alternative if we just concentrated on the conservative goals or gave them extra weight, which in this case would be national security. Likewise, what would be the winning alternative if we just concentrated on the liberal goals or gave them extra weight, which in this case would be having a higher GNP with full employment and lots of consumer goods. One exciting characteristic of super-optimum solutions is that they win even when one only uses conservative weights or when one only uses liberal weights. The reason here, and often in other SOS situations, is that the SOS alternative does better than the other alternatives on every individual goal, not just better on the overall total. There are ways of systematically arriving at super-optimum solutions. See S. Nagel and M. Mills, 'Generating Super-Optimum Solutions', in Marc Holzer (ed.), *Public Productivity Handbook* (Marcel Dekker, 1992).

DISPUTES BETWEEN CONTROLLING COUNTRIES AND COLONIES OR QUASI-COLONIES

The problem of the American military bases in the Philippines is an especially challenging problem. Problems need to have the following characteristics in order to qualify as SOS problems.

1 There should be at least one conservative alternative and at least one liberal alternative. If there is only one alternative for dealing with the problem, there is no problem since there is no choice, although one could say that there is still a go/no-go choice as to whether that one alternative should be adopted.
2 There should be at least one conservative goal and at least one liberal goal. If all the goals are conservative, then the conservative alternative should easily win. Likewise, if all the goals are liberal, then the liberal alternative should easily win.
3 The conservative alternative should do better on the conservative goal, with the liberal alternative doing better on the liberal goal. That is the tradeoff requirement. If either alternative does better on both kinds of goals, that alternative should easily win.
4 It should be possible to say meaningfully that conservatives give relatively more weight to the conservative goals and relatively less weight to the liberal goals, and vice versa for the assigning of weights by liberals. If that is not so, it is not so meaningful to talk about a conservative total with conservative weights and a liberal total with liberal weights.
5 There should be a super-optimum solution that does better than the previous conservative alternative on the conservative totals with conservative weights, and also does better than the previous liberal alternative on the liberal totals with liberal weights. This is the most difficult to achieve of these five characteristics, but it is still manageable.

The problem of what to do about the American military bases in the Philippines is especially difficult because it goes beyond the usual dilemma of choosing between (1) a liberal alternative that clearly wins with liberal weights, and (2) a conservative alternative that clearly wins with conservative weights. An analysis of Table 6.3 tends to show that the liberal alternative barely squeaks by the conservative and neutral alternatives on the liberal totals, and the conservative alternative barely squeaks by the other two alternatives on the conservative totals. We thus have a dilemma that is even tighter than usual between the liberal and conservative alternatives.

Table 6.3　The Philippine–US military bases

Criteria Alternatives	L Goal Liberal concerns	C Goal Conservative concerns	L Goal Sovereignty	N Total (neutral weights)	L Total (liberal weights)	C Total (conservative weights)
C Alternative 　Bases & more 　money	3	4	2	18	19	17*
L Alternative 　No bases	3	2	4	18	23*	13
N Alternative 　Phase out	3	3	2	16	18	14
SOS Alternative 　Bases & massive 　credits to 　upgrade 　economy	5	5	3	26	29**	23**

The alternatives

Working backwards from these totals to the alternatives, the conservative alternative is basically to allow the American bases to remain, but to ask for more money. The liberal alternative is to throw the bases out. The neutral alternative is something in between, generally a gradual phasing out of the bases. Other in-between positions might involve throwing out the Clark Air Base but keeping the Subic Naval Base, or vice versa. Another possibility is allow the bases, but with more Philippine flags and other symbols of Philippine sovereignty at the bases. A recently proposed middling position is to allow the bases, but to give the Philippine government more say in how the planes should be used, especially with regard to putting down an attempted coup.

The phasing out idea is probably the most common middling alternative. It, however, blends into both the conservative and the liberal alternatives. The conservatives are willing to tolerate the bases, but they are going to be eventually phased out to some extent anyhow as the cold war decreases even further. They are also going to be phased out to some extent because they have probably already become rather obsolete in light of modern defense technology. Few, if any, of the planes or ships could ever get anywhere without being destroyed by modern missiles. The Russian equivalent of nuclear-armed Trident submarines in the Pacific Ocean could probably wipe out both the naval base and the air base almost before the alarm could ring. There are also bases that are possibly relatively more welcome by the nearby Okinawans and Koreans.

Likewise, the liberal alternative of throwing out the bases would have to be achieved by phasing out. They cannot be thrown out within a matter of hours. For one thing, the liberal and conservative members of the Philippine House of Representatives would not tolerate a rushed departure without allowing for substitute employment opportunities and some substitution for the large amounts of money that are spent by Americans associated with the bases. The Philippine Senate is elected at large and is not so sensitive to pressures from the Luzon constituency, where the bases are located.

One might therefore think there is really one alternative here, namely to phase out the bases. This problem, however, illustrates the importance of symbolism and language in political controversy. Whether the liberals really mean it or not, they talk about throwing out the bases now, not phasing them out. Whether the conservatives really mean it or not, they talk about retaining the bases indefinitely. Thus the controversy needs to be resolved in terms of what each side argues, not necessarily in terms of the realities beneath the surface. Perceptions, value judgments and symbolism are often more important in resolving political controversies than empirical reality, especially in the short run.

The goals

As for goals, Table 6.3 lists the first goal as 'Liberal concerns'. That means a whole set of interests that liberals are especially sensitive to, including workers rather than employers, consumers rather than merchants, tenants rather than landlords, small farmers/businesses rather than big farmers/ businesses, debtors rather than creditors, minority ethnic groups rather than dominant ethnic groups, and in general the relatively less well-off segments within society. The second goal is listed as 'Conservative concerns'. That means a set of interests to which conservatives are especially sensitive, including employers, merchants, landlords, big farmers, big businesses, creditors and dominant ethnic groups. One useful aspect of this problem is that it goes to the heart of liberal versus conservative interests and constituencies, as contrasted to lower-impact problems.

The third goal is national sovereignty. In some contexts, this can be a conservative goal, as when Russia nationalists talk about restraining the Lithuanians, expelling the Jews, or otherwise discriminating against citizens of the Soviet Union who are not ethnic Russians. In other contexts, sovereignty can be a liberal left-wing goal, as when Vietnamese advocated becoming independent of China, France, Japan, France again, the United States and China again, during various points in Vietnamese history. Likewise, it is a liberal concept in the Philippines when Filipinos talk about getting rid of the Spanish colonialists or the American imperialists, including what they consider to be military-base imperialism. This makes sovereignty in this analysis a relatively liberal goal. Obviously, the goal of conservative concerns is a conservative goal, and the goal of liberal concerns is a liberal one.

Scoring the relations

As for scoring the relations of the alternatives on the goals, both the liberal and conservative concerns are to some extent favorably benefitted by the present and additional American dollars. Those dollars benefit both workers and employers, consumers and merchants, tenants and landlords, small and large farmers, small and large businesses, debtors and creditors, and both minority and dominant ethnic groups. The amount of money is quite substantial. The Philippines is one of the top three recipients of American foreign aid in the world, along with Israel and Egypt, whose aid is lessening. The liberal and conservative concerns, however, do not benefit equally. The American presence has a conservative influence. The United States tends to be supportive of conservative pro-American politicians, especially in a country that has American military bases, such as Korea, Greece, Turkey, West Germany, Spain and the Philippines.

To be more specific, the conservative alternative of retaining the bases with even more money is a bit of a wash (or approximately a neutral tie or a 3 on a 1–5 scale) with regard to liberal concerns. The money is at least a 4 on liberal concerns, but the conservative influence of the United States is a 2 or lower. Those two sub-scores average a 3. On the conservative concerns, the conservative alternative of the bases and more money gets at least a 4.

On sovereignty, the conservative alternative is at least a 2 on a 1–5 scale, which is the equivalent of a –1 on a –1 to +2 scale.

The liberal alternative also produces a washed-out 3 (approximately a neutral score of 3) on liberal concerns. It gets a 4 with regard to getting rid of some of the American conservative influence, but it gets a 2 on losing the American money. The liberal alternative of no bases gets a 2 or lower on conservative concerns. It does relatively well on sovereignty, as both liberals and conservatives can recognize, although they may disagree on the relative weight of sovereignty in this context.

The neutral phase-out approach is about middling on liberal concerns. It provides some money for a while, which is good, but not as good as a lot of money for a long time. It provides a diminishing of American conservative influence, but not as fast as the liberals would like, and not as slow as the conservatives might like. By allowing the Americans to retain the bases even under a phase-out arrangement, the neutral alternative does have a negative effect on Philippine sovereignty, although not as negative as the conservative alternative. We could show that difference by giving the neutral alternative a 2.5 on sovereignty or the conservative alternative a 1.5. Either way, the overall results are not affected.

A super-optimum solution

These overall results are that the liberal alternative wins on the liberal totals and the conservative alternative wins on the conservative totals, although not by much, as previously mentioned. Finding a super-optimum solution may be especially difficult where the alternatives are so nearly tied and where the problem is so filled with emotional symbolism. A possible super-optimum solution would involve two key elements. The first is a recognition (as much as possible on all sides) that the bases are probably going to be phased out in the future. This will not be due to the United States surrendering or to the Philippines overcoming the US opposition. It will be due more to defense technology changes (as mentioned above) that makes these bases about as meaningful as the Maginot Line in France in 1940, Pearl Harbor in the United States in 1941, or the guns of Singapore pointing to the sea in 1942. The phasing out will also be due to recent world changes that seem to greatly decrease the likelihood of a world war between the former Soviet Union, eastern Europe and China on the one hand, and the United States and its allies on the other. The probability seemed even less as of 1999 when global economic competition and the seeking of mutual customers, sources of supply, and investment have replaced the Cold War.

More important than a natural rather than a forced phase-out is a second key element of a possible super-optimum solution. This element emphasizes massive credits to upgrade the Philippine economy. It could involve no payment of cash whatsoever on the part of the United States and yet provide tremendous economic benefits to the Republic of the Philippines. It involves a number of elements. First of all, the United States makes available an amount of credits that, when expressed in dollars, would be about twice as many dollars as the United States would be willing to pay in the form of rent or a cash payment. The United States would be willing to pay more in the form of credits for the following reasons.

1 It is normally a lot easier to give credit than to pay cash. An example might be returning merchandise to a store and asking for cash. One may receive various negative reactions from an employee arguing that the merchandise should be kept. If, however, one asks for a credit slip, the decision maker is likely to be much more accommodating.
2 The American economy would benefit substantially if the credits could only be used in the United States to buy American products and services. That would benefit the United States more than paying out cash that is then spent in Japan or elsewhere. At the same time, it does not substantially hamper the Philippines in buying products and services needed for upgrading its economy.
3 The US economy would also substantially benefit indirectly from an upgrading of the Philippine economy, since that would enable the Philippines to buy even more American products and services in the future.

As for what the credits would be for, that is where the Philippines could especially benefit. The shopping list might include such things as the following:

1 credits to pay for personnel and facilities for on-the-job training and adult education to upgrade worker productivity;
2 relevant credits for upgrading Philippine higher education, especially in fields that relate to engineering and public policy which could have high marginal rates of return;
3 relevant credits for upgrading elementary and secondary education as part of a large-scale investment in human resource development;
4 relevant credits for seeds, pesticides, herbicides and farm equipment to make land reform programs more successful, including the hiring of experts for training programs;
5 relevant credits for subsidizing suburban job opportunities, regional cities and overseas employment opportunities;

6 relevant credits to improve energy and electricity production in the Philippines which is such an important aspect of improving the gross national product;

7 relevant credits for buying technologies that can improve productivity along with upgraded skills, including modern assembly-line technologies;

8 relevant credits for health care and housing that can be shown to be related to increased worker productivity;

9 other credits for buying American products and services that relate to upgrading the Philippine economy, as contrasted to buying consumer goods or other products and services that have little increased productivity payoff.

There are additional benefits for both sides that should be mentioned. (By both sides in this context is meant the Republic of the Philippines and the United States. Both sides also refers to the liberals and conservatives within the Philippines.)

1 By providing credits rather than cash, there is a minimum of loss due to corruption. It is a lot easier to pocket money than it is to pocket a new schoolhouse or an expert consultant in on-the-job training.

2 By providing credits that are earmarked for upgrading the economy, there is a minimum of loss due to wasteful expenditure including bureaucratic administration.

3 Waste is not going to be completely eliminated. We would not want a straitjacket system that discourages experimentation with innovative ideas for increasing productivity. If innovation is going to be encouraged, some waste must be expected, since not all innovative ideas work out well.

4 This could set a precedent for future American aid to other countries and future aid by other developed countries to developing countries. The key aspect of the precedent is emphasizing credits for upgrading the economy, as contrasted to an emphasis on food, shelter, clothing and other traditional charitable 'do-gooderism'.

5 In that regard, we are talking about teaching people how to fish, rather than giving them a fish. The fishing analogy is endorsed by liberals who founded the Peace Corps and conservatives who believe in jobs for welfare recipients rather than charitable handouts. Actually we are talking about teaching people how to develop and apply new technologies for doing such things as fishing, growing crops, manufacturing products, transporting commuters and making public policy decisions.

6 The kind of programs that most win friends and influence people in favor of the United States might be programs that involve bringing left-

wing anti-Americans to the United States to receive training or having American trainers go to work with Philippine union leaders or Mindinao farmers. People acquire a much more favorable attitude toward Americans in that context than by receiving a sack of flour labeled 'Made in the USA'.

It might be noted that, if the Filipinos emphasize how obsolete the bases are becoming, they may succeed in getting rid of the bases faster. On the other hand, it might be wise to emphasize how valuable the bases are in order to get even more credits as payment for retaining them. On the third hand, the United States is not so unaware of the empirical realities, and it is not so unaware of bargaining techniques. This idea of retaining the bases along with an inevitable, at least partial, phase-out and massive credits for upgrading the Philippine economy should not be approached as a matter of traditional negotiation and game playing. Rather, it should be approached as a matter that can be resolved to the mutual benefit of all sides in the sense of a super-optimum solution with all major viewpoints coming out ahead.

DISPUTES BETWEEN CENTRAL GOVERNMENTS AND SECESSIONIST PROVINCES

Super-optimizing applied to Russian secession

Table 6.4 which follows shows the application of SOS analysis to the problem of the proposed secession of Chechnya from the Russian Soviet Federated Socialist Republic (RSFSR). This application was developed in collaboration with Edward Ojiganoff, the Head of the Policy Analysis Division of the Supreme Soviet of the RSFSR. The Chechnya problem is partly analogous to the proposed secession of Croatia from Yugoslavia or the secession of any ethnic region from a larger country of which it has been a part.

The *alternatives* in the RSFSR–Chechnya situation are (1) to deny independence to Chechnya: this can be considered the relatively conservative position because it seeks to conserve the country, state or political unit as it is; (2) to grant independence to Chechnya: this can be considered the relatively liberal position because it is more tolerant of dissident attitudes; (3) to retain Chechnya as a sub-unit within the RSFSR but grant Chechnya more autonomy than it has at present. This can be considered the relatively neutral position.

As for the *goals*, a key conservative goal is to favor greater Russia and seek a high national income for Russia; a key liberal goal help for Chechnya, including a high national income for that country. More goals can be added

Table 6.4   Secession of Chechnya from the RSFSR

Alternatives	C Goal Greater Russia & high RSFSR GNP	L Goal Chechnya independence & high Chechnya GNP	N Total (neutral weights)	C Toal (conservative weights)	L Total (liberal weights)
C Alternative Deny independence	3	1	4	7*	5
L Alternative Grant independence	1	3	4	5	7*
N Alternative More autonomy	2	2	4	6	6
SOS Alternative Economic union	≥2.5	≥2.5		≥7.5**	≥7.5**

Note: Unlike most of the SOS tables, this simpler SOS table involves relations scores on a 1–3 scale rather than a 1–2 scale. A 3 means conducive, 2 means neither conducive or adverse, and a 1 means adverse. Likewise, the weights are on a 1–2 scale rather than a 1–3 scale. Under such a scale, a weight of 2 is high and a weight of 1 is low. To calculate the total using neutral weights, simply add the relation scores without any weights.

later, possibly with more alternatives. For the sake of simplicity, however, we will begin with three basic alternatives and two basic goals.

The *relations* between the three alternatives and the two goals can be expressed in terms of a 1 to 3 scale. In that context, a 3 means that the alternative is relatively conducive to the goal. A 2 means neither conducive nor adverse. A 1 means relatively adverse or negative to the goal. Relations can also sometimes be expressed in dollars, miles, 1–10 scales, question marks or other units.

Denying independence to Chechnya is perceived as being at least a mildly positive 3 on the goal of favoring greater Russia. Granting independence to Chechnya is perceived as being at least a mildly negative 1 on favoring greater Russia. More autonomy is in between, with a neutral score of 2. On the other hand, granting independence to Chechnya is scored a 3 on the goal of helping Chechnya. Denying independence is scored a 1 on helping Chechnya. More autonomy is in between on that goal, too, with a neutral score of 2. These perceptions and scores are likely to be approximately held by both conservatives and liberals in this context.

There are three *total scores* that can be generated from this data. They are neutral, conservative or liberal, depending on the relative importance of the two goals. If the two goals are considered to be of equal importance, the neutral totals are 4 for each of the alternatives. If the conservative goal is considered more important than the liberal goal, we can count the conservative column twice. That results in totals of a 7 for denying independence (3 + 3 + 1), a 5 for granting independence (1 + 1 + 3) and a 6 for more autonomy (2 + 2 + 2). Thus, with conservative weights for the goals, the conservative alternative wins on the conservative totals.

Likewise, if the liberal goal is considered more important, we can count the liberal column twice. That results in totals of a 5 for denying independence (3 + 1 + 1), a 7 for granting independence (1 + 3 + 3) and a 6 for more autonomy (2 + 2 + 2). Thus, with liberal weights for the goals, the liberal alternative wins on the liberal totals. The single asterisk shows the winning alternative on each total column before the SOS alternative or super-optimum solution is taken into consideration.

Finding a super-optimum solution

The object is to find a super-optimum solution which will simultaneously win on the conservative totals over the conservative alternative and win on the liberal totals over the liberal alternative. That means being better than both the conservative best and the liberal best using their own goals and weights to judge what is best. In terms of the simple scoring system, such a solution needs to score positively or better than a neutral 2 on a 1–3 scale on both goals. It also means going above traditional tradeoff reasoning. The conservative alternative usually does well on the conservative goal, but not so well on the liberal goal. The liberal alternative usually does well on the liberal goal, but not so well on the conservative goal. The SOS alternative does at least mildly well on both goals.

Doing well on both goals does not require being a winner on each separate goal. It means being a winner on each of the two main totals. These totals involve using conservative weights and liberal weights, respectively. If the suggested SOS alternative receives a 2.5 on each goal, then it will receive a 7.5 on the conservative total (2.5 + 2.5 + 2.5). That is higher than the 7 received by the conservative alternative. Likewise, the suggested SOS alternative will receive at least a 7.5 on the liberal total (2.5 + 2.5 + 2.5).

A proposed SOS solution to the problem of Chechnya seceding from the RSFSR is to allow Chechnya its independence, but as part of an economic union with the RSFSR and possibly other autonomous regions within the

RSFSR and other neighboring political units. This is analogous to the RSFSR, the Ukraine and Byelorussia withdrawing from the USSR and forming an economic union or commonwealth. Such an economic union can benefit both the RSFSR and Chechnya by facilitating a profitable interchange of goods, capital, workers and ideas. It can lead later to developing a more meaningful division of labor than previously existed, with the possibility of well-directed subsidies and incentives from the economic union to make the division of labor even more successful.

An alternative SOS might be to retain Chechnya within the RSFSR, but seek to achieve the benefits of an economic union through immediate subsidies. Such an alternative may not be economically feasible from the perspective of the currently hard-pressed RSFSR. It may also not be politically feasible from the perspective of the independence-seeking Chechnya. To be a meaningful SOS requires satisfying the following criteria:

1   the SOS must win on the conservative totals;
2   it must also win on the liberal totals;
3   it must win by a safe enough margin for the SOS to retain first place regardless of reasonable changes in scoring the relations between the alternatives and goals or in indicating the relative weights of the goals;
4   the SOS must be politically feasible, so that it is capable of being adopted;
5   the SOS must be administratively feasible so that it is capable of being successfully implemented, including backing by sufficient funds.

DISPUTES BETWEEN CONFLICTING NATIONS WITHIN A COUNTRY

Super-optimizing applied to civil war in Yugoslavia

The above analysis can be applied to Yugoslavia through reasoning by analogy. Some special points worth noting include the following. Each republic and autonomous province of Yugoslavia could become a separate sovereign nation, or at least each republic could. They would each have a population and a national income that would be within a low to middle range among members of the United Nations. They would be joined together in an economic union of six republics. This would be analogous to the joining of the seven former republics of the Soviet Union in the Commonwealth of Independent States or the approximately ten nations in the European Union. The so-called Eurasian Economic Union is more relevant, since the members were formerly part of one country.

The new economic union could be referred to as the Yugoslavia Economic Union or the South Europe Economic Union, for example. The latter would allow for other South European countries to join, such as Greece. An alternative would be to have a Yugoslavia Economic Union consisting of the six Yugoslavian republics, but having the Yugoslavia Economic Union later join in a larger economic union covering southern or possibly central Europe.

The Yugoslavia Economic Union could add to its unity by having a constitutional monarchy. The precedent for doing so is the former British Commonwealth. It is now the Commonwealth of Nations, but many of those nations still have a relationship to Queen Elizabeth which gives them more unity, tradition and stability than they otherwise would have. In the case of Yugoslavia, a democratic constitutional monarchy could serve a unifying peacemaking role. Crown Prince Alexander does evoke a favorable response from many Serbs, Croats, Slovenes and other Yugoslavian ethnic groups. He probably evokes a more favorable response than the Yugoslavian national or federal presidency or other governmental institutions.

As of 1999, there are increasing case studies and experiences regarding the benefits and processes related to forming an economic union. Such unions are becoming increasingly important in such places as western Europe, the Soviet Union and the trilateral pact between the United States, Canada and Mexico. The idea is also taking root in South America, Sub-Sahara Africa, South Asia and elsewhere. Moving toward establishing such a union may make more sense in ending the civil war in Yugoslavia than trying to achieve a lasting ceasefire or a military solution.

At first the economic union can emphasize the unhindered exchange of goods, people, capital and ideas across all the boundaries of the former republics. It can also emphasize equality of opportunity for all ethnic groups in terms of equal treatment regardless of origins in matters of rights that relate to politics, criminal justice, education, employment, housing and consumer rights. The economic union can later develop appropriate divisions of labor in terms of making the best use of the land, labor and capital of each former republic. That kind of division or specialization can be facilitated by well-directed subsidies and incentives available to the economic union.

Such an economic union is a super-optimum solution since it enables conservative nationalists and separatists to achieve more national identity and stature than they otherwise would have. At the same time, it satisfies the liberal emphasis on quality of life in terms of jobs and consumer goods. It makes more sense than each country going off on its own, without the benefits of the economic interaction associated with an economic union. It likewise makes more sense than forcing nations into a regional government above the member nations, or even a world government.

Some of these ideas are summarized in Table 6.5. This makes use of a 1–5 system of scoring relations, rather than 1–3. It also uses a 1–3 system for weighting goals, rather than 1–2. These are general ideas with much potential for Yugoslavia in terms of peace, prosperity and political reform. They need to be further developed in collaboration with policy makers,

Table 6.5 International economic communities and super-optimum solutions

Criteria Alternatives	C Goal National identity & stature C=3 L=1	L Goal Quality of life in terms of jobs and consumer goods C=1 L=3	N Total (neutral weights)	L Total (liberal weights)	C Total (conservative weights)
C Alternative Nationalism & separatism	12 ④ 4	2 ② 6	12	10	14*
L Alternative One world or world govt	6 ② 2	4 ④ 12	12	14*	10
N Alternative Regional govt	9 ③ 3	3 ③ 9	12	12	12
SOS Alternative Economic community	15 ⑤ 5	5 ⑤ 15	20	20**	20**

Notes:

1 The relations between each alternative and each goal are shown on a 1–5 relations scale or circled score. A 5 means highly conducive to the goal, a 4 means mildly conducive, a 3 means neither conducive nor adverse, a 2 means mildly adverse and a 1 means highly adverse to the goal.

2 The conservative goal (C column 2) is given a weight or multiplier of 3 by conservatives (upper left-hand corner, e.g. 12) on a 1–3 scale of weights, but a weight of 1 by liberals (lower right-hand corner, e.g. 4).

3 The liberal goal (L column 3) is given a weight or multiplier of 1 by conservatives (upper left-hand corner, e.g. 2), but a weight of 3 by liberals (lower right-hand corner, e.g. 6).

4 A single asterisk shows the alternative that wins on the liberal totals (column 5) and the conservative totals (column 6) before considering the SOS alternative.

5 A double asterisk shows the alternative that wins after the SOS super-optimum solution is considered. The SOS should score higher than the former conservative winner on the conservative totals (column 6) and simultaneously higher than the former liberal winner on the liberal totals (column 5).

political scientists, economists and other relevant people, mainly in Yugo-slavia.

The most appropriate next step may be to engage quickly but meaning-fully in that collaboration in order to develop and implement a worthwhile plan for creating a Yugoslavia Economic Union of six sovereign states, possibly including a constitutional monarchy as a peacemaking unifying force. It could bring together Serbs, Croats, Slovenes, Muslims, Albanians, Macedonians, Montenegrins and other Yugoslavians.

Post-civil war dispute resolution*

The situation here in Croatia is now different than before. It does seem that the peace is holding and that UN forces will be sent to Croatia. Croatia is internationally recognized by more than 40 states (including Russia) and we hope that federal troops and the Serbian army will pull out from this region. Constitutional law on protection of the minorities has been passed and I hope it will be enforced.

It is now time to think about the future and in this general aim 'to maximize the greatest happiness' I do agree with you. There are some elements that are now more clear than before. Republics of the former Yugoslavia are separate states and, by the ruling of the arbitrary expert commission of the Hague peace conference, there is no republic or state that can claim to inherit the mantle of Yugoslavia in the sense of international law.

In this respect there is no provision for a Serbian king. And, please, once again, let me stress that the only favorable response the royal family might have is among Serbs. Princess Katherine of Serbia was in Belgrade last week at the ceremony of reconciliation between the orthodox Serbian church in the country and out of exile for the first time after 1945. She was welcomed by the crowd: 'We want the king!' I can see in your comments to my letter that you have decided not to pursue this line of political integra-tion. Now with the peace conference under Lord Carrington in Brussels I do not see a real need to have them to 'call upon Bush and Yeltsin to call for a conference'. I also doubt that Croatian politicians would agree to this kind of initiative.

I must say that I do not imply that doing anything 'that might make queen and king look good that he is willing to have the war continue if the small price one has to pay is to give them some prestige for helping to end it'. I am ready to pay a much bigger price to stop this war. But the problem is that

---

*   This section is contributed by Ivan Grdesic.

there is no feasible way to use their good will without political implications. The royal family are not you and me, that can be private persons. The king and queen are always political figures and political figures bring opposition or support. Even more so when they publicly declare their being ready to come back and be the monarchs of Serbia. And I think you still have the false impression that Croats and Slovenes have a favorable response toward them. I think that most of the people just do not care as long as this matter stays within Serbia.

There is no neutrality in the relationship between victim and aggressor. In this situation one can speak about neutrality only on an abstract level ('overall utilitarian goal') and then one has to disregard causes and consequences of the conflict, take a long time perspective. If one rises high enough on abstract level, there is ground for neutrality for everything.

I must admit that it is really very hard to 'go above traditional tradeoff reasoning'. But then we are dealing more or less with the postwar situation and the economic cooperation will come one way or another; money is the strongest force. Under this presupposition we can work on SOS in economic terms: unhindered exchange of goods, people and capital. But not in the near future with the monetary union or central banking system. Right now the only economic issue between Serbia and Croatia, on both sides, is the war reparations and damage compensation.

The economic interest of Croatia toward Serbia and other less developed states of former Yugoslavia is to expand the market for industrial production, and that can be seen as neocolonialism, as it was in the days of Yugoslavia. But the real economic interest of a Croatian service and tourism-oriented economy is the economic integration with western states through regional integration such as 'Alpe-Adria' and 'Pentagonale' (Italy, Austria, Hungary, Slovenia, Croatia). So I see this as only one of the possible ways of cooperation but probably not the primary one upon which one can build with much expectation. The best principle to provide enduring peace in this part of Europe is to recognize the existing borders, human rights and minority rights.

I think I agree with Danica about the political side of this initiative. I am not willing to join any kind of project oriented to (a) establishing any form (symbolic or 'real') of Yugoslavia (not even as a Yugoslav economic community), (b) introducing the Serbian royal family into the picture, and (c) approaching the problem in the neutrality attitude. I am willing to work on some form of post facto analysis that will be only this and not the platform for political initiative, which I do not see as a viable option.

A brief reply by S. Nagel

I do not think I need to prepare a formal response since the above ideas are quite constructive: 'we can work on SOS in economic terms: unhindered exchange of goods, people and capital [but] not in the near future'. By 'near future', Grdesic means within the next few weeks. The most immediate issue is war reparations and damage compensation. But then comes the need 'to expand the market for industrial production of Croatia' toward 'Serbia and other less developed states of former Yugoslavia', and especially for Croatia toward Germany, Italy, Austria, Hungary and Slovenia. Germany is the best place for customers, suppliers, and investment money although Grdesic did not mention Germany. Germany is also an important ally of Croatia partly because they both have a high percentage of Roman Catholics.

What Grdesic may be saying is that he likes the idea of an economic community, but one based on Yugoslavia is too small, especially since Croatia is the most prosperous unit, although tied to Slovenia, and does not want to be supporting the 'other less developed states of former Yugoslavia'. He says that those other places might view Croatia's taking the lead in an economic community as a form of neocolonialism. There is an element of snobbiness in that. I think the gulf between Croatia and Serbia is not exactly the same as the gulf between Britain and Uganda. It is about the same as the gulf between Illinois and Kentucky or Missouri. If Illinois sells products to Kentucky, they do not think that is neocolonialism.

On the other hand, Grdesic belittles Croatia's potential by overemphasizing tourism and service industries. Tourism can be a profitable business that does require sophisticated hotel management, but Croatia should have more to offer the world than some ancient museum places. Service industries are also capable of high technology. McDonald's uses the highest hamburger-making technology there probably is. Croatia is capable of getting into electronics and computers. The countries Grdesic mentions are the big players if one includes Germany and the European Union. I think I added Germany: he did not specifically mention Germany. He mentions Italy, Austria, Hungary, and Slovenia. Maybe he deliberately left Germany out because liberal Croatians have not forgiven Germany for the way it treated Croatia in World War II. The Nazis encouraged a Nazi–Croatian party called Ustache which committed atrocities against other Croatians, Yugoslavians, and Jews.

PART III
INSTITUTION BUILDING IN
DEVELOPMENTAL POLICY
STUDIES

7   Policy-making Institutions

REFORMING BRANCHES OF GOVERNMENT

Parliamentary versus presidential government

Table 7.1 involves five differently weighted goals and three alternative policies, thereby yielding a 15-cell matrix. The alternatives are parliamentary, presidential and autocratic government. The goals are multiple sources of ideas, national coordination, local responsiveness, stability and flexibility.

If the goals were equally weighted, the unweighted sums would be close to being tied. If, however, one considers national coordination and multiple sources of ideas in this context to be especially important, presidential government scores 4 points higher on the weighted sum. On the other hand, the threshold weights show that, if one considers local responsiveness and flexibility to be especially important, parliamentary government may score higher on the weighted sum. The goals favoring parliamentary government, however, have to be given more extra weight (a 5 apiece) than the goals favoring presidential government (a 2 or 3) in view of the relation scores and the fact that three of the five goals favor presidential government.

This is the fundamental political science dispute between parliamentary and presidential governments, which is applicable to all countries.

The alternatives

The conservative position is generally to support presidential government because it gives greater stability, which conservatives like. The liberal position is to support parliamentary government, largely because it is more responsive and liberals have traditionally been more interested in responsiveness, at least with regard to economic issues (although not necessarily with regard to civil liberties issues). The neutral position is to try to find a middle position, which is not so easy. (See Table 7.2.) One can make it easier to remove the president through impeachment, but that has never

Table 7.1 Evaluating alternative ways of relating legislatures to chief executives

Goals ╲ Policies	Multiple sources of ideas W=2 (-2)	National coordination W=3 (-1)	Local responsiveness W=1 (5)	Stability W=1 (-3)	Flexibility W=1 (5)	Unweighted sum	Weighted sum	Gap
Parliamentary government	3 6 (5)	3 9 (4.33)	4 (8)	3 (7)	4 (8)	17	26	
Presidential government	4 8 (2)	4 12 (2.67)	3	4	3	18	30	4
Autocratic government	1 2	5 15	(-1) 2	(0) 3	(-1) 3	14	25	

Notes:

1. Democracy involves universal adult voting rights and minority political rights. Dictatorship involves the absence of rights, or at least the absence of minority political rights.
2. Universal voting rights means all adults have the right to vote, but only one vote per person, and candidates are chosen by majority vote. Minority political rights especially refer to the right of minority viewpoints to have access to the media in order to try to convert the majority.
3. Democracy is generally defined as universal voting rights accompanied by minority political rights. Pure dictatorship involves no majority rule and no rights of minorities to convert the majority. Between these two categories are Policies 2 and 3, which involve various combinations of majority rule and minority rights.
4. With the above three goals, the policy of universal voting rights and minority political rights scores the best, even if the goals are unweighted. If the goals are weighted with more weight to multiple source of ideas and popular responsiveness, Policy 4 will win by an ever wider margin.

Notes applicable to many of the tables:

1 Each number in the center of a cell is the score of a policy on a goal on a 1–5 scale. The meaning of each 1–5 category is: 1 = highly adverse to achieving the goal; 2 = mildly adverse to achieving the goal; 3 = neither conducive nor adverse; 4 = mildly conducive to achieving the goal; and 5 = highly conducive to achieving the goal.

2 Each number to the right of the center of a cell is the weighted score. It consists of the unweighted score multiplied by the weight associated with the goal, as indicated at the top of the column. No weighted scores are shown if W=1.

3 Each number in parentheses below the center of the cell is the threshold value of the relation. If the perceived value of the relation changes upwards or downwards to the threshold value, there will be a tie between the second place (or other) alternative and the first place alternative.

4 Each number in parentheses to the right of a goal weight is the threshold value of the weight. If the perceived value of the weight changes upwards, or downwards to the threshold value, there will be a tie between the second place (or other) alternative and the first place alternative.

5 The gap at the right-hand side of the table refers to the difference between the weighted sum of the first place alternative and the weighted sum of the second place alternative. The gap is shown physically between the two weighted sums. Where all the goals have a weight of 1.00, the sum and the weighted sum are the same.

Table 7.2   Presidential versus parliamentary government

Alternatives \ Criteria	C Goal Continuity	L Goal Responsiveness	N Total (neutral weights)	L Total (liberal weights)	C Total (conservative weights)
C Alternative Presidential government	4	2	12	10	14*
L Alternative Parliamentary government	2	4	12	14*	10
N Alternative Compromise	3	3	12	12	12
SOS Alternative Right to continuous economic growth & right to upgraded work	5	5	20	20**	20**

been done. One can try to give parliamentary government more stability by saying that it takes a two-thirds vote to bring down the prime minister rather than a mere majority vote, but that has never been done. One can have a presidential government with short terms and no provision for re-election to get more responsiveness. Or one can likewise have long terms for members of parliament in order to get more stability.

The goals

The conservative goal should be referred to as continuity, not as stability. Stability sounds like stagnation. Continuity implies growth, but smooth growth rather than jerky growth. Continuity can imply change, but change in accordance with some kind of predictability based on previously developed trends. The key liberal goal is responsiveness, which is broad enough to include more than just electoral responsiveness. This could be an example of raising one's goals so as to broaden the notion of responsiveness, like broadening the notion of unemployment and also broadening the notion of continuity.

The super-optimum solution

The SOS is to say that it is not especially important whether one has a chief executive who is chosen directly by the people, or indirectly by the people through the Parliament. What is needed is a constitutional or statutory commitment on the part of the chief executive and the government in general to responsiveness and stability.

Responsiveness A responsiveness is needed that goes beyond merely reading the public opinion polls in order to get re-elected. Responsiveness in the parliamentary context instead of traditional political context has meant that it is easy to throw the government out of power. That is more a process designed to bring about responsiveness than responsiveness in itself. Responsiveness should mean such things as that the government is sensitive to people who are displaced as a result of new technologies or reduced tariffs; that is, the government is responsive to their need for new jobs. A government is much more responsive if it sees to it that displaced workers find new jobs, even though the president is a president for life and cannot be thrown out of office, than would be a government in which the prime minister can be replaced by 10 per cent of the Parliament saying they want to get rid of him. Responsiveness should mean that, when people are hurting, the government does something about it other than changing prime ministers.

Stability On the matter of stability, we do not want stagnant stability. We want continuity. We want continuous growth. Growth is change, not stability. We want statutes and constitutional provisions that will require the government, regardless of whether it consists of Republicans or Democrats, to engage in policies that guarantee about 6 per cent growth per year. We do have a 1946 Employment Act and a 1970 Humphrey–Hawkins Act that say unemployment should not get above 3 per cent, or that inflation should not get above 3 per cent, but such laws mean nothing because they provide no provision for enforcement. Worse, they provide no provision for achieving these goals. They are akin to King Canute asking the waves to stop, which can be done by the Army Corps of Engineers building appropriate dams, but not simply by issuing a 'there shalt not be' statement.

A pair of constitutional provisions

The SOS would be a set of statutes or a pair of statutes (or better yet, a pair of constitutional provisions).

Continuous economic growth   This would require 6 per cent a year continuous growth. That is a minimum. There is nothing wrong with doing
better than that, even if it is jerky (one year 10 per cent, another year 5 per
cent, another year 12 per cent). This sounds very unstable, but neither
conservatives nor liberals would object to that kind of instability. Nobody is
likely to object to their income being highly unstable with one year $1
million, the next year $20 million. When people talk about instability they
mean jumping from positive to negative, or positive to zero, but not from
very high positive to positive and back.

Upgrading skills   The second statute or constitutional right is an obligation
for displaced workers to be retrained and/or relocated. This is like two new
constitutional rights. Traditional constitutional rights have related to free
speech, equal protection and due process. Modern constitutional rights have
related to social security, minimum wage, safe workplace and, more recently, clean air. What we are proposing is a constitutional right to economic
growth and to be relocated if one is a displaced worker. On its own the word
'relocated' sounds too much like moving a person from one city to another.
We are also talking about upgrading skills so one can get a better job
without moving to another city. Instead of talking about the right to relocation, we should talk about the right to upgraded work. It is not the right to
work, a phrase that has been ruined by people who use it to mean the right
not to be in a union. A problem with the concept of the right to upgraded
work is that there is nothing in that concept that confines it to displaced
workers, although that is not necessarily bad. Perhaps all workers should
have a right to upgraded work, but especially those who have no work at all
as a result of technological change or tariff reductions. If there were really a
meaningful right to economic growth and upgrade work, that kind of SOS
would score high on continuity. To emphasize this, we need to talk about
continuous economic growth.

Making these rights meaningful

A key point is that these rights are not made meaningful merely by being
stated in statutes or constitutions. Nor are they made particularly meaningful by saying that someone who feels he has been denied one of them
can sue Congress or the president. They are made meaningful by establishing institutions like the Ministry of International Trade and Industry,
that has a mandate, a budget, personnel and sub-units that are meaning-
fully relevant to promoting continuous economic growth. One could establish a separate government agency to enforce the right to upgraded
work. The rights become meaningful when you have institutions in place

to enforce them, not just words in place in a statute or a constitution. The courts cannot enforce them. It requires specialized administrative agencies. The courts can enforce due process by reversing convictions that violate due process; they can enforce free speech and equal protection by issuing injunctions ordering the police to cease interfering with speakers or marchers, or ordering the schools to cease operating segregated classrooms; but they have no power to award well-directed subsidies or tax breaks which are needed for economic growth and upgraded work. That requires appropriate administrative agencies.

Legislative supremacy versus judicial review

Table 7.3 is a relatively simple analysis, since there are only two goals and three alternatives. The alternatives are no constitutional review, concurrent review and judicial review. The goals are popular responsiveness and sensitivity to minority rights. Having no constitutional review drops out, since it is outscored by concurrent review on both goals. There is, however, a tradeoff between concurrent review and judicial review, since concurrent review does better on popular responsiveness, but judicial review does better on sensitivity to minority rights. The table tentatively shows a weight of 3 for minority rights compared to a weight of 1 for popular responsiveness. This causes judicial review to have a higher weighted sum, by 4 points. One can see, however, that giving minority rights just slightly more weight than popular responsiveness would be enough to enable judicial review to have a higher weighted sum, since the relation scores for the two alternatives are the same in magnitude, but opposite in placement.

One useful way of doing a threshold analysis is to start with equal weights for all the goals, and then see what changes would be needed to bring the second-placed or another alternative up to a tie with the first-place alternative. That kind of analysis can be especially helpful in revealing how shaky or secure the first-place alternative is. It can also be helpful in dealing with missing information concerning a weight or relation score. It is usually much easier to decide whether a weight or a relation score is above or below a threshold value than it is to decide the exact value of a subjective weight or unclear relation.

Table 7.4 provides an example of using the P/G% software to arrive at a conclusion as to what policy ought to be adopted in light of a set of goals to be achieved. The subject matter is what is the best institutional structure for determining whether government acts comply with or violate the constitution. The table shows three alternatives. In practice, no constitutional review at all means that the chief executive can largely do as he or she

Table 7.3   Evaluating alternative ways of relating courts to legislatures–executives

Policies \ Goals	Popular responsiveness W=1 (3)	Sensitivity to minority rights W=3 (1)		Unweighted sum	Weighted sum	Gap
1 No constitutional review	3	1	3	4	6	
2 Concurrent constitutional review	4 (8)	2 (3.33)	6	6	10	
3 Judicial constitutional review	2 (–2)	4 (2.67)	12	6	14	4

Notes:
1   Under judicial review, the courts are authorized to declare legislative and executive acts unconstitutional. Under concurrent review, all three branches of government have equal responsibility for upholding the constitution.
2   Judicial review is especially important if one gives more weight to minority rights than to popular responsiveness in this context. One does not have to weight minority rights three times as much as popular responsiveness: just twice as much would mean that judicial review would have a weighted sum of 10 versus an 8 for concurrent review. The threshold weight (where they are tied) is equal weight for both goals. See also notes 1–5 below Table 7.1.

pleases. It thus means constitutional determination by the president, the king, the prime minister, the dictator or whatever the chief executive is called. This is the prevailing practice in many developing countries, in eastern Europe, and in some American states prior to the US Supreme Court's determination that the states have an obligation to comply with the federal constitution.

Concurrent constitutional review means in theory that the legislature or parliament and the courts have an equal say in determining constitutionality. In practice, it means legislative supremacy, since the legislature generally has more power to enforce its interpretation than the courts. This is the system that prevails in Great Britain and to some extent in countries that have been influenced by Britain. It is also the prevailing system in other western European democracies.

With judicial constitutional review, the courts, especially the national supreme court, have the last word on what is constitutional, regardless of the subject matter. This system exists only in the United States and to some extent in West Germany and Japan, as a result of American occupation. The

Table 7.4   Constitutional law: judicial review

Criteria / Alternatives	C Goal Popular responsiveness	L Goal Sensitivity to minority rights	N Total (neutral weights)	L Total (liberal weights)	C Total (conservative weights)
C Alternative No constitutional review	3	1	8	6	10
L Alternative Concurrent constitutional review	4	2	12	10	14*
N Alternative Judicial constitutional review	2	4	12	14*	10
SOS Alternative Sensitize legislators, administrators & public	5	5	20	20**	20**

wording of some Latin American constitutions provides for judicial review, but in practice the courts tend to bow to the will of the chief executive and the legislature.

Table 7.4 shows two key goals that are relevant to deciding among the three alternatives: popular responsiveness and sensitivity to minority rights. Each alternative policy is scored on each of those goals using a 1–5 scale. On such a scale, a 5 means highly conducive to the goal, 4 means mildly conducive, 3 means neither conducive nor adverse, 2 means mildly adverse, and 1 means highly adverse to the goal.

On the goal of popular responsiveness, concurrent review receives a higher score than the other two alternatives. This is so in view of its emphasis on legislative supremacy and democratically chosen legislatures. Judicial review receives a lower score than the other two alternatives. This is so in view of its association in the United States with a federal judiciary that is appointed for life and is thus not so responsive to public opinion. Having no constitutional review at all is generally between the other two alternatives on popular responsiveness, although some chief executives may be less or more responsive to public opinion than others.

On the goal of sensitivity to minority rights, judicial constitutional review does better than the other two alternatives. This is so because, in the American context, appointment for life has enabled federal judges to be more capable of deciding in favor of minority free speech, minority equal treatment and due process rights for people on trial who otherwise would have few rights if left to the legislatures or public opinion. This is defining minority rights in a broader sense than just rights for blacks or non-dominant ethnic groups. It is defining minority rights as being synonymous with the civil liberties aspects of free speech, equal protection and due process. On that goal, no constitutional review tends to be highly adverse, and concurrent constitutional review tends to be at least mildly adverse.

Thus we have a tradeoff problem, with some alternatives doing better on one goal and some doing better on the other. If the goals are weighted equally, the first summation column shows a tie between concurrent review and judicial review. If, however, sensitivity to minority rights is given slightly more weight than popular responsiveness, judicial review wins over concurrent review. On the other hand, if popular responsiveness is given slightly more weight than minority rights, concurrent review wins over judicial review. The weighted sum column shows the results if sensitivity to minority rights is considered more important than popular responsiveness and 'more important' is interpreted as a weight of 2, rather than a weight of 1. Under those circumstances, judicial review is the winner over both other alternatives.

The problem thus reduces to the question of which is more important, sensitivity to minority rights or popular responsiveness. One does not have to decide how much more important one goal is than the other, just which is more important. A weight of 1 for each goal can be considered a threshold weight or a tie-causing weight, because at that weight there is a tie between the two top alternatives. The question thus becomes whether the more desirable weight for sensitivity to minority rights is greater than 1 or less than 1 if popular responsiveness is anchored at a weight of 1.

This kind of analysis can be used not only for deciding among alternative public policies, but also for explaining why one policy rather than another is adopted. In this context, there are three policies to be explained. The explanations which the table generates are the following.

1   A country is likely to adopt or retain judicial review if it considers sensitivity to minority rights to be more important than popular responsiveness. That is more likely to be the case in a country that has many religions, ethnic groups and other pluralistic social divisions, as does the United States.

2   A country is likely to adopt or retain legislative supremacy if it considers

popular responsiveness to be more important than sensitivity to minority rights. That is more likely to be the case in a country that has one dominant religion and ethnic group, as England traditionally has.

3   A country is likely to adopt or retain the approach of having no constitutional review if it places a negative value on popular responsiveness and a negative value on minority rights. If both those goals are given weights of −1, the weighted summation scores are −4, −6 and −6. That makes no constitutional review the winner since −4 is a higher number than −6. This is more likely to be the case in dictatorships, where the dictator puts his or her own will ahead of public opinion, and where the dictator is insensitive to minority rights, especially free speech, but also to ethnic minority rights, as part of a possible divide-and-conquer policy.

If one were to apply the approach of removing the causes of this problem, it would mean socializing legislators and administrators to a higher sensitivity with regard to abiding by the constitution so that there would be no need for constitutional review. It should not be necessary for the courts to have to tell Congress or the president that they are violating the constitution. They should be aware of that themselves.

The problem is that they are aware, but public pressure pushes them to adopt an unconstitutional alternative. This has been the case almost every year in the 1970s and 1980s, in the state of Illinois where the Illinois legislature adopts unconstitutional abortion restrictions which every year the governor vetoes. The legislature overrides his veto, and then the courts declare the legislation unconstitutional. That happened once again in 1989, except that the legislature withdrew its appeal before the Supreme Court before even the conservative Supreme Court could uphold the lower court. On that particular issue, politics has recently changed and maybe the legislature will not do the same thing again. The conservative Republican candidate for the US Senate is strongly in favor of freedom of choice on abortion; so are the Republican candidate for governor and the Democratic candidate for governor. That may end this particular kind of unconstitutional legislation, but it does not have anything to do with unconstitutional legislation in general.

Really, the SOS is not just to sensitize legislators and administrators, but to sensitize the general public. The legislators and administrators are doing unconstitutional things because they think that is what the general public wants. In that regard, some administrators, including president George Bush, have deliberately perverted public opinion into applauding unconstitutionality. That occurred in the debate between presidential candidates George Bush and Michael Dukakis when Bush derogatorily referred to Dukakis as a card-carrying member of the ACLU (the American Civil Liberties Union).

Subsequently, ACLU literature says that, as a result of Bush's attacking card-carrying supporters of the constitution, it has now become a stigma bordering on communistic to be in favor of the Bill of Rights or the constitution. Bush has never abandoned that position. This may be one of the worst role-model examples he has provided. The ACLU is able to recruit middle-class people and intellectuals by sending them scare letters about the general public now thinking that what the ACLU stands for is communistic.

This does not solve the problem, however, for the ACLU to be able to use that to increase its membership. What was needed was for some people in the Bush administration who were known members of the ACLU to come out and say so. That would include the Attorney General, Thornburg, who was president of the Philadelphia chapter and helped to recruit a lot of members. He backed off in a very cowardly manner, though, and said that that was in his younger, more radical days (it was about five years before). The senator from Philadelphia, Arlen Spector, a mildly conservative Republican senator, is on the ACLU national board. He has never said anything against Bush's position. There are other prominent Republicans who had not encouraged Bush to be a better example. Some future president may have the courage, although it should not take that much courage to come out in favor of the Bill of Rights.

REFORMING LEVELS OF GOVERNMENT

Unitary government versus federalism

Table 7.5 is slightly more complicated. The alternatives are unitary, federal and confederate government. The goals are multiple sources of ideas, national coordination/economies of scale and local responsiveness. The goals are tentatively given weights of 2, 3 and 1, respectively, reflecting how a reasonable society might give relative weights to such goals. The raw scores for each goal are then multiplied by the relative weight or importance of the goal. The key sum is then the weighted sum, rather than the unweighted sum. Looking at the weighted sum column, federalism scores highest, followed by unitary government and then confederate government.

There are many conceptually feasible ways of filling the two-point gap between the 20 points of federalism and the 18 points of unitary government. The easiest way to explain why the second-place alternative is favored by some people is generally to look at the threshold weights, rather than the threshold relation scores. That is also generally the best way of arguing that the second-place alternative should be the first-place alternative, since the weights tend to be more subjective than the relation scores. The threshold

Table 7.5 Evaluating alternative ways of relating national governments to provinces

Goals \ Policies	Multiple sources of ideas W=2 (1)	National coordination and economies of scale W=3 (5)	Local responsiveness W=1 (–1)	Unweighted sum	Weighted sum	Gap
1 Unitary government	2 (3) 4	4 (4.67) 12	2 (4)	8	18	2
2 Federal government	4 (3) 8	3 (2.33) 9	3 (1)	10	20	
3 Confederate government	5 10	1 3	4	10	17	

Notes:

1 Under unitary government, all power goes to the national government to delegate to the provinces as it sees fit. Under confederate government, all power goes to the provinces to delegate to the national government, as they see fit. Federalism involves a constitution which specifies that some powers go to the national government and some to the provinces.

2 If national coordination were the only goal, unitary government would be best. If one adds the goals of multiple sources of ideas and local responsiveness, federal government is best even if national coordination is given the most weight.

analysis on the weights tells us that any one of three changes would bring unitary government up to a tie with federalism: (1) downgrading the weight of multiple sources of ideas from 2 to 1, (2) upgrading the weight of national coordination from 3 to 5 or (3) downgrading local responsiveness from +1 to –1. That third change, however, seems unreasonable. Perhaps the most reasonable explanation for some people favoring unitary government (other than that they are accustomed to it) is a combination of a slightly lowered value on multiple sources of ideas and a slightly increased value on national coordination.

The computer program is not only helpful in instantly indicating the threshold values even when differential weights are involved; it is also useful for testing what combination of changes in the weights will produce a tie. Various combinations can be expressed in terms of an indifference curve where two weights are involved, or in terms of a pair of indifference curves where three weights are involved. Those curves can be plotted by an advanced version of the P/G% program.

REFORMING POLITICAL PARTIES

Table 7.6 shows how a one-party, a two-party and a multiple party system score on two relevant criteria, namely choice for the voters and ability to govern effectively and efficiently. Like the system of no constitutional review, the one-party system drops out because it is outscored by the two-party system on both voter choice and effective government. Two parties tend to provide more choice than one party, although the one party may have contending factions which provide some choice. A two-party system tends to govern more effectively because the parties provide a more competitive stimulus toward greater effectiveness and efficiency than a one-party system normally provides. Multiple parties provide still more choice, but generally the least effective governing, owing to instability and lack of responsible government when no party has a majority.

One could do a threshold analysis between (1) one party and two parties, (2) two parties and multiple parties, and (3) one party and multiple parties. One could likewise do multiple threshold analyses like those with the alternatives in the tables 7.1, 7.3, 7.5, 7.6 and 7.11. One pair of alternatives, however, generally stands out as being worth comparing, usually the first- and second-place alternatives. The gap between these in Table 7.6 is only one point, which is a smaller gap than any of the other tables have. The gap would be substantially bigger if governing effectively were weighted more than choice for the voters. On the other hand, if choice were given twice the weight of governing effectively, multiple parties would be tied on desirabil-

Table 7.6 Evaluating alternative political party systems

Policies \ Goals	Choice for the voters W=1 (2)	Ability to govern effectively and efficiently W=1 (0.5)	Sum	Gap
1 One-party system	2	3	5	
2 Two parties or two blocks	4 (3)	4 (3)	8	
3 Multiple parties	5 (6)	2 (3)	7	1

Notes:
1 Multiple parties provide more choices, but too much diffusion of responsibility.
2 One party-systems provide virtually no choice except between party factions. They are also less likely to govern well without the stimulus which party competition provides.
3 The two-party bloc provides both choice and a competitive stimulus to more effective and efficient government.
4 The two goals here are approximately equal in importance.

ity with the two-party system. That might explain why some political systems favor multiple parties: the society wants more diverse choice and is willing to sacrifice some effective governing.

REFORMING POLITICAL COMMUNICATION FROM INTEREST GROUPS AND PUBLIC OPINION

As for the free speech element of democracy, there are a number of points that can be made in favor of minority rights to convert the majority as being conducive to societal productivity. In matters of science, the free circulation of popular, unpopular and extremely unpopular ideas allows the truth to have a better chance of being accepted. A dramatic example of a dictatorial society being severely damaged by restricting freedom of scientific speech was Nazi Germany with regard to the development of nuclear weapons. In the 1930s, Einstein physics was looked upon by Hitler as Jewish physics and not to be encouraged. As a result, Nazi Germany lost time in the development of nuclear energy and weapons. In the meantime, Einstein helped persuade President Roosevelt to develop the atomic weapons that helped the United States win World War II. That was a high opportunity cost for Nazi Germany to pay. A dramatic example of a dictatorial socialistic society being severely damaged by restricting freedom of speech was Communist Russia with regard to development of hybrid grains. In the 1950s, Mendelian genetics was looked upon by Stalin as Catholic biology and not to be encouraged. As a result, the Soviet Union encouraged an approach of growing crops that emphasized providing a good environment more than good genes. Environmentalism was in conformity with Stalin's interpretation of Marxism. Those were the years in which the Soviet Union declined from being the bread-basket of Europe to an importer of foreign grains, to the substantial detriment of its economy and its international trade, from which it still may not have fully recovered.

In matters of policy rather than science, freedom of speech allows the most effective means in achieving given ends to have a better chance of being adopted. A dramatic example of this from within the United States is the prohibition on advocating the abolition of slavery, which existed in the South in the 1800s prior to the civil war. Those restrictions on a minority viewpoint may have helped delay the conversion of the southern economy from a slave economy to a free economy, and that delay may have facilitated the occurrence of the civil war. More importantly, the legacy of prolonged slavery was probably a key factor in holding back the South for many years after the civil war. Even now, the legacy of prolonged slavery may be a key factor responsible for at least some of the race relations problems of the United States. The occurrence of slavery is highly correlated with having a relatively unproductive, inefficient economy that provides little incentive for introducing modern labor-saving technology that can greatly raise standards of living. The poorest parts of the world are those that practise slavery, serfdom, peonage and related forms of human bondage, and that generally place restrictions on advocating alternative economic systems.

Freedom of speech also provides a check on leadership that is corrupt, inefficient and not complying with the legal system. The US Supreme Court has recognized in some of its opinions that freedom of speech may be the most important right in the Bill of Rights. The other rights are less meaningful if one cannot inform others that the rights are being violated. Even the dictatorial Soviet Union at the height of the Stalin era encouraged people to speak out against corrupt and inefficient leadership, at least at the lower and middle leadership levels, so long as the basic principles of communism were not attacked. The government has provided a subsidized periodical called *Krokodil* that carries articles and reports critical of bureaucrats who are not properly carrying out five-year plans and other Soviet policies.

Free speech is indirectly responsible for higher standards of living to the extent that free speech promotes scientific discovery and dissemination, more effective means toward given societal goals and more effective governmental personnel. Some of the positive correlation is also due to the reciprocal fact that higher standards of living create a more tolerant middle class, which allows still more freedom of speech.

Some critics of free speech argue that it leads to political instability and revolution. The empirical data tend to show just the opposite relation. This relation is partly attributable to the fact that free speech facilitates non-violent change, particularly by providing more peaceful outlets through which potential revolutionaries can make themselves heard and win converts without resorting to revolution. The positive relation between free speech and non-violent change is also partly attributable to the fact that free speech and non-violent change are partly co-effects of having a large tolerant middle class. The correlation between permissiveness and stability, however, is not as high as the correlation between permissiveness and modernity.

Policies toward lobbies or political action groups

The conservative alternative for dealing with lobbies or political action groups has traditionally been to have unrestricted spending and unreported spending. That accords with conservative opposition to government regulation and also with the fact that political action groups tend to be disproportionately conservative. The liberal alternative has been to have restrictions on spending and also to have reporting requirements. The neutral compromise favors required reporting, but not restrictions on spending.

Relevant goals include creativity and equality. As with virtually all the goals in SOS analysis, they are favored by both conservatives and liberals, since they are positive goals. Liberals, however, tend to emphasize equality more than conservatives. Conservatives, on the other hand, tend to emphasize creativity, especially entrepreneurial creativity, more than liberals. This is a classic tradeoff or symmetrical tradeoff situation. The conservative alternative produces relatively positive results on the conservative goal, but negative results on the liberal goal. The liberal alternative produces relatively negative results on the conservative goal, but positive results on the liberal goal. The neutral alternative produces middling results on both goals.

The SOS alternative of government funding of elections achieves more equality than a system of broad spending restrictions and reporting that are difficult to enforce. Government funding also allows for considerable creativity, assuming the funding is large enough for creative advertising. The creativity of political advertising is more in the ideas than in the expensive repetition.

In light of the relation scores, the conservative alternative wins on the conservative totals, and the liberal alternative wins on the liberal totals, before considering the SOS alternative. Government funding of elections wins overall on both totals, even if its creativity and equality scores are lowered slightly. The reason for government funding of elections not being more widely adopted is partly the conservative goal of favoring conservative political action committees, as mentioned above, although that goal is not explicitly included in Table 7.7. Government funding of elections has been adopted in the United States only when there was a big enough campaign spending scandal, like the Watergate scandal, which resulted in government funding of presidential elections. Once such reforms are adopted, it is difficult for politicians to reverse them and reinstitute a system of heavy private-sector campaign contributions. Unfortunately, the undesirability of relying so strongly on such campaign contributions may have to increase before SOS reforms can be adopted.

Table 7.7 Evaluating policies toward lobbies

Criteria Alternatives	C Goal Creativity	L Goal Equality	N Total (neutral weights)	L Total (liberal weights)	C Total (conservative weights)
C Alternative Unrestricted & unreported spending	4	2	12	10	14*
L Alternative Spending restrictions & reporting	2	4	12	14*	10
N Alternative Reporting but no spending restrictions	3	3	12	12	12
SOS Alternative Government funding of elections	5	5	20	20**	20**

Public opinion

Table 7.8 is a policy analysis table showing alternative ways of dealing with freedom of speech on the rows, goals on the columns, relations between alternatives and goals in the cells, and overall totals at the far right. The conservative alternative involves restricted free speech. The liberal alternative involves virtually unrestricted free speech. The neutral or compromise alternative, as adopted by the US Supreme Court, involves some restrictions where conflicting constitutional rights are involved, such as (1) restrictions on campaign spending under the equal treatment clause, (2) restrictions on newspaper reporting of pending trials under the due process clause, and (3) restrictions on defaming non-public figures as part of one's right to privacy.

The super-optimum solution emphasizes (1) free speech for business, including the right to advertise low prices and better quality than one's competitors; (2) free speech for labor, including the right to recruit union members and publicize management wrongdoing; (3) government-subsidized access to mass media, such as equal free TV time for political candidates and requirements that cable TV owners make time available for minority interest groups; and (4) more education and socialization at the elementary–secondary levels regarding the value of free speech for both conservative and liberal viewpoints.

REFORMING ELECTORAL PROCEDURES

Voter registration and turnout and SOS solutions

Table 7.9 applies super-optimum solutions analysis to the electoral reform problem of voter registration and turnout. See section on Electoral Reform in Part I, Chapter 4. The conservative alternative is to leave the procedures the way they are. The liberal alternative is to facilitate easier registration, especially through registration by postcard, as proposed by the Democrats in the House and the Senate in 1990. The neutral or compromise position is milder reforms that relate to such matters as allowing registration in the precincts (as contrasted to having to go to city hall) and providing for permanent registration (as contrasted to periodically requiring reregistration).

Three goals in particular are mentioned in discussing the alternatives. One is preventing non-eligibles from registering and voting. A second goal is to keep the tax costs down for whatever system of registration and voting is adopted. A third is decreasing the number of eligibles who do not register and vote. Conservatives are especially sensitive to the goal of blocking non-eligibles. Liberals are especially sensitive to the goal of facilitating participation by eligibles. Keeping the cost down is a relatively neutral goal.

There is a tradeoff present, in that leaving things as they are tends to block *non*-eligibles but also interferes with eligibles registering and voting. Postcard registration, on the other hand, could result in more *non*-eligibles

Table 7.8 Evaluating ways of handling freedom of speech

Criteria / Alternatives	C Goal Government stability	L Goal More creative ideas	L Goal More constructive criticism of government	N Goal More DP, EP & privacy	N Goal Lower tax costs	N Goal Political or constitutional feasibility	N Total (neutral weights)	L Total (liberal weights)	C Total (conservative weights)
C Alternative Restricted free speech	2	2	2	3	3	2	28	30	26
L Alternative Unrestricted free speech	2	4	4	2	3	2	34	40	28
N Alternative Some restrictions for EP, DP & privacy	3	3	3	4	3	3	38	41*	35*
SOS Alternative Free speech for Business & Labor, with access to mass media	4	5	5	3	2	3	44	50**	38**

Notes:

1 The neutral position does well on both the liberal totals and conservative totals, better than a more liberal or conservative position. This may be so because free speech is not an issue that divides liberals and conservatives the way economic issues do.

2 A policy that involves government funding and facilities for minority viewpoints would facilitate creative ideas and constructive criticism of government, but it seems politically unfeasible since the Supreme Court does not require it and a majoritarian Congress is not so likely to appropriate funds. The closest provision is probably requiring radio and TV stations to give minority parties free time when the major parties receive free time, and likewise with federal presidential funding, provided that the minority parties are substantial.

3 Unlimited free speech would allow invasions of privacy, prejudicial pre-trial publicity and unlimited campaign expenditures, which neither the courts nor Congress endorse. Those rights of privacy, due process and minimum equality in political campaigning are the fundamental rights which allow free speech limitations under Alternative 3.

4 Examples of limitations under Alternative 1 include pornography, libel, false pretenses and advocacy that leads to physical harm. All these free speech exceptions have been substantially limited over the last 20 or so years.

245

Table 7.9   Evaluating policies toward voting registration and turnout

Criteria / Alternatives	C Goal Reduce non-eligible registration & voting	N Goal Reduce tax cost	L Goal Increase registration & voting	N Total (neutral weights)	L Total (liberal weights)	C Total (conservative weights)	L Goal Increase Democratic voters	C Goal Increase Republican voters	N Total (neutral weights)	L Total (liberal weights)	C Total (conservative weights)
C Alternative Leave as is	4	4	2	20	18	22*	2	4	32	28	36**
L Alternative Postcard registration	3	2	4.5	19	20.5*	17.5	4	2	31	34.5*	27.5
N Alternative Precinct, registration, permanent registration	3	2	4	18	19	17	3	3	30	31	29
SOS Alternative On site or census & vote anywhere	3	4	5	24	26**	22**	4	2	36	40**	32

Notes:

1 The first set of totals involves only working with the first three non-partisan goals. The second three totals involve working with all five goals, including the two partisan goals.

2 The super-optimum solution wins on both the liberal and conservative totals when the first three non-partisan goals are used. The super-optimum solution loses on the conservative total when the two partisan goals are added.

registering, but it does facilitate eligibles doing so. The middling alternatives of precinct registration and permanent registration have middling relation scores.

The super-optimum solution might be to allow on-site registration, whereby voters register at the time they arrive to vote. The SOS package might also include voting at any polling location that is convenient. That system would facilitate more registration and voting than the liberal alternative of postcard registration. It would do worse than the present system with regard to blocking non-eligibles, but probably not very much worse. This is so partly because crooked politicians do not win elections by arranging for non-eligibles to register and vote. Rather, they win elections by stuffing the ballot boxes, miscounting the vote, lying to the voters or using other easier methods.

The conservative alternative wins on the conservative total, before considering the SOS alternative. Likewise the liberal alternative wins on the liberal total. The SOS alternative, however, wins on both totals, making it an SOS alternative. The liberal total involves giving the liberal goal a weight of 3, the conservative goal a weight of 1 and the neutral goal a weight of 2. The conservative total involves giving the liberal goal a weight of 1, the conservative goal a weight of 3 and the neutral goal a weight of 2.

Columns 8 and 9 help explain why the SOS alternative has not been adopted. A big part of the answer is that Republican members of the House and Senate perceive electoral reforms that facilitate registration and voting as disproportionately resulting in more votes for Democratic candidates. As a result, when the goals of increasing Democratic voters or Republican voters are taken into consideration, the conservative alternative then wins over the SOS alternative on the conservative totals.

Perhaps more Republican legislators could be persuaded to vote in favor of electoral reform if they were to recognize that the non-voters are disproportionately young people. Those people are now leaning more toward Republican national candidates than they have in the past. This is partly because they have only known Republican presidents since 1968, with the somewhat uninspirational exception of Democratic President Carter. Perhaps a more realistic way of getting the SOS alternative adopted is to wait until the political cycle brings the Democrats sufficiently into power. Once the reforms are made, the Republicans are not likely to be able to change them back without appearing to be disenfranchising voters.

Legislative redistricting

Table 7.10 indicates that the conservative alternative is to provide as many safe Republican districts as possible in legislative redistricting. The liberal

Table 7.10   Evaluating policies toward legislative redistricting

Criteria / Alternatives	L Goal Proportionality	C Goal Competitiveness	N Total (neutral weights)	L Total (liberal weights)	C Total (conservative weights)
C Alternative Safe Republican districts	2	2	8	8	8
L Alternative Safe Democratic districts	2	2	8	8	8
N Alternative Randomized districts	2	2	8	8	8
SOS Alternative Proportional & competitive districts	5	5	20	20**	20**

alternative is to provide as many safe Democratic districts as possible. The neutral or compromise alternative is to randomize the allocation of districts so that effects on Republican and Democratic representation are ignored.

There are two key goals involved. Liberals tend to be especially sensitive to equity or proportionality. Conservatives tend to be relatively more sensitive to the idea of competition, although more so in the marketplace than in the voting place. Concentrating on having safe Republican districts receives at least a mildly negative score on both goals. Likewise, concentrating on having safe Democratic districts also gets negative scores. Randomizing the districts is not as likely to produce proportionality or competitiveness as deliberately trying through computerized redistricting to maximize or at least achieve proportionality and competitiveness.

If there were ten districts and 60 per cent of the voters are Democrats and 40 per cent are Republicans, then one could set aside six districts for all the Democrats and four districts for all the Republicans. That would give proportionality but not competitiveness. One could arrange for nine of the districts each to have 50 per cent Democrats and 50 per cent Republicans, and then put all the remaining Democrats in the tenth district. That would give a lot of competitiveness, but could result in bad proportionality if the wind is blowing in either a Democratic or Republican direction on election day.

It is possible with computerized redistricting to move the precincts (or building blocks out of which the districts are made) in such a way as to obtain as high a composite score on proportionality and competitiveness as possible. Proportionality can be measured by deviation from the Democrats dominating 60 per cent of the districts. Competitiveness can be measured by deviation from the average district being 50 per cent Democrats and 50 per cent Republicans. The composite score would be the multiplied product of those two deviations. One would multiply (rather than add) to obtain the composite score because two different scales are involved.

We do not have SOS redistricting like that largely because redistricting tends to be controlled by incumbent legislators who prefer to get re-elected from safe districts, rather than have proportionality or competitiveness. Sometimes the courts are involved in redistricting and demand more objectively, but usually only with regard to equal population per district. As the courts become more concerned with political malapportionment in addition to population malapportionment, SOS redistricting may become a more realistic alternative.

REFORMING DEMOCRACY

Benefits and costs

Democracy includes both majority rule and minority rights to try to convert the majority to minority viewpoints. As for the former element, there are a number of points that can be made in favor of majority rule as being conducive to societal productivity. People almost genetically have a desire to exert control over their destinies. Democracy gives them at least the feeling that they are playing some part in controlling the government. Democracy thereby tends to make people feel happier in that regard, assuming all other things are held constant. The more people participate in government and politics, the greater is the leadership pool and the innovation potential. Thus, if an individual with valuable ideas and leadership qualities is in one of the disenfranchised groups in a society that does not enfranchise virtually all adult groups, that person's abilities may not be put to good use.

A democratic form of government is more efficient because if it is not, it can be more easily voted out of office. A government that is not subject to being removed by majority rule may be less likely to improve itself. It may change only by shifting office holders through the equivalent of palace revolutions, but not change in terms of basic principles.

A democratic government in the hands of the people more quickly finds out about complaints, and it can thus better remedy the source of those complaints. By remedying those complaints and thereby obtaining more popular support, society is likely to have a more productive population than one that feels antagonistic toward the government and society. Democratic governments tend to rely on an educated citizenry in order to function well, but they also tend to encourage citizens to become more politically enlightened by providing them with learning experiences through participating in governmental activities, especially at the local level.

Democracies are sometimes criticized because they move more slowly in making decisions by virtue of their governmental structures, which require more approval by representatives of the people. That delay may, however, be more than justified if the decisions reached are more effective and efficient than they otherwise would be. Democracies are also sometimes criticized because majoritarian rule can mean a lot of authority giving to those who lack expert knowledge, a favorable orientation toward new ideas or favorable attitude toward being especially productive. That may be a largely irrelevant point, though, if the leadership does tend to be reasonably knowledgeable, receptive toward innovation and oriented toward societal productivity.

Tabular analysis

Table 7.11 evaluates alternative ways of relating government to the electorate. The ways involve two dimensions. One relates to whether or not there are universal voting rights for all adults regardless of ethnic groups, gender, economic class, region or other characteristics not relevant to being able to choose candidates who reflect one's interests. The second dimension relates to whether there are minority political rights, especially the right to try to convert the majority to minority viewpoints. The relevant societal goals include (1) multiple sources of ideas, (2) popular responsiveness, and (3) fast, unquestioned decisions. The numbers in each cell show how each policy alternative scores on each goal using a 1–5 scoring system. Under such a system, a 1 means the policy is highly adverse to achieving the goal, a 2 means mildly adverse, a 3 means neither adverse nor conducive, a 4 means mildly conducive and a 5 means highly conducive to achieving the goal.

If one sums across the tentative scores for each alternative, one observes that dictatorship receives a summation score of only 6 points, whereas democracy receives 12 points. A useful question to ask is what it would take to bring dictatorship up to the desirability level of democracy: that is, what it would take to cover the 6-point gap between their two sums. In parentheses are the threshold values for the relation scores and the weights which would be

Table 7.11 Evaluating alternative ways of relating government to the electorate

Goals / Policies	Multiple sources of ideas W=1 (-0.5)	Popular responsiveness W=1 (-0.5)	Fast, unquestioned decisions W=1 (4)	Sum	Gap
1 No universal voting rights and no minority political rights	1 (7)	1 (7)	4 (10)	6	
2 Universal voting rights, but no minority political rights	2	4	3	9	
3 Minority political rights, but no universal voting rights	4	1	3	8	6
4 Universal voting rights and minority political rights	5 (-1)	5 (-1)	2 (-4)	12	

Notes:

1 Democracy involves universal adult voting rights and minority political rights. Dictatorship involves the absence of both kinds of rights, or at least the absence of minority political rights.

2 Universal voting rights means all adults have the right to vote, but only one vote per person, and candidates are chosen by majority vote. Minority political rights especially refer to the right of minority viewpoints to have access to the media in order to try to convert the majority.

enough to bring the dictatorship alternative up to 12 points. All those values are impossible to achieve on a 1–5 scale for the relations scores. For example, if dictatorship could receive a score of 7 on multiple sources of ideas, that would fill the gap, but 5 is the maximum score possible.

Likewise, if multiple sources of ideas were to receive a negative weight of –0.5, then there would be a tie because dictatorship would receive a summation score of 5 minus 0.5, and democracy would receive a score of 7 minus 2.5. They would thus be tied at 4.5 apiece. It is unreasonable to think a society would place a negative value on multiple sources of ideas. The input item that seems most subject to enough reasonable change to result in a tie is the weight of fast, unquestioned decisions. If that goal is given a weight of 4, while the other goals have weights of 1, then there will be a tie. Thus people who support dictatorship rather than democracy may do so because they highly value fast, unquestioned decisions and place relatively little value on multiple sources of ideas or popular responsiveness. That analysis may also explain why in wartime (when fast, unquestioned decisions are needed more), democracies tend to institute restrictions on free speech and criminal procedure.

Democratic competition

The East German economy has been a relative failure compared to the West German economy since World War II. This has been used as a factor to show the superiority of capitalism over socialism. Some contrary evidence is the fact that the Swedish socialistic economy has flourished since World War II in spite of relatively few people and resources. The Spanish capitalistic economy has been a much greater failure than the East German socialistic economy since World War II. One can get much greater predictability out of knowing whether a society has a competitive economy and political system (versus a monopolistic one) than out of knowing whether it is a capitalistic private–ownership economy (or a socialistic government–ownership economy).

Both East Germany and Spain have been failures in terms of providing high standards of living for their people. They both have one-party monopolistic political systems, although one was communist and the other was fascist. They both have monopolistic economic systems which try to keep out foreign goods through high tariffs, with government–favored business firms, although one had government–owned firms and the other had privately–owned firms.

Both West Germany and Sweden have been successes in terms of providing high standards of living for their people. They both have competitive political systems, with strong two-party competition, whereby the out-party is constantly trying to offer better ideas than the in-party. They both encourage competition among business firms and allow foreign competition. Thus comparing East Germany and West Germany does point to ways in which public policy can improve the quality of life, but it is a public policy that encourages competition over monopoly, not necessarily one that encourages capitalism over socialism.

Table 7.12 shows that political and economic competition relate to a high degree of prosperity. Both kinds of competition have been present in prosperous West Germany and Sweden. Until relatively recently, both kinds of competition have been absent in relatively impoverished East Germany and Spain.

REFORMING CONSTITUTIONAL RIGHTS OF MINORITIES

Race

Equal treatment under the law in the American context mainly relates to prohibitions on ethnic group discrimination, particularly discrimination against blacks. Discrimination refers to denying someone, because of his or her race, various opportunities for which they would otherwise be qualified. Discrimination can take many forms, including governmental discrimination, with regard to criminal procedure, school access and voting, or private discrimination, with regard to housing, public accommodations and employment. A form of discrimination exists when the dominant group forces segregation or involuntary separation on the minority group, but not when minority group members voluntarily choose to live together or to be distinctive. What are the effects of discrimination on the whole society, particularly the dominant racial group, not just the group discriminated against?

Discrimination probably has a substantial effect on decreasing the gross national product by failing to make full use of the actual and potential skills that blacks have. Long-established discrimination by the building trade unions is a good example. Likewise, housing discrimination may prevent qualified blacks from living where there are suburban job openings to which they might otherwise lack meaningful access. Past school discrimination and inferior black school facilities greatly lessen the chances that potential black professionals will achieve their potential.

Another kind of societal economic effect comes from segregated school and housing facilities. Segregated school systems may involve duplicate costs, as with the special Texas black law school or the Tennessee black medical school, which were established with only a few students to avoid

Table 7.12   Political and economic competition as key causes of prosperity

		Competition (Causal variable)	
		No (in politics and economics)	Yes (in politics and economics)
Prosperity or high standard of living (Effect variable)	Yes		West Germany (capitalism) Sweden (socialism)
	No	East Germany (socialism) Spain, Pre-1980 (capitalism)	

Notes:
1 The table only includes industrial nations. A separate table could be made for developing nations.
2 Among industrialized nations, those that provide for competition in politics and economics have more prosperity than those which do not provide for competition in both activities. Industrialized nations that provide for competition is only one of the two activities are likely to have middling prosperity, although competition in politics may be more important to prosperity than competition in economics.
3 The table is mainly designed to relate political and economic competition as key causes in prosperity. One could also interpret it as tending to show that countries that have economic competition are more likely to have political competition and vice versa.
4 One could also interpret the table as tending to show that industrialized nations are more likely to have a higher standard of living than non-industrialized nations, regardless of political and economic competition.
5 A final conclusion which the table generates is that whether a country has capitalistic private ownership or socialistic government ownership is virtually irrelevant to prosperity in comparison to political–economic competition and industrialization.

integrating white southern universities, although these two schools may have recently become economically viable institutions. Segregated housing patterns combined with employment discrimination can lead to ghetto slums with their disproportionately high costs for police, fire protection and welfare recipients. These unnecessarily high costs of segregation should especially worry conservative taxpayers.

Discrimination against a minority group frequently has a depressive effect on weaker members of the majority group. Thus low wages paid to blacks tend to keep down the wages of whites in occupations that blacks might enter. Black strike-breaking labor can also deter more aggressiveness on the part of white unions. Likewise, depressed standards of police behavior in dealing with blacks are sometimes hard to change when the police deal with whites, especially poor whites.

Psychologically speaking, discrimination against blacks can create a false sense of superiority on the part of some whites. This may partly account for the lack of education and occupational ambition of many white southerners who have their race to fall back on to compensate for their lack of education and job status. Discrimination can also cause guilt feelings and anxieties on the part of whites, especially if their behavior and attitudes toward blacks conflict with democratic ideals that are preached in their society, thereby creating the American dilemma. Discrimination can, of course, have severe psychologically disturbing effects on blacks, but the emphasis in this impact analysis is on the effects on the whole society in general and the majority whites in particular.

With regard to US foreign and military policy, domestic discrimination decreases the ability of the United States to win influence in Africa, Asia and Latin America. Domestic discrimination may also decrease the morale of blacks in the armed forces, especially in a war against non-Caucasian people, and it may increase interracial friction within the armed forces, as indicated by numerous clashes in the late 1960s.

An especially important effect of discrimination is the antagonism and hatred that it generates on the part of blacks toward whites. Such emotional incidents can flare up into intra-ghetto riots and possibly eventually into inter-neighborhood riots. Discrimination also divides whites themselves – between those who advocate faster removal of discriminatory barriers and those who advocate retention or slower removal. This intra-white hostility sometimes manifests itself in student and other youthful protest activities.

Miscellaneous effects of discrimination include the loss of new manufacturing developments by discriminatory communities, which business executives consider to have an undesirable environment for raising their families. Discrimination by reducing black income can also reduce black consumer purchasing power, thereby hurting white business concerns. Finally, the presence of discrimination often deters non-discriminatory behavior on the part of whites who do not want to discriminate, but who feel compelled to comply with what they perceive to be the dominant viewpoint unless the dominant viewpoint is made illegal by anti-discrimination legislation.

In addition to mentioning various phenomena that behavioral scientists tend to agree are effects of discrimination, some alleged effects that have no scientific acceptance should also be mentioned. For example, the ab- sence of discrimination may lead to increased inter-marriage. No accepted biological study has supported the view that the children of a racially mixed marriage are in any sense biologically defective. In fact, lessening the skin color purity of the races may bring a lessening of friction between them. In addition, the children of a racially mixed marriage are likely to have access to more societal opportunities than children of a wholly black background.

It is sometimes alleged that integrating schools will have the effect of lowering the learning level of white students without necessarily raising the level of black students. The Coleman Report, however, tends to show that economic class integration or racial integration along class lines (poor blacks with middle-class whites, poor whites with middle-class blacks, poor blacks with middle-class blacks, or poor whites with middle-class whites) does not generally lower the learning level of middle-class children but does raise the learning level of the poorer children.

Some whites in more frank moments correctly allege that their jobs would be in jeopardy if discrimination barriers were dropped. In this regard, dropping discrimination against blacks is like dropping tariff discrimination against foreign products. It may mean a temporary relocation of marginal less-efficient employees, but the total national economy benefits from the lowered consumer prices and from the more efficient use of its labor. Like- wise, in the long run, removing inefficient racial discrimination can raise the gross national product, decrease government costs attributable to slums and duplicative facilities, increase depressed wages, make for more efficient geographical allocation of industry, and increase consumer purchasing power, as has been previously mentioned.

Although this discussion of equal protection under the law has empha- sized racial discrimination, many of the same social consequences described would apply to much of the discrimination that is based on sex, religion, ancestral nationality, economic class or other characteristics that usually lack sufficient correlation with ability to be meaningful criteria for allocat- ing employment and other social opportunities.

Table 7.13 is a policy analysis table showing alternative ways of dealing with race relations on the rows, goals on the columns, relations between alternatives and goals in the cells, and overall totals at the far right. A conservative alternative is to have no affirmative action in hiring or educa- tion admissions, but to outlaw discrimination. The liberal alternative is to allow for preferential hiring of minorities. The neutral or compromise alter- native, as adopted by the US Supreme Court, is to allow for temporary preferential hiring where firms or government agencies had previously been guilty of racism, until a balance is provided.

Table 7.13   Alternative public policies toward race relations

Policies / Goals	Stimulating minority advancement	Always favoring the one with the higher score	Never favoring one who is unqualified	Sum
1 Requiring segregation or discrimination C2	1	1	1	3
2 Allowing discrimination (same as doing nothing) C1	2	2	2	6
3 Outlawing discrimination N	4	4	4	12
4 Requiring affirmative action L1	5	4	4	13*
5 Requiring preferential hiring L2	4	2	4	10
6 Allowing reverse racism L3	2	2	2	6

Notes:
1   Discrimination in this context means requiring or allowing a white with a score of 40 to be preferred over a black with a score of 60, where 50 is the minimum score for one who is qualified, or where both are qualified but the white is preferred even though the black applicant is substantially more qualified.
2   Affirmative action in this context means only hiring blacks who are qualified, but actively seeking qualified blacks through (a) advertising, (b) locating one's physical plant, (c) removing requirements that are racially correlated, but not correlated with job performance, and (d) providing on-the-job training for all, but especially to overcome lack of training of blacks.
3   Preferential hiring means only hiring blacks who are qualified, but preferring qualified blacks over moderately less qualified whites, generally as a temporary measure to offset prior discrimination.
4   Reverse racism is the same as discrimination, except blacks are favored.
5   The summation column tends to indicate that the optimum policy for achieving the desired goals is to move away from discrimination to requiring affirmative action, but not to requiring preferential hiring, except as a short-term remedy for prior discrimination.

The super-optimum solution where everyone comes out ahead is to emphasize the upgrading of skills of minority members so that they can qualify for better job opportunities without needing preferential hiring. The upgrading of skills can occur as part of elementary–secondary education (K–12), on-the-job-training (OJT) and special opportunities industrialization centers (OIC), which train functionally illiterate people in such basic skills as the completing of employment applications.

Ethnic groups

Dealing with relatively low-income ethnic groups in Russia and elsewhere

There are two conservative positions toward minority ethnic groups. One is to force assimilation so as to make the group disappear; the other is to allow the group to preserve its culture, but discriminate against members of the group with regard to employment and educational opportunities. There are basically two liberal positions toward minority ethnic groups. One is to allow voluntary separatism; the other is to give minority group members affirmative action or preferences regarding employment or educational opportunities.

The professed conservative goal is judging people on the basis of their merit. Any policy that discriminates or shows preference runs contrary to that goal. Separatism also decreases the ability of minority members to move into positions in the larger society for which they can qualify. The professional liberal goal is equity or fairness across the minority and majority groups, and also responsiveness to the desires of both groups. Policies that repress minority cultures are not responsive to their desires. The policies that discriminate or show preferences are lacking in equity, at least in the long run.

The SOS alternative is to upgrade the skills of members of low-income ethnic groups so they can better qualify for employment and educational opportunities without preferences or affirmative action. They are also more likely to want to be part of a larger society if they can qualify for better opportunities. See Table 7.14.

SOME CONCLUSIONS: SUPER-OPTIMUM PERSPECTIVES ON IMPROVING GOVERNMENT

Something should be said about the way democracy, federalism, judicial review, separation of powers and the two-party system appeal to both liberals and conservatives. As regards democracy, liberals like the majoritarian element partly because it means economic liberalism. They like the elements of free speech especially for liberal ideas. Conservatives like the majoritarian element partly because it means conservatism on civil liberties

Table 7.14 Dealing with relatively low-income ethnic groups in Russia and elsewhere

Goals Alternatives	C Goal Merit	L Goal Equity and responsiveness	N Total (neutral weights)	L Total (liberal weights)	C Total (conservative weights)
C1 Alternative Repress culture	4	2	12	10	14*
C2 Alternative Discriminate	2	2	8	8	8
L1 Alternative Autonomous voluntary separatism	2	4	12	14*	10
L2 Alternative Preferences	2	2	8	8	8
N Alternative Encourage integration, but preserve culture	3	3	12	12	12
Non-preferential affirmative action	2	2	8	8	8
SOS Alternative Upgrade skills	>3.5	>3.5	>14	>14**	>14**

matters. They like the elements of free speech especially for conservative ideas.

Liberals like federalism as an improvement on a confederate form of government, but also to provide multiple sources of liberal ideas. Conservatives like federalism as an improvement on a unitary form of government, but also to provide multiple sources of conservative ideas. Liberals like judicial review for protecting free speech, equal protection and due process. Conservatives like judicial review for protecting property rights and also free speech, equal protection and due process in the business context.

Liberals like separation of powers because it enables a relatively liberal president to succeed over a conservative Congress. It also provides multiple sources of liberal ideas. Conservatives like separation because it enables a relatively conservative president to succeed over a liberal Congress. It also provides multiple sources of conservative ideas.

Finally, as regards the two-party system, liberals like it because they like the liberal side of the system, while conservatives like it because they like the conservative side of the system.

On the matter of improving government structures, that mainly means attracting good people to government jobs, both elected and appointed. One thing about super-optimum solutions is that a lot of good people could be attracted to government and public policy positions by the excitement of doing innovative, super-optimum things. This can be contrasted to a traditional image of government as being stodgy and bureaucratic, and behind the private sector with regard to developing new ideas.

The government structures the United States has are more conducive to prosperous business than almost any alternative, regardless of how much complaining business does about them. To a considerable extent, American productivity is due to American democracy. There are a lot of factors, but that is one of the most important. When we talk about super-optimum solutions, we are generally not talking about changing the way the president is elected or the structure of Congress or the Supreme Court. Those are almost givens that are too difficult to change, since they require constitutional amendments. Even if there were better ways of electing the president, it is not worth expending a lot of effort changing the system, and likewise with the courts and Congress. We are better off concentrating on improving the way in which we deal with other economic, social and technological policy problems within the existing constitutional structure.

8   Policy Analysis Institutions

INSTITUTIONALIZING IMPROVED POLICY ANALYSIS

It is one thing to talk about the desirability of super-optimizing policy analysis. It is another thing to talk about establishing or improving a set of institutions for more effectively arriving at super-optimum solutions in public policy analysis. The discussion below is also applicable to institutionalizing improved policy analysis that seeks to find the best alternative, combination or allocation among various alternatives without necessarily arriving at super-optimum solutions.

In Table 8.1 there are five activities listed on the columns: training, research, funding, publishing and associations. There are three basic institutions listed along the rows, consisting of universities, independent institutes or private-sector entities, and government agencies. There are also three basic concepts on the lower rows, consisting of trends, examples from developing nations and SOS solutions for synthesizing the work of the three basic institutions on each of the five policy analysis activities.

Five policy analysis activities and three institutions

The first column deals with *training*. The cells within each column emphasize what each institution can do best on the activity that is associated with the column. On the matter of training, universities are best on career preparation. That includes university programs in public policy, public administration, political science or another social science where the program is geared toward training practitioners or academics who will spend a substantial amount of their time evaluating alternative public policies or other forms of policy analysis. Government agencies are especially good at on-the-job training (OJT). An example would be a training program within the Department of Housing and Urban Development to teach policy analysts or other HUD employees how to evaluate applications for urban development grants or alternative public housing proposals. Independent entities are those

Table 8.1 Institutions for policy studies activities

Institutions & concepts \ Activities	Training (3 tracks)	Research (3 tracks)	Funding (for training & research)	Publishing (books and journals)	Association (mutual interactions)
Universities	Career preparation	Generalized or basic research	1 Career training 2 Basic research	1 University presses 2 Scholarly journals	Scholarly associations
Independent institutes & private sector	Continuing policy education (CPE)	Intermediate or mid-level research (evaluation research)	1 Continuing education 2 Mid-level research	1 Commercial publishing 2 Commercial journals	Interest groups
Government agencies	Job-specific (OJT)	Task-specific (program evaluation)	1 Job-specific 2 Task-specific	1 Internal reports 2 Internal periodicals	Government agencies
Trends	1970s schools 1980s texts 1990s CPE	1970s centers 1980s texts 1990s CPE	1970s up 1980s down 1990s ?	1970s new 1980s plateau 1990s plateau	1970s new 1980s plateau 1990s plateau
Developing nations	Examples: Beijing Univ. NSA Ministry	Examples: Zambia Univ. CAFRAD UN Commmission	Examples: MUCIA Ford Found. AID & World Bank	Examples: Macmillan PSO journals	Examples: EROPS UNUSA PRC
SOS solutions	All	All	All	All	All

which are neither universities nor government agencies. They may include the American Society for Public Administration conducting pre-conference workshops designed to upgrade the skills of governmental decision makers, or the American Bar Association conducting continuing legal education (CLE) programs. The abbreviation CPE for continuing policy education programs is used in the table.

The second column deals with *research* activities. The universities are especially oriented toward generalized or basic research. They are also most appropriate if one wants to emphasize innovative creativity. In-house government research is especially effective for more specific tasks from an insider's perspective. It is research that has a good chance of being adopted, just as OJT training has a good chance of leading to a higher job. The independent institutes range from high-quality policy institutes like the Brookings Institution and the American Enterprise Institute to institutes that are sometimes referred to as the beltway bandits who specialize in good packaging but possibly shallow substance at high prices. The independent institutes do well on complying with time and subject matter specifications.

The third column is concerned with *funding* activities. Much of the policy training and research at universities is funded internally through legislative appropriations, alumni contributions and student tuition, but also by government grants and foundations. The independent sector can include policy institutes and also funding sources like the Ford Foundation. Both may benefit from endowments. Most independent institutes, however, rely on soft money (or non-recurring grants), and they usually do better financially on business training and research than on governmental training and research. The government agencies tend to rely almost exclusively on taxes to fund their training and research activities. They could rely more on the willingness of many academics to participate in training and research activities for only the out-of-pocket cost, in view of the interest of policy academics in insightful experiences and in making a worthwhile contribution.

The fourth column relates to *publishing* as a policy studies activity, including both books and journals. Universities provide university presses, which publish some policy-relevant books, although they tend to be concerned with more abstract matters or more geographically narrow matters. Some universities publish relevant scholarly journals, such as the *Policy Studies Journal* (*PSJ*) and the *Policy Studies Review* (*PSR*), which have been published at various universities since they began. The private sector publishes policy-relevant books series, such as those published by Greenwood, Macmillan, JAI Press, Marcel Dekker, Lexington and Sage. Many of the relevant journals are commercially published; these include the *Journal of Policy Analysis and Management* (*JPAM*), which is published by Wiley.

Government agencies do relevant publishing in the form of internal reports and internal periodicals. The Government Accounting Office does both.

The fifth column deals with *associations* as forms of mutual interaction and networking. People at universities tend to be associated with scholarly associations, such as the American Political Science Association or the Policy Studies Organization. The private sector tends to be organized into interest groups that take a strong interest in public policy, such as the various trade and professional associations. The private sector also includes public-interest groups like Common Cause or more partisan groups like the Americans for Democratic Action. People from government agencies often belong to specialized associations which might emphasize public works, criminal justice or education. They also join more general practitioner groups which also include academics like the American Evaluation Association or the American Society for Public Administration.

Trends, developing nations and SOS

On the matter of *trends*, the following points may be made.

1   Training in the 1970s emphasized the development of new schools like the Kennedy School of Government at Harvard or the Graduate School of Public Policy at Berkeley. The 1980s emphasized the development of new public policy textbooks, starting with books by Edward Quade and by Stokey and Zeckhauser. The 1990s saw more emphasis on continuing policy education with the upgrading of skills through workshops and OJT, as in other industries.

2   Research in the 1970s emphasized the establishment of research centers like the American Enterprise Institute. The 1980s saw an outpouring of books from such centers, as well as other sources such as the Policy Studies Organization. The 1990s saw more research and publishing that is relevant to providing materials for continuing policy education, rather than so much emphasis on textbooks and trade books.

3   Trends in funding were upward in the 1970s, when money was more readily available for policy research from the Carter administration, but downward in the 1980s when it was less available from the Reagan administration. The 1990s saw an increase in policy analysis funding as part of the peace dividend and the increased interest in industrial policy and the role of the government in stimulating the marketplace.

4   There were new journals in the 1970s including *PSJ*, *PSR* and *JPAM*. There has been a leveling-off in the 1980s, although at a high level. That has continued in the 1990s although the newsletter journal has become

an important new form of scholarly periodicals. That includes the *Policy Evaluation Newsletter–Journal* and the *Developmental Policy Studies Newsletter–Journal*. Both were established in the 1990s.

5 Associations tend to be related to journals. The 1970s saw new policy associations established, such as PSO, APPAM (Association for Public Policy Analysis and Management) and AEA (American Evaluation Association). There has been a leveling-off in the 1980s and 1990s. One upsurge, though, has been the expansion of policy associations toward being more cross-national. The Policy Studies Organization has thus established regional PSOs in Asia, Africa, East Europe and Latin America.

The above analysis has tended to use American examples. We could also discuss each of the five activities in terms of examples from *developing nations*.

1 Policy analysis training in China as elsewhere involves universities, independent institutes and government agencies. Beijing University has an excellent program on foreign policy and international relations. The National School of Administration is a semi-independent training institute which has links with the People's University and also the government. A good example of in-house government training is the Ministry of Machinery and Electronics, which has its own training campus.

2 One can use Africa to illustrate the role of universities, institutes and government agencies in research. The Political Science Department of Zambia University does policy-relevant research on electoral reform and other matters. The African Training and Research Centre in Administration for Development (CAFRAD) is a policy institute which does excellent research and publishing on African policy problems. A relevant government agency might be the UN Economic Commission on Africa, or the Commonwealth Secretariat. Both also encourage relevant conferences and research.

3 Funding for training and research in developing nations include university programs like the Midwest University Consortium for International Affairs (MUCIA). Good examples of the semi-private sector funding training and research are the Ford, the Asia and the Rockefeller Foundations. Important government agencies include the Agency for International Development (AID) and the World Bank. Both have recently taken an increased interest in the importance of democratic institutions and systematic public policy analysis.

4 There are a number of book publishers, such as Macmillan, M.E. Sharpe and Kumerian, who have specialized series that deal with developing nations. There are many journals, such as the *Journal of Commonwealth*

and Comparative Politics, the *Journal of Asian Studies*, the *Journal of Development Studies*, *African Affairs* and the *Latin American Research Review*, that specialize in developing nations.

5　An example of a scholarly association concerned with developing nations is the Eastern Regional Organization of Public Administration (EROPA). It is the Asian regional organization for the International Association of Schools and Institutes of Administration. A relevant interest group is the UNUSA, an American organization that supports the activities of the United Nations, including those directed toward economic, social, technological, political and legal development. An example of a government agency in a developing nation context might be the People's Republic of China (PRC) Ministry of Foreign Affairs, which seeks to bring students to China from developing nations of Africa and elsewhere in Asia.

The last row of the table addresses the question of what is a *super-optimum* way of resolving the division of labor between universities, independent private institutes and government agencies, in dealing with policy training, research, funding, publishing and associations. One could say that emphasizing the private sector is the conservative way; emphasizing government agencies is the liberal way; emphasizing universities is relatively neutral, although some universities are governmental and some are private. The super-optimum solution is not a compromise that involves giving more to the neutral position: that would defeat the purpose of getting the separate benefits of each type of institution. Rather, the SOS solution seeks to expand the policy activities of universities, independent institutes and government agencies, all simultaneously. There is plenty of room for that kind of three-way expansion, given the need for better policy analysis in order to have better public policies and a better quality of life in industrial and developing nations. That means more and better policy training, research, funding, publishing and associations through universities, independent institutes and government agencies.

SOME INTEGRATING CONCLUSIONS

Some of the *integrating ideas* that are relevant to this chapter on the need for improved policy analysis in developing regions are considered in what follows. Improved policy analysis involves the ability to deal with multiple goals, multiple alternatives, missing information, spreadsheet-based decision-aiding software, a concern for successful adoption and implementation, and the striving for super-optimum solutions whereby conservatives, liberals and other major viewpoints can all come out ahead of their best initial expectations simultaneously.

Improved policy analysis requires more than a systematic analytic methodology. It also requires a system of institutions such as universities, independent institutes and government agencies performing essential functions with regard to training, research, funding, publishing and networking.

On a higher level of integration, there is a need to emphasize more the *interdependence* of effective policy analysis methods and effective policy analysis institutions. The development of a methodology that is capable of determining an optimum or even a super-optimum alternative, combination or allocation does not mean much unless the following activities are also occurring.

1   The methodology is being taught to students who are preparing for careers that involve policy analysis. It is also being taught to practitioners who have already gone beyond their college training.
2   The methodology is being applied in systematically evaluating alternative public policies that relate to economic, social, technological, political and legal problems.
3   Funding is available to conduct the relevant training and the relevant research.
4   Books and journals are being published to facilitate the training activities by way of developing teaching materials. Books and journals are also being published to disseminate the results of the research and to share experiences on how future research and teaching can be improved.
5   Associations hold regular meetings in which papers are presented and roundtable discussions are held to indicate what is happening at the cutting edge of policy analysis activities and also to establish mutually beneficial collaborative contacts.

The development of strong institutions with good potential for training, research, funding, publishing and associations does not mean much if systematic policy analytic methodologies are not also being simultaneously developed. Otherwise there will be a number of regrettable outcomes.

1   The training programs will have nothing meaningful to teach or at least less than the optimum which they could be teaching.
2   The research activities are not so likely to develop results that are as insightful as they otherwise could be.
3   Much of the funding may be wasted on largely irrelevant or ineffective training and research.
4   The publishing may go through the motions of generating books and

journals, but policy analysts who are academics or practitioners may be disappointed at how little value the books and journals might have.

5   The papers presented at associational meetings might overemphasize 'number crunching', unrealistic mathematical models, unnecessary jargon and other forms of modern scholasticism which have afflicted many professional associations. This is contrasted to a concern for dealing in a meaningful way with many important goals and alternatives in order to arrive at super-optimum or other conclusions which are relevant to improving the quality of life through better public policy in developing regions.

Perhaps the reciprocal nature of policy analysis methods and policy analysis institutions will seem obvious. Nevertheless, one can find important literature that may overemphasize one at the expense of the other. For example, the publications of the World Bank, the Commonwealth Secretariat and the African Association for Public Administration and Management on the subject of African capacity building may overemphasize building institutions without an adequate concern for building analytic methods. The methodology books, on the other hand, almost never talk about policy analysis institutions. The classic volumes by Edward Quade (E.S. Quade, *Analysis for Public Decisions* (North Holland, 1989) of the Rand Corporation, or Edith Stokey and Richard Zeckhauser (Edith Stokey and Richard Zeckhauser, *A Primer for Policy Analysis* (W.W. Norton, 1978) of the Harvard Kennedy School, have a lot to say about variations on management science, operations research and decision analysis, but there is no mention in these books about training methods, research utilization, funding sources, publishing outlets or relevant associations.

One does not have to incorporate all the ideas of a chapter into its short title. Perhaps, however, the title could be expanded to 'The Need for Improved Policy Analysis Methods and Institutions in Developing Nations and Elsewhere'. More important than the title and the contents is the idea that there are these joint needs. It is hoped that this chapter will be a step in the right direction of clarifying and suggesting ways in which those needs can be met.

APPENDIX ALLOCATING $100 MILLION TO POLICY ANALYSIS ACTIVITIES AND INSTITUTIONS

The allocation budget of $100 million comes from page 27 of *The African Capacity Building Initiative: Toward Improved Policy Analysis and Development Management in Sub-Saharan Africa* (World Bank, 1991). The exact quote is, 'Financial resources will be needed to implement capacity building action programs ... an ACB fund will be created initially of $100 million.' See Table 8.2.

Training and research are given greater weight than funding, publishing and associations, since the second set of activities mainly serve to facilitate the first. The $100 million is allocated to the five activities in proportion to their weights. Going down each activity separately, each institution is scored using *relative scoring*. Such scoring involves first deciding which institution is (relatively speaking) the least important of the three types of institutions. This is given an anchor score of 1. One then scores the middling institution as being twice as important as the base and half as important as the most important institution, unless a more precise scoring system is needed and is available. These relative scores are then converted to part or whole percentages by adding down to determine the total of each column. The score in each cell is then divided by the total score of the column. The decimal equivalents of those part or whole percentages are then multiplied by the total allocated to each activity in order to determine the dollar allocations for each type of institution on each activity.

The total dollar allocations for each type of institution are determined by adding across the five separate allocations. The total allocation percentages for each institution are determined by adding across the weighted percentages and dividing by the sum of the weights. All dollar amounts in the table are in millions of dollars. As a result of rounding to the nearest million dollars, the percentages may sometimes add to slightly more or less than 100 per cent. The dollar amounts may also add up to slightly more or less than $100, $28 or $14.

This allocation analysis is not meant to be final. It is meant to be stimulus to thinking systematically about how (on a relatively high level of generality) $100 million might best be allocated to various activities and institutions for improving African capacity building, especially with regard to systematic public policy analysis.

Table 8.2 Allocating World Bank funds to policy analysis activities and institutions

Institutions \ Activities	Training (3 tracks) W=2	Research (3 tracks) W=2	Funding (for training & research) W=1	Publishing (books & journals) W=1	Associations (mutual interactions) W=1	Allocations
L Universities	Career preparation 4 (56% = $16)	Generalized or basic research 4 (56% = $16)	1 Career training 2 Basic research 4 (56% = $8)	1 University presses 2 Scholarly journals 1 (14% = $2)	Scholarly associations 4 (56% = $8)	(50% = $50)
C Independent institutes & private sector	Continuing policy education (CPE) 1 (14% = $4)	Intermediate or mid-level research (evaluation research) 1 (14% = $4)	1 Continuing education 2 Mid-level research 1 (14% = $2)	1 Commercial publishing 2 Commercial journals 4 (56% = $8)	Interest groups 2 (28% = $4)	(22% = $22)
N Government agencies	Job-specific (OJT) 2 (28% = $8)	Task-specific (program evaluation) 2 (28% = $8)	1 Job-specific 2 Task-specific 2 (28% = $4)	1 Internal reports 2 Internal periodicals 2 (28% = $4)	Government agencies 1 (14% = $2)	(26% = $26)
Totals	7 (100% = $28)	7 (100% = $28)	7 (100% = $14)	7 (100% = $14)	7 (100% = $14)	(100% = $100)

BUDGET = $100 MILLION

This allocation analysis may not lend itself to an SOS allocation, since all the goals are ideologically neutral. None of the goals is relatively conservative or relatively liberal. Thus the alternative institutions receive only one set of allocation percentages and amounts, rather than a conservative and liberal set that need to be exceeded. One can say that emphasizing universities is relatively liberal, and emphasizing private sector institutes is relatively conservative, with government agencies in the middle. One needs ideological goals as well as alternatives, however, in order to have an ideological controversy subject to a super-optimum solution, as contrasted to an optimum solution. The latter finds the best allocation in light of the goals, alternatives and relations with only one set of weights. The SOS solution finds an alternative that does better than the conservative alternative with conservative weights, and simultaneously does better than the liberal alternative with liberal weights.

NOTES

1 On improved policy analysis, see Edward Quade, *Analysis for Public Decisions* (North-Holland, 1988); John Mullen and Byron Roth, *Decision Making: Its Logic and Practice* (Rowman & Littlefield, 1991); John Arnold, *The Art of Decision Making* (American Management Associations, 1978); S. Nagel, *Professional Developments in Policy Studies* (Greenwood Press, 1992); S. Nagel, *Developing Nations and Super-Optimum Policy Analysis* (Nelson-Hall, 1992).

2 On socialistic policy analysis, see Michael Harrington, *Why We Need Socialism in America* (Dissent, 1971); Paul Sweezy, *Socialism* (McGraw-Hill, 1949). On the Chinese population problem, see Judith Banister, *China's Changing Population* (Stanford University Press, 1987); Jean Robinson, 'Of Family Policies in China', in Richard Hula and Elaine Anderson (eds), *The Family and Public Policy* (Greenwood Press, 1991).

3 On capitalistic policy analysis, see Milton Friedman, *Capitalism and Freedom* (University of Chicago Press, 1963); George Gilder, *Wealth and Poverty* (Basic Books, 1980). On land reform and agricultural policy as it pertains to developing countries, see William Browne and Don Hadwiger (eds), *World Food Policies: Toward Agricultural Independence* (Lynne Reinner, 1986); John Mellor, 'Agriculture on the Road to Industrialization', in John Lewis and Laleriana Kallab (eds), *Development Strategies Reconsidered* (Transaction books, 1986); Raid El-Ghonemy, *The Political Economy of Rural Poverty: The Case of Land Reform* (Routledge, Chapman and Hall, 1991).

4 On institutionalizing policy analysis (including training, research, funding, publishing and networking institutions), see John Crecine, *The New Educational Programs in Public Policy: The First Decade* (JAI Press, 1982); Ilene Bernstein and Howard Freeman, *Academic and Entrepreneurial Research: The Consequences of Diversity in Federal Evaluation Studies* (Russell Sage, 1975); Virginia White, *Grants: How To find Out About Them and What To Do Next* (Plenum, 1975); Carolyn Mullins, *A Guide to Writing and Publishing in the Social and Behavioral Sciences* (Wiley, 1977); UNESCO, *International Organizations in the Social Sciences* (UNESCO, 1981); S. Nagel, *The Policy Studies Handbook* (Lexington-Heath, 1980).

5   For additional literature on the subject of capacity building regarding policy analysis institutions in developing nations, see Edward Jaycox, *The African Capacity Building Initiative: Toward Improved Policy Analysis and Development Management in Sub-Saharan Africa* (World Bank, 1991); Mohan Kaul and Gelase Mutahaba, *Enhancement of Public Policy Management Capacity in Africa* (Commonwealth Secretariat and African Association for Public Administration and Management, 1991); Vasant Moharir, 'Capacity Building Initiative for Sub-Saharan Africa', in J. Pronk (ed.), *Sub-Saharan Africa: Beyond Adjustment* (Netherlands Ministry of Foreign Affairs, 1990). For additional literature on the subject of allocating scarce resources among alternative activities, see S. Nagel, 'Allocating Scarce Resources', *Decision-Aiding Software: Skills, Obstacles and Applications* (Macmillan, 1991); S. Nagel, 'Super-Optimum Solutions and Allocation Problems', *Policy Analysis Methods, Process and Super-Optimum Solutions* (Greenwood Press, 1992).

Index

DATE DUE

			Printed in USA

HIGHSMITH #45230